Mastering IT Leadership and Management, Strategies for Success in the Digital Age

Dedication 12

Acknowledgments 12

About the Book 13

About the Author 14

Preface 17

Purpose of the Book --- 18

Target Audience -- 18

Overview of IT Leadership and Management ---------------------------- 18

Importance of IT Leadership in Today's Digital World ------------------ 18

Part 1: Foundations of IT Leadership 19

"Leadership is not about being in charge. It's about taking care of those in your charge." ...19

Chapter 1: The Evolving Role of IT Leaders -------------------------- 20

"The only constant in technology is change, and the true mark of leadership is the ability to adapt, innovate, and guide others through that change." 20
Historical Perspective of IT Leadership 20
The Transition from Technical Expert to Strategic Leader 20
Key Competencies of Modern IT Leaders 22
Industry Case Study: The Transformation of IT Leadership at General Motors (GM) 23
Best Practices 25
Lessons Learned 26
Conclusion 27
Quizzes 28
   I.   Multiple Choice Questions: 28
  II.   True/False Questions: 28
Exercises 29
   I.   Case Study Analysis: 29
  II.   Role Reflection: 29
 III.   Vision Development Exercise: 29
 IV.   SWOT Analysis: 29
  V.   Group Discussion: 30

Chapter 2: IT Leadership vs. IT Management ---------------------- 31

"Management is doing things right; leadership is doing the right things." 31
Defining Leadership and Management in the IT Context 31
Differences and Overlaps Between Leadership and Management 32
Balancing Leadership and Management Responsibilities 33
Industry Case Study: Microsoft's Dual Approach to IT Leadership and Management 34
Best Practices 36

Mastering IT Leadership and Management, Strategies for Success in the Digital Age

Lessons Learned 37
Conclusion 38
Quizzes 39
    I.   Multiple Choice Questions: 39
    II. True/False Questions: 39
Exercises 40
    I.   Case Study Reflection: 40
    II. Leadership vs. Management Role-Playing: 40
    III. Vision and Execution Planning: 40
    IV. Self-Assessment: 40
    V. Group Discussion: 41

Chapter 3: Building a Vision for IT -- 42

"The best way to predict the future is to create it." 42
Creating a Strategic IT Vision 42
Aligning IT Strategy with Business Objectives 44
Communicating the Vision to Stakeholders 45
Industry Case Study: IBM's Strategic Vision for IT Transformation 46
Best Practices 48
Lessons Learned 49
Conclusion 50
Quizzes 51
    I.   Multiple Choice Questions: 51
    II. True/False Questions: 51
Exercises 52
    I.   SWOT Analysis Exercise: 52
    II. Vision Statement Workshop: 52
    III. Stakeholder Engagement Plan: 52
    IV. IT Vision Communication Strategy: 52
    V. Case Study Analysis: 53
Conclusion of Part 1: Foundations of IT Leadership 54

Part 2: Essential Skills for IT Leaders _____ 55

"The single biggest way to impact an organization is to focus on leadership development. There is almost no limit to the potential of an organization that recruits good people, raises them up as leaders, and continually develops them." 55

Chapter 4: Leading IT Teams --- 56

"The strength of the team is each individual member. The strength of each member is the team." 56
Building and Nurturing High-Performance IT Teams 56
Leadership Styles in IT 58
Empowering and Motivating IT Professionals 60
Industry Case Study: Leading High-Performance IT Teams at Google 61
Best Practices 63
Lessons Learned 64
Conclusion 65

Mastering IT Leadership and Management, Strategies for Success in the Digital Age

Quizzes..66
    I.   Multiple Choice Questions:..66
    II.   True/False Questions:..66
Exercises 67
    I.   Team Dynamics Analysis:..67
    II.   Leadership Style Reflection: 67
    III. High-Performance Team Workshop:...67
    IV. Conflict Resolution Simulation:..67
    V.   Continuous Development Plan:...68

Chapter 5: Effective Communication --69

"The art of communication is the language of leadership."......................................69
Bridging the Gap Between IT and Non-IT Stakeholders..69
Presenting Technical Concepts to Executive Leadership...71
Negotiation and Conflict Resolution in IT..72
Industry Case Study: Effective Communication at Amazon Web Services (AWS)....73
Best Practices..75
Lessons Learned 76
Conclusion 77
Quizzes..78
    I.   Multiple Choice Questions:..78
    II.   True/False Questions:..78
Exercises 79
    I.   Audience Analysis Exercise:..79
    II.   Role-Playing: Bridging IT and Non-IT Communication:..............................79
    III. Storytelling Workshop: 79
    IV. Active Listening Practice:..79
    V.   Visual Communication Design: 80

Chapter 6: Decision-Making and Problem-Solving-----------------------------81

"In the end, we are our choices. Build yourself a great story."..................................81
Strategic Decision-Making in IT 81
Data-Driven Decision-Making...83
Problem-Solving Techniques for IT Leaders..84
Industry Case Study: Decision-Making and Problem-Solving at Netflix...................85
Best Practices..87
Lessons Learned..88
Conclusion 89
Quizzes..90
    I.   Multiple Choice Questions:..90
    II.   True/False Questions: 90
Exercises 91
    I.   Root Cause Analysis Exercise:..91
    II.   Data-Driven Decision-Making Workshop: 91
    III. Creative Problem-Solving Session: 91

Mastering IT Leadership and Management, Strategies for Success in the Digital Age

    IV. Decision-Making Under Pressure Simulation: 91
    V. Stakeholder Engagement Plan: 92

Chapter 7: Managing Change in IT--93

"Change is the law of life. And those who look only to the past or present are certain to miss the future." 93
Leading IT Change Initiatives 93
Overcoming Resistance to Change 95
Change Management Frameworks and Models 96
Industry Case Study: Managing Change at Procter & Gamble (P&G) through IT Leadership 97
Best Practices 99
Lessons Learned 100
Conclusion 102
Quizzes 103
    I. Multiple Choice Questions: 103
    II. True/False Questions: 103
Exercises 104
    I. Change Management Strategy Development: 104
    II. Case Study Analysis: 104
    III. Resistance Management Role-Play: 104
    IV. Stakeholder Communication Plan: 104
    V. Continuous Monitoring and Adjustment: 105
Conclusion of Part 2: Essential Skills for IT Leaders 106

Part 3: Strategic IT Management _____107

"Strategy is not the consequence of planning, but the opposite: its starting point." 107

Chapter 8: IT Governance and Compliance---------------------------------108

"Good governance is the art of putting wise thought into prudent action in a way that advances the well-being of those governed." 108
Implementing IT Governance Frameworks 108
Ensuring Compliance with Industry Regulations 110
Ensuring Compliance with Industry Regulations 111
Understanding Regulatory Requirements 111
Developing a Compliance Strategy 111
Integrating Compliance into IT Governance 112
Conclusion 113
Risk Management in IT 114
Industry Case Study: IT Governance and Compliance at JPMorgan Chase 115
Best Practices 117
Lessons Learned 119
Conclusion 121
Quizzes 122
    I. Multiple Choice Questions: 122
    II. True/False Questions: 122

Mastering IT Leadership and Management, Strategies for Success in the Digital Age

Exercises 123
    I.   Governance Framework Selection: 123
    II.   Compliance Audit Simulation: 123
    III. Risk Management Integration: 123
    IV. Compliance Culture Assessment: 123
    V.   Technology in Governance and Compliance: 124

Chapter 9: IT Project and Portfolio Management --------------------------- 125

"A project is complete when it starts working for you, rather than you working for it." 125
Principles of IT Project Management 125
Managing IT Portfolios for Strategic Alignment 127
Best Practices in IT Project Delivery 129
Industry Case Study: IT Project and Portfolio Management at Cisco Systems 132
Best Practices 134
Lessons Learned 135
Conclusion 137
Quizzes 138
    I.   Multiple Choice Questions: 138
    II.   True/False Questions: 138
Exercises 139
    I.   IT Portfolio Analysis Exercise: 139
    II.   Project Risk Management Workshop: 139
    III. Agile Methodology Simulation: 139
    IV. Stakeholder Engagement Plan: 139
    V.   Post-Project Review Exercise: 140

Chapter 10: Financial Management for IT Leaders ------------------------- 141

"Financial management is not just about managing money; it's about managing the business that creates and uses money." 141
Budgeting and Cost Management in IT 141
Understanding IT Financial Metrics 143
Making the Case for IT Investments 145
Industry Case Study: Financial Management at Intel Corporation 148
Best Practices 150
Lessons Learned 152
Conclusion 154
Quizzes 155
    I.   Multiple Choice Questions: 155
    II.   True/False Questions: 155
Exercises 156
    I.   IT Budget Development Exercise: 156
    II.   Cost Management Simulation: 156
    III. ROI and TCO Calculation Workshop: 156
    IV. Business Case Development Exercise: 157
    V.   Long-Term Financial Planning Exercise: 157
Conclusion of Part 3: Strategic IT Management 158

Mastering IT Leadership and Management, Strategies for Success in the Digital Age

Part 4: Navigating the Digital Transformation 159

"It is not the strongest companies that survive, nor the most intelligent, but those most responsive to change." 159

Chapter 11: Digital Leadership in the Age of Transformation---------------160

"The greatest danger in times of turbulence is not the turbulence—it is acting with yesterday's logic." 160

Defining Digital Leadership 160
Leading Digital Transformation 161
Fostering a Culture of Innovation 162
Empowering Teams in the Digital Age 163
Navigating Ethical Challenges in Digital Leadership 164
Industry Case Study: Digital Leadership in the Age of Transformation at General Electric (GE) 165
Best Practices 167
Lessons Learned 169
Conclusion 171
Quizzes 172
    I. Multiple Choice Questions: 172
    II. True/False Questions: 172
Exercises 173
    I. Strategic Vision Development: 173
    II. Innovation Culture Workshop: 173
    III. Cross-Functional Collaboration Exercise: 173
    IV. Adaptability and Resilience Simulation: 173
    V. Ethical Digital Leadership Case Study: 174

Chapter 12: Navigating Digital Transformation ----------------------------175

"It is not the strongest of the species that survive, nor the most intelligent, but the one most responsive to change." 175
Setting the Vision for Digital Transformation 175
Driving Innovation Through Technology 176
Managing Cultural Change in Digital Transformation 177
Executing Digital Transformation Initiatives 178
Sustaining Digital Transformation 179
Industry Case Study: Navigating Digital Transformation at Honeywell 180
Best Practices 182
Lessons Learned 184
Conclusion 186
Quizzes 187
    I. Multiple Choice Questions: 187
    II. True/False Questions: 187
Exercises 188
    I. Digital Transformation Vision Exercise: 188
    II. Innovation Workshop: 188

Mastering IT Leadership and Management, Strategies for Success in the Digital Age

    III.   Cultural Change Management Simulation: 188
    IV.   Data-Driven Decision-Making Exercise: 189
    V.   Continuous Improvement Plan: 189

Chapter 13: Building a Cybersecurity Strategy ---------------------------------190

"Security is not a product; it is a process." 190
Understanding the Cybersecurity Landscape 190
Conducting a Cybersecurity Risk Assessment 191
Developing a Comprehensive Cybersecurity Strategy 192
Building an Incident Response Plan 193
Fostering a Culture of Security 194
Industry Case Study: Building a Cybersecurity Strategy at Equifax 195
Best Practices 197
Lessons Learned 199
Conclusion 201
Quizzes 202
    I.   Multiple Choice Questions: 202
    II.   True/False Questions: 202
Exercises 203
    I.   Cybersecurity Risk Assessment Exercise: 203
    II.   Incident Response Planning Workshop: 203
    III.   Building a Security-Aware Culture Exercise: 203
    IV.   Layered Defense Strategy Development: 204
    V.   Cybersecurity Innovation Investment Proposal: 204
Conclusion of Part 4: Navigating the Digital Transformation 205

Part 5: Leading in a Hybrid and Remote Work Environment _____206

"The measure of intelligence is the ability to change." 206

Chapter 14: IT Leadership in a Hybrid Work World--------------------------207

"The key to success is not just managing work, but managing how and where work happens." 207
Enabling Remote Work Technologies 207
Fostering a Strong Organizational Culture 208
Ensuring Security in a Hybrid Work Environment 209
Supporting Employee Well-Being and Work-Life Balance 210
Leading with Empathy and Inclusion 211
Industry Case Study: IT Leadership in a Hybrid Work World at Microsoft 212
Best Practices 214
Lessons Learned 216
Conclusion 218
Quizzes 219
    I.   Multiple Choice Questions: 219
    2.   True/False Questions: 219
Exercises 220

Mastering IT Leadership and Management, Strategies for Success in the Digital Age

- I. Remote Work Technology Evaluation: 220
- II. Hybrid Meeting Inclusivity Workshop: 220
- III. Security Awareness Training Simulation: 220
- IV. Employee Well-Being Plan Development: 221
- V. Building a Sense of Belonging Exercise: 221

Chapter 15: Talent Management and Development —————————————— 222

"The growth and development of people is the highest calling of leadership." 222
Recruiting Top IT Talent 222
Developing IT Skills and Competencies 223
Retaining Top IT Talent 224
Managing and Developing IT Leadership 225
Creating a Culture of Engagement and Retention 226
Industry Case Study: Talent Management and Development at Google 227
Best Practices 229
Lessons Learned 231
Conclusion 233
Quizzes 234
- I. Multiple Choice Questions: 234
- II. True/False Questions: 234

Exercises 235
- I. Talent Acquisition Strategy Development: 235
- II. Continuous Learning Program Design: 235
- III. Employee Retention Analysis: 235
- IV. Diversity and Inclusion Initiative: 236
- V. Leadership Development Plan: 236

Conclusion of Part 5: Leading in a Hybrid and Remote Work Environment 237

Part 6: Future Trends in IT Leadership _____ 238

"The future of IT leadership belongs to those who not only embrace emerging technologies but also foresee the ethical, strategic, and human impacts of innovation. True leaders will navigate the digital frontier with vision, agility, and a deep commitment to guiding their organizations through uncharted territories." 238

Chapter 16: The Future of IT Leadership ————————————————— 239

"The future belongs to those who prepare for it today." 239
Evolving Role of IT Leaders 239
Navigating Emerging Technologies 240
Addressing Ethical and Social Implications 241
Developing Future IT Leaders 242
Building Resilience and Agility 243
Industry Case Study: The Future of IT Leadership at IBM 244
Best Practices 246
Lessons Learned 248
Conclusion 250
Quizzes 251

Mastering IT Leadership and Management, Strategies for Success in the Digital Age

    I.   Multiple-Choice Questions 251
    II. True/False Questions 252
Exercises 253
    I.   Reflective Essay:..253
    II. Case Study Analysis:...253
    III. Group Discussion: 253
    IV. Scenario-Based Role Play: 253
    V. Strategic Planning Exercise: 253

Chapter 17: Continuous Learning and Adaptation --------------------------254

"In a world that is constantly changing, the greatest skill is the ability to learn." 254
The Importance of Continuous Learning 254
Fostering a Culture of Continuous Learning 255
Strategies for Organizational Adaptation 256
Preparing for Future Challenges 257
Embracing Lifelong Learning 258
Industry Case Study: Continuous Learning and Adaptation at IBM 259
Best Practices 261
Lessons Learned 263
Conclusion 265
Quizzes..266
    I.   Multiple Choice Questions:..266
    II. True/False Questions:...267
Exercises 268
    I.   Reflective Essay: 268
    II. Case Study Analysis: 268
    III. Group Discussion:..268
    IV. Action Plan Development: 268
    V. Scenario-Based Role Play: 268
Conclusion of Part 6: Future Trends in IT Leadership 269

Conclusion _____270

Recap of Key Concepts --270
Chapter 1: The Evolving Role of IT Leadership...270
Chapter 2: Building a Visionary IT Strategy..270
Chapter 3: IT Governance and Compliance..270
Chapter 4: Managing IT Operations and Infrastructure 271
Chapter 5: Cybersecurity Leadership 271
Chapter 6: Data Management and Analytics 271
Chapter 7: IT Project and Portfolio Management..271
Chapter 8: Financial Management for IT Leaders 272
Chapter 9: Building a Cybersecurity Strategy..272
Chapter 10: Talent Management and Development..272
Chapter 11: Digital Leadership in the Age of Transformation............................272
Chapter 12: Financial Management for IT Leaders...273

Mastering IT Leadership and Management, Strategies for Success in the Digital Age

Chapter 13: IT Leadership in a Hybrid Work World 273
Chapter 14: Talent Management and Development 273
Chapter 15: The Future of IT Leadership..273
Chapter 16: Continuous Learning and Adaptation 274
Chapter 17: Fostering a Culture of Continuous Learning 274
Conclusion 274

The Ongoing Journey of IT Leadership — 275
Embracing Lifelong Learning..275
Adapting to Change and Driving Innovation..275
Building and Leading High-Performing Teams 276
Navigating Ethical and Social Responsibilities 276
Preparing for the Future of IT Leadership...276
Conclusion 277

Call to Action for Aspiring IT Leaders — 278
Embrace Continuous Learning..278
Cultivate a Visionary Mindset...278
Build Strong Relationships 278
Drive Innovation and Embrace Change..278
Uphold Ethical Standards 279
Focus on Talent Development...279
Lead with Purpose 279
Conclusion 279

Appendices — 280

Appendix A: IT Leadership Frameworks and Models — 280
1. COBIT (Control Objectives for Information and Related Technologies)............280
2. ITIL (Information Technology Infrastructure Library).....................281
3. TOGAF (The Open Group Architecture Framework) 281
4. Balanced Scorecard 282
5. Lean IT..282
6. Agile 283
7. DevOps..283
Conclusion 284

Appendix B: Tools and Resources for IT Leaders — 285
1. Project Management Tools...285
2. Cybersecurity Tools..286
3. Data Management and Analytics Tools...286
4. Collaboration and Communication Tools...287
5. Continuous Learning and Development Resources 287
6. Strategic Planning and Decision-Making Tools................................288
7. Leadership and Management Resources..289
Conclusion 289

Appendix C: Glossary of IT Leadership and Management Terms — 290

Mastering IT Leadership and Management, Strategies for Success in the Digital Age

A 290
B 290
C 291
D 291
E 292
F 293
G 293
H 294
I 294
J 295
K 295
L 296
M 297
N 298
O 298
P 299
Q 300
R 300
S 301
T 302
U 302
V 303
W 303
X 303
Y 304
Z 304
Conclusion 304

References 305

Case Studies and Frameworks -- 305

Leadership and Strategy Resources -- 305

Cybersecurity Tools -- 306

Data Management and Analytics Tools --- 306

Learning and Development Resources --- 307

Collaboration and Communication Tools ------------------------------------- 307

Strategic Planning and Decision-Making Tools ------------------------------ 307

Mastering IT Leadership and Management, Strategies for Success in the Digital Age

Dedication

To my cherished parents, whose unwavering support and guidance have shaped my journey and instilled in me the values of hard work, perseverance, and the significance of family. Your enduring influence has engraved in my soul a profound understanding of morality and justice. May I strive to uphold these ideals to meet your highest standards and expectations.

To my amazing wife, thank you for your unwavering support, love, and faith in my aspirations. You inspire me every day to strive for greater heights.

To my lovely daughters, for filling my life with joy and laughter. Your strength and resilience inspire me to be the best version of myself. May you always continue to add light, color, and flavor to my life.

To my son, whose curiosity and zest for life remind me of the importance of learning and growing continuously. May you continue to be a much better version of myself on all aspects.

This book is dedicated to all of you, as you have been my greatest motivation and support throughout this journey. Thank you for being my pillars of strength.

Acknowledgments

I would like to express my heartfelt gratitude to those who have supported me throughout the journey of learning and those who assisted me in writing this book.

First and foremost, I would like to acknowledge my managers and mentors throughout my long career, whose wisdom and guidance have been invaluable. Their insights and encouragement have shaped my understanding of IT leadership and management, and I am very grateful for the time they invested in my development. Thank you for believing in my potential and supporting me in reaching new heights.

I extend my appreciation to my friends and colleagues, whose collaboration and support have enriched my personal and professional experiences. Working alongside such talented individuals has not only inspired me but has also provided me with diverse perspectives that have greatly influenced the content of this book. Your dedication and commitment to excellence in the field of information technology continue to motivate me.

I also wish to thank my customers for their trust and partnership. Your real-world challenges and feedback have informed much of the practical advice and strategies presented here. It is through our shared experiences that I have gained the insights necessary to create a meaningful and relevant resource for others in the industry.

To everyone mentioned and to those who have played a role in my journey—thank you for your support, encouragement, and belief in me. This book is as much yours as it is mine.

Mastering IT Leadership and Management, Strategies for Success in the Digital Age

About the Book

"Mastering IT Leadership and Management, Strategies for Success in the Digital Age" is an essential resource for both current and aspiring leaders in the field of information technology. This book addresses the unique challenges faced by IT professionals in an ever-evolving digital landscape and offers actionable strategies to enhance leadership effectiveness and management skills.

In this comprehensive guide, readers will discover how to align IT initiatives with overarching business objectives, ensuring that technology serves as a catalyst for organizational growth and innovation. The book delves into crucial topics such as fostering a culture of collaboration, managing change, and navigating the complexities of digital transformation.

Drawing on real-world case studies and best practices, the author provides valuable insights into the art of communication between technical and non-technical stakeholders, enabling leaders to bridge gaps and drive successful outcomes. Readers will also learn the significance of developing resilient teams that are equipped to adapt to rapid changes in technology and market demands.

Whether you are an experienced IT executive looking to refine your leadership approach or a newcomer seeking foundational knowledge in IT management, this book serves as a comprehensive guide to mastering the skills needed for success in the digital age. Equip yourself with the tools and insights necessary to lead effectively and make a lasting impact in your organization.

Mastering IT Leadership and Management, Strategies for Success in the Digital Age

About the Author

Ashraf Hamed
Information Technology Governance Consultant | Governance Proponent | Strategist | Technology Advocate | Technology and Vendor Agnostic

Location: Based in Cairo, Africa Serving South Europe, Middle East, and Africa

Bio: Ashraf Hamed is a distinguished IT Consultant and Auditor with an impressive tenure, in US government & multi-national corporations, exceeding 35 years, specializing in IT Governance, Risk, and Compliance (GRC).

With an expansive career that bridges various industries and business vectors, Ashraf has become a trusted advisor and strategic asset to multinational corporations seeking robust IT frameworks and compliance strategies.

His expertise is deeply rooted in designing and implementing comprehensive IT governance models that ensure alignment with business goals, enhance operational efficiency, and mitigate risk.

A relentless advocate for the strategic integration of technology, Ashraf has led numerous enterprises through complex compliance landscapes, adapting to both regional and international regulatory standards.

Ashraf's career is marked by his commitment to fostering secure, compliant, and resilient IT environments, while adhering to the highest levels of professional and personal ethics.

His strategic insights are particularly sought after in dynamic and diverse markets such as South Europe, the Middle East, and Africa, where he has successfully navigated varying compliance challenges and technological advancements.

A notable thought leader, Ashraf has contributed to several industry panels and forums, sharing best practices in IT risk management and governance frameworks.

His work not only underscores the critical nexus between technology and business strategy but also highlights his ability to translate intricate IT concerns into clear, actionable strategies tailored to each client's unique context.

Mastering IT Leadership and Management, Strategies for Success in the Digital Age

Credentials and Certifications:
Business Continuity & Cloud
- ISO/IEC 22301 Lead Implementer
- Certified Cloud Security Professional (CCSP)

Data Governance, Protection & Privacy
- Certified Information Privacy Manager (CIPM)
- Data Governance and Stewardship Professional (DGSP)

Information Security Governance, Management & Audit
- Certified Information Security Manager (CISM)
- COBIT5 for Security Practitioner
- Implementing the NIST Cybersecurity Framework Using COBIT 2019
- ISO/IEC 27001 Lead Auditor/Practitioner

Information Technology Audit
- Certified Information Systems Auditor (CISA)
- COBIT5 for Assurance Practitioner

Information Technology Governance:
- Certified in the Governance of Enterprise IT (CGEIT)
- Control Objectives for Information and related Technology (COBIT 2019) Practitioner

Portfolio, Program & Project Management:
- Agile Certified Practitioner (ACP)
- DSDM Advanced Practitioner
- Kanban Coaching Professional (KCP)
- Microsoft's Sure Step Project Management Methodology
- PRINCE2 Practitioner /Agile Practitioner
- Project Management Professional (PMP)
- SAP Activate Methodology

Risk Management
- Certified Risk and Information Systems Control (CRISC)
- COBIT5 for Risk Practitioner
- Management of Risk Practitioner M_o_R

Service Management
- ITIL Expert
- ISO/IEC 20000 Lead Auditor/Practitioner
- CMMI for Services (CMMI-Svc), by Software Engineering Institute, Carnegie Mellon
- Kepner Tregoe Resolve
- Unified Service Management, The USM Method Practitioner

Skills Management
- Skills Framework for the Information Age (SFIA)

Track record of relentless pursuit of over-achievement. Distinguished post-graduate studies in international Technology and Management.

Professional Philosophy:
"Navigating the complexities of IT governance requires not just adherence to standards, but also foresight that anticipates future challenges and opportunities. My role is to equip businesses with GRC frameworks that are not only compliant but also enable growth and innovation across diverse geographical landscapes."

Engagement and Contributions:
- Regular contributor to the IT GRC Forum
- Guest lecturer at multiple universities in the Middle East and Europe
- Frequent speaker at international conferences specializing in IT security and governance

Mastering IT Leadership and Management, Strategies for Success in the Digital Age

Ashraf is dedicated to leveraging his extensive experience and foresight to drive organizations' IT strategy forward, ensuring resilience, compliance, and competitive advantage in the global market.

Fluency in Arabic, English, French, German and Turkish languages

ashraf.hamed@consultia.co | http://www.consultia.co | GSM +20 100 133 335 2 | https://www.linkedin.com/in/ashamed

Mastering IT Leadership and Management, Strategies for Success in the Digital Age

Preface

In today's fast-paced and ever-evolving digital landscape, effective leadership and management in the field of information technology have never been more crucial. As organizations rely increasingly on technology to drive innovation, streamline operations, and enhance customer experiences, the demand for skilled IT leaders who can navigate this complex environment continues to grow.

This book, **"Mastering IT Leadership and Management, Strategies for Success in the Digital Age,"** is born out of my passion for the field and my desire to share insights and best practices that I have gathered over my years of experience. Throughout my career, I have witnessed firsthand the challenges that IT professionals face, from aligning technology with business objectives to managing teams and fostering a culture of collaboration. My goal in writing this book is to provide a comprehensive guide that addresses these challenges head-on and equips readers with the strategies necessary for success.

Each chapter delves into key aspects of IT leadership, offering practical tools, frameworks, and real-world examples to illustrate essential concepts. Whether you are a seasoned executive or just beginning your journey in IT management, this book aims to provide valuable insights that you can apply in your daily work.

I am grateful to my mentors, colleagues, and customers who have inspired me and contributed to my understanding of effective IT leadership. Their support has been instrumental in shaping the content of this book. I hope that the knowledge shared within these pages not only enhances your leadership skills but also encourages you to cultivate a mindset of continuous learning and growth.

As you embark on this journey through the chapters, I encourage you to reflect on your own experiences and apply the strategies outlined here to your unique context. Together, we can master the art of IT leadership and management, driving meaningful change in our organizations and contributing positively to the industry.

Thank you for taking the time to explore this book. I look forward to hearing about your journey as you implement these strategies in your own professional life.

— **Ashraf Hamed**

Mastering IT Leadership and Management, Strategies for Success in the Digital Age

Purpose of the Book
The primary aim of this book is to serve as a comprehensive guide for IT professionals aspiring to become successful leaders in their organizations. Whether you are a seasoned IT manager looking to refine your leadership skills or a budding leader eager to take on new challenges, this book will provide you with the tools and insights necessary to navigate the complexities of IT leadership in today's digital landscape.

Target Audience
This book is intended for IT professionals at all levels of leadership, from team leads and managers to CIOs and IT directors. It is also valuable for those transitioning into leadership roles from technical positions, as well as business leaders who want to better understand the strategic role of IT within their organizations.

Overview of IT Leadership and Management
IT leadership is more than just managing technology; it's about guiding teams, driving innovation, and aligning IT initiatives with business goals. In today's dynamic environment, IT leaders must be strategic thinkers, effective communicators, and change agents capable of leading their organizations through digital transformation. This book explores the multifaceted nature of IT leadership, covering foundational principles, essential skills, and the strategic management of IT resources.

Importance of IT Leadership in Today's Digital World
The digital age has transformed how businesses operate, making IT leadership a critical component of organizational success. As technology continues to advance at a rapid pace, IT leaders must be prepared to tackle new challenges, such as cybersecurity threats, the integration of emerging technologies, and the shift to remote and hybrid work environments. This book highlights the importance of adaptability, continuous learning, and the ability to lead with a forward-thinking mindset.

By the end of this book, you will gain a deeper understanding of what it takes to be an effective IT leader and how to apply these principles to drive success in your organization. The journey to mastering IT leadership is ongoing, but with the right tools and knowledge, you can confidently lead your team and organization into the future.

Mastering IT Leadership and Management, Strategies for Success in the Digital Age

Part 1: Foundations of IT Leadership

"LEADERSHIP IS NOT ABOUT BEING IN CHARGE. IT'S ABOUT TAKING CARE OF THOSE IN YOUR CHARGE."

— Simon Sinek

Mastering IT Leadership and Management, Strategies for Success in the Digital Age

Chapter 1: The Evolving Role of IT Leaders

"THE ONLY CONSTANT IN TECHNOLOGY IS CHANGE, AND THE TRUE MARK OF LEADERSHIP IS THE ABILITY TO ADAPT, INNOVATE, AND GUIDE OTHERS THROUGH THAT CHANGE."

— **The Author**

Historical Perspective of IT Leadership

The role of IT leadership has undergone a profound transformation over the past few decades. In the early days of computing, IT leaders were primarily technical experts, often referred to as "IT managers" or "chief technologists." Their responsibilities centered on managing hardware and software, ensuring the organization's systems were operational, and troubleshooting technical issues. The focus was largely on maintaining the status quo—keeping the lights on and ensuring the technology infrastructure was reliable.

During the 1980s and 1990s, as businesses began to recognize the strategic importance of information technology, the role of IT leaders started to shift. They were no longer just the custodians of technology; they were becoming integral to business strategy. IT leaders began to be involved in decisions about which technologies to adopt, how to integrate them into business processes, and how to use technology to gain a competitive edge. The title "Chief Information Officer" (CIO) emerged during this period, reflecting the growing importance of IT leadership at the executive level.

As the 21st century dawned, the pace of technological change accelerated dramatically. The rise of the internet, the advent of mobile computing, the proliferation of data, and the emergence of cloud computing fundamentally altered the IT landscape. IT leaders were now expected not only to manage technology but also to drive innovation, lead digital transformation initiatives, and ensure that technology investments were aligned with business goals. The role of IT leadership had evolved from a back-office function to a critical enabler of business success.

The Transition from Technical Expert to Strategic Leader

The evolution of IT leadership from a technical focus to a strategic role has been driven by the increasing complexity and centrality of technology in business operations. Today, IT leaders are expected to wear multiple hats: they must be technologists, strategists, communicators, and change agents. This transition requires a shift in both mindset and skill set, moving from a focus on technical proficiency to a broader understanding of how technology can create value for the organization.

1. **Understanding the Business Context:** Modern IT leaders must deeply understand the business context in which they operate. This includes understanding the organization's goals, challenges, and competitive landscape. IT leaders need to articulate

Mastering IT Leadership and Management, Strategies for Success in the Digital Age

how technology initiatives will support business objectives, whether by improving efficiency, enhancing customer experience, or enabling new business models.

2. **Strategic Thinking:** Strategic thinking is now a core competency for IT leaders. They must be able to look beyond immediate technical challenges and consider the long-term implications of technology decisions. This includes anticipating future technology trends, understanding potential risks and opportunities, and aligning technology investments with the organization's strategic priorities.

3. **Communication and Collaboration:** As IT leaders become more integrated into the business, the ability to communicate effectively with non-technical stakeholders is increasingly important. IT leaders must translate technical concepts into business terms, build relationships with other executives, and collaborate across departments to drive technology initiatives.

4. **Leading Change:** In today's fast-paced business environment, IT leaders are often at the forefront of change. Whether implementing a new enterprise resource planning (ERP) system, migrating to the cloud, or launching a digital transformation initiative, IT leaders must be adept at managing change. This includes not only the technical aspects but also the human aspects—ensuring that employees are engaged, trained, and ready to adopt new technologies.

Mastering IT Leadership and Management, Strategies for Success in the Digital Age

Key Competencies of Modern IT Leaders

The modern IT leader must possess a diverse set of competencies that go beyond traditional technical skills. These competencies are critical for navigating the complex and rapidly changing technology landscape and for leading organizations to success in the digital age.

1. **Technical Acumen:** While the role of IT leaders has expanded, technical expertise remains a foundational competency. IT leaders must stay current with emerging technologies, understand how to apply them in a business context, and ensure that their organization's technology infrastructure is robust, secure, and scalable.

2. **Business Acumen:** IT leaders must have a strong grasp of business principles, including financial management, marketing, operations, and customer service. They need to understand how different parts of the business interconnect and how technology can support and enhance business functions.

3. **Leadership and People Management:** Leading IT teams requires strong leadership and people management skills. IT leaders must be able to inspire and motivate their teams, manage performance, and foster a culture of innovation and continuous improvement. They must also navigate organizational politics and build consensus around technology initiatives.

4. **Risk Management:** As the guardians of their organization's digital assets, IT leaders must be vigilant in managing risks. This includes cybersecurity risks, compliance risks, and operational risks. IT leaders must have a deep understanding of the threat landscape and be able to implement strategies to mitigate risks and protect the organization's data and systems.

5. **Strategic Vision:** Finally, IT leaders must have a strategic vision for how technology can drive business success. This includes identifying emerging technologies that could disrupt the industry, leveraging data for competitive advantage, and being able to pivot quickly in response to changing market conditions.

Mastering IT Leadership and Management, Strategies for Success in the Digital Age

Industry Case Study: The Transformation of IT Leadership at General Motors (GM)

Situation:
In the early 2000s, General Motors (GM) faced significant challenges as the automotive industry began to undergo rapid technological changes. The rise of digital technology, data analytics, and connected vehicles meant that GM needed to rethink its approach to IT. At that time, the IT department was largely reactive, focusing on maintaining existing systems rather than driving innovation. The company recognized that, to remain competitive, it needed to elevate the role of IT from a support function to a strategic partner.

Task:
The task was to transform GM's IT leadership into a more strategic role that would drive digital innovation and support the company's broader business objectives. This required a shift from focusing on managing technology infrastructure to leading digital transformation initiatives that could enhance customer experience, optimize operations, and position GM as a leader in the automotive industry.

Action:
In 2012, GM appointed Randy Mott as CIO, a seasoned IT leader known for his strategic vision and leadership in digital transformation. Mott initiated a comprehensive overhaul of GM's IT strategy, which included:

1. **Insourcing IT Operations:** Mott reversed GM's long-standing practice of outsourcing IT operations, bringing more than 90% of IT work back in-house. This move was designed to give GM greater control over its technology initiatives and enable faster innovation.

2. **Building a Strategic IT Workforce:** Mott focused on recruiting top IT talent and building a team capable of driving innovation. He emphasized the importance of aligning IT talent with the company's strategic goals and fostering a culture of continuous learning and development.

3. **Digital Transformation Initiatives:** Under Mott's leadership, GM launched several digital initiatives, including the development of the OnStar telematics system, which provided customers with connected vehicle services. This project required close collaboration between IT and business units to ensure that technology aligned with customer needs and business objectives.

4. **Data-Driven Decision Making:** Mott prioritized the use of data analytics to drive decision-making across the company. By leveraging big data, GM gained insights into customer behavior, optimized supply chain operations, and improved product development processes.

Result:
As a result of these efforts, GM successfully transformed its IT function into a strategic asset that played a central role in the company's digital transformation. The insourcing of IT operations enabled faster innovation and greater agility, while the focus on building a

Mastering IT Leadership and Management, Strategies for Success in the Digital Age

strategic IT workforce ensured that the company had the talent needed to lead in a rapidly changing industry. The OnStar system became a significant competitive advantage, enhancing GM's brand and providing valuable services to customers. Overall, GM's approach to IT leadership allowed the company to navigate the complexities of the digital age and maintain its position as a leader in the automotive industry.

This case study illustrates the evolving role of IT leaders from technical experts to strategic business leaders who drive innovation and align technology with organizational goals. It highlights the importance of vision, strategic thinking, and the ability to lead change in achieving successful digital transformation.

Mastering IT Leadership and Management, Strategies for Success in the Digital Age

Best Practices

1. **Embrace Strategic Thinking:** IT leaders must evolve from being merely technical experts to becoming strategic thinkers. This involves understanding the broader business context, aligning technology initiatives with organizational goals, and anticipating future trends. Leaders should prioritize strategic decisions that drive long-term value rather than focusing solely on immediate technical challenges.

2. **Foster Continuous Learning and Adaptation:** The rapid pace of technological change demands that IT leaders cultivate a culture of continuous learning within their teams. Leaders should encourage their teams to stay updated on emerging technologies and industry trends, ensuring that their skills and knowledge remain relevant.

3. **Develop Strong Communication Skills:** Effective IT leaders must translate technical jargon into business terms that are easily understood by non-technical stakeholders. Building relationships with business leaders and fostering cross-functional collaboration are critical to ensuring that IT is fully integrated into the organization's strategic objectives.

4. **Lead with a Vision:** Successful IT leaders articulate a clear, compelling vision for how technology will drive business success. This vision should be aligned with the organization's goals and communicated effectively to all stakeholders. Leaders should set strategic objectives that guide the IT function toward achieving this vision.

5. **Promote Innovation and Change:** IT leaders should not only manage existing technology but also drive innovation and lead digital transformation initiatives. This involves staying informed about emerging technologies, understanding their potential impact on the business, and fostering a culture that embraces change.

Mastering IT Leadership and Management, Strategies for Success in the Digital Age

Lessons Learned

1. **Shift from Technical to Strategic Focus:** The evolution of IT leadership from a technical role to a strategic one has been driven by the increasing complexity of technology in business operations. Modern IT leaders are expected to contribute to business strategy and drive innovation, rather than simply maintaining IT infrastructure.

2. **Importance of Business Acumen:** IT leaders who understand business principles, including financial management, operations, and customer service, are better equipped to align technology initiatives with business goals. This holistic understanding allows them to make informed decisions that benefit the entire organization.

3. **The Role of IT in Digital Transformation:** As exemplified by the transformation at General Motors under Randy Mott's leadership, IT leaders play a critical role in driving digital transformation. By insourcing IT operations, building strategic IT teams, and prioritizing data-driven decision-making, IT leaders can turn technology into a competitive advantage.

4. **Managing Change is Key:** IT leaders are often at the forefront of organizational change, whether it's implementing new technologies or leading digital transformation. Successfully managing change requires not only technical expertise but also the ability to engage and motivate teams, communicate effectively, and address the human aspects of change.

By incorporating these best practices and lessons learned, IT leaders can effectively navigate the complexities of modern technology and drive their organizations toward success in the digital age.

Mastering IT Leadership and Management, Strategies for Success in the Digital Age

Conclusion

The role of IT leaders has undergone a profound transformation, evolving from a purely technical focus to a strategic one that is integral to the success of modern organizations. As explored in this chapter, IT leaders are no longer just the custodians of technology; they are key drivers of business innovation, growth, and competitive advantage.

The historical perspective provided a foundation for understanding how IT leadership has shifted in response to technological advancements and the increasing importance of IT in business strategy. The transition from technical expert to strategic leader highlights the expanding scope of responsibilities for IT leaders, requiring them to balance their technical expertise with business acumen, leadership skills, and a forward-thinking mindset.

Key competencies of modern IT leaders, such as strategic vision, communication, and change management, are now essential for navigating the complexities of today's digital landscape. IT leaders must be adept at aligning technology initiatives with business goals, fostering collaboration across departments, and leading their teams through continuous change and innovation.

As we conclude Chapter 1, it's clear that the role of IT leaders will continue to evolve as technology advances and business environments become more dynamic. Those who embrace this evolution, develop the necessary skills, and remain adaptable will be well-positioned to lead their organizations to success in the digital age. The journey of IT leadership is ongoing, and the insights gained in this chapter provide a strong foundation for exploring the further complexities and challenges that lie ahead in subsequent chapters.

Mastering IT Leadership and Management, Strategies for Success in the Digital Age

Quizzes

I. Multiple Choice Questions:

1. **What was the primary focus of IT leaders in the early days of computing?**

    A. Driving innovation
    B. Managing hardware and software
    C. Aligning IT with business strategy
    D. Leading digital transformation

2. **The transition from a technical expert to a strategic leader in IT involves:**

    A. Focusing solely on technical proficiency
    B. Maintaining the status quo in IT operations
    C. Understanding how technology creates value for the organization
    D. Managing hardware and software issues

3. **Which of the following is NOT a key competency of modern IT leaders?**

    A. Technical Acumen
    B. Business Acumen
    C. Risk Management
    D. Product Development

4. **The transformation of IT leadership at General Motors (GM) under Randy Mott involved which key initiative?**

    A. Outsourcing IT operations
    B. Focusing solely on hardware management
    C. Insourcing IT operations to drive innovation
    D. Ignoring digital transformation initiatives

II. True/False Questions:

1. IT leaders today are expected to be both technologists and strategists. (True/False)
2. The role of IT leaders has remained the same since the early days of computing. (True/False)
3. Strategic thinking is not necessary for modern IT leaders. (True/False)
4. Effective communication with non-technical stakeholders is increasingly important for IT leaders. (True/False)

Mastering IT Leadership and Management, Strategies for Success in the Digital Age

Exercises

I. Case Study Analysis:
   - **Objective:** Analyze the transformation of IT leadership at General Motors (GM) as described in the chapter.
   - **Instructions:**
     1. Summarize the key actions taken by Randy Mott to transform IT leadership at GM.
     2. Identify the challenges GM faced before this transformation and how the changes addressed these challenges.
     3. Discuss the outcomes of these initiatives and what lessons can be applied to your own organization.

II. Role Reflection:
   - **Objective:** Reflect on the transition from a technical expert to a strategic leader.
   - **Instructions:**
     1. Consider your current role or a role you aspire to in IT leadership.
     2. Write a brief reflection on how you can shift your focus from technical proficiency to strategic leadership.
     3. Identify three actions you can take to develop key competencies of a modern IT leader, such as strategic vision, business acumen, and risk management.

III. Vision Development Exercise:
   - **Objective:** Practice developing a strategic vision for an IT department.
   - **Instructions:**
     1. Imagine you are the CIO of an organization undergoing digital transformation.
     2. Draft a strategic vision for the IT department that aligns with the organization's business goals.
     3. Outline the key steps you would take to communicate this vision to your team and other stakeholders.

IV. SWOT Analysis:
   - **Objective:** Conduct a SWOT analysis based on the role of IT leadership.
   - **Instructions:**
     1. Identify the Strengths, Weaknesses, Opportunities, and Threats associated with the evolving role of IT leaders in your organization.
     2. Discuss how you would leverage strengths and opportunities to overcome weaknesses and threats.
     3. Present your analysis to a peer or mentor and gather feedback.

Mastering IT Leadership and Management, Strategies for Success in the Digital Age

V. Group Discussion:
- **Objective:** Facilitate a group discussion on the key competencies of modern IT leaders.
- **Instructions:**
    1. Organize a discussion group with colleagues or peers in IT leadership roles.
    2. Discuss the key competencies outlined in the chapter, such as technical acumen, business acumen, and leadership skills.
    3. Each participant should share examples from their own experience that demonstrate these competencies in action.
    4. Conclude the discussion by identifying common challenges and strategies for further developing these competencies.

These quizzes and exercises are designed to reinforce the concepts covered in Chapter 1 and help learners apply these ideas in practical, reflective, and collaborative ways.

Mastering IT Leadership and Management, Strategies for Success in the Digital Age

Chapter 2: IT Leadership vs. IT Management

"MANAGEMENT IS DOING THINGS RIGHT; LEADERSHIP IS DOING THE RIGHT THINGS."

— Peter Drucker

Defining Leadership and Management in the IT Context

In the realm of Information Technology (IT), the roles of leadership and management are often intertwined, yet they serve distinct functions. Understanding the differences between these roles is crucial for IT professionals who aspire to excel in both capacities.

Leadership in IT: Leadership is primarily about setting a vision, inspiring and motivating teams, and driving change. IT leaders are responsible for creating a strategic direction for the technology function, aligning IT goals with the broader objectives of the organization, and fostering a culture of innovation. Leadership in IT is forward-looking—anticipating future trends, identifying opportunities for growth, and ensuring that the organization is prepared to meet the challenges of an evolving technological landscape.

Management in IT: On the other hand, management focuses on the execution of strategies, the organization of resources, and the efficient operation of IT functions. IT managers are responsible for planning, budgeting, staffing, and controlling day-to-day operations. They ensure that projects are completed on time and within budget, that systems are reliable and secure, and that the IT department operates smoothly. Management in IT is about maintaining stability—ensuring that the organization's technology infrastructure supports business operations effectively and efficiently.

While leadership and management are distinct, both are essential to the success of an IT organization. Effective IT professionals must be able to both lead and manage—setting a strategic direction while ensuring that day-to-day operations run smoothly.

Mastering IT Leadership and Management, Strategies for Success in the Digital Age

Differences and Overlaps Between Leadership and Management

Vision vs. Execution: The most fundamental difference between leadership and management lies in their focus. Leadership is visionary—it's about setting a direction for the future and inspiring others to follow that direction. Management, by contrast, is about execution—turning that vision into reality through careful planning, organization, and control. While IT leaders focus on where the organization is going, IT managers focus on how to get there.

Innovation vs. Stability: Leadership often involves driving change and innovation. IT leaders are tasked with identifying new technologies, spearheading digital transformation initiatives, and encouraging a culture of creativity and experimentation. Management, however, is more concerned with maintaining stability. IT managers are responsible for ensuring that existing systems are reliable, processes are efficient, and the organization can continue to operate smoothly even as it undergoes change.

Inspiration vs. Supervision: Leadership involves inspiring and motivating teams. IT leaders must be able to communicate a compelling vision and persuade others to buy into it. They build relationships, foster collaboration, and create an environment where team members are motivated to achieve their best. Management, on the other hand, involves supervising and controlling. IT managers are responsible for setting objectives, monitoring performance, and ensuring that team members meet their goals.

Change vs. Continuity: Leadership is inherently about change. IT leaders act as agents of change, pushing the organization to innovate, adapt, and grow. Management, by contrast, is about continuity. IT managers ensure that the organization's operations are consistent, predictable, and reliable. They focus on maintaining the status quo while implementing the leader's vision.

Strategic vs. Tactical: Leadership is strategic, focusing on long-term goals and the big picture. IT leaders think about where the organization needs to be in the future and what must be done to get there. Management is tactical, focusing on short-term objectives and the details of execution. IT managers concentrate on what needs to be done today to meet the organization's immediate needs.

While these differences are significant, it's important to recognize that leadership and management are not mutually exclusive. In fact, the most effective IT professionals are those who can blend leadership and management skills, balancing the need for vision and innovation with the need for execution and stability.

Mastering IT Leadership and Management, Strategies for Success in the Digital Age

Balancing Leadership and Management Responsibilities

For IT professionals, finding the right balance between leadership and management responsibilities is key to success. This balance is not always easy to achieve, especially in fast-paced environments where both strategic direction and operational efficiency are crucial.

1. Understanding Your Role: The first step in balancing leadership and management responsibilities is understanding your role within the organization. Are you primarily responsible for setting strategic direction, or are you more focused on managing day-to-day operations? Knowing where your primary responsibilities lie will help you allocate your time and energy appropriately.

2. Delegating Effectively: Effective delegation is critical for balancing leadership and management. As an IT leader, you may be tempted to involve yourself in the details of project management or technical troubleshooting. However, it's important to delegate these tasks to your team, allowing you to focus on higher-level strategic activities. Trusting your team and empowering them to take ownership of their tasks will free you up to concentrate on leadership responsibilities.

3. Staying Grounded in Operations: While it's important to focus on leadership, IT leaders cannot afford to be completely disconnected from operations. Understanding the day-to-day challenges your team faces and staying informed about the status of key projects will help you make better strategic decisions. It's a delicate balance—staying grounded in operations without becoming bogged down in the details.

4. Continuous Learning and Adaptation: The balance between leadership and management will shift over time, depending on the needs of the organization. IT professionals must be willing to adapt and learn, continuously developing both their leadership and management skills. This includes staying up to date with industry trends, seeking out mentorship and coaching, and being open to feedback.

5. Building a Strong Team: Finally, balancing leadership and management is easier when you have a strong team in place. Surround yourself with capable managers who can handle the operational aspects of IT, allowing you to focus on strategic leadership. At the same time, cultivate leaders within your team who can take on leadership responsibilities as needed. A strong, capable team will help you achieve the right balance between leadership and management.

Mastering IT Leadership and Management, Strategies for Success in the Digital Age

Industry Case Study: Microsoft's Dual Approach to IT Leadership and Management

Situation:
In the early 2010s, Microsoft faced several challenges that necessitated a clear distinction between IT leadership and IT management. The company was contending with the rapid evolution of technology, changing consumer behaviors, and increased competition from rivals like Apple and Google. Simultaneously, its existing IT infrastructure required consistent maintenance and optimization to support ongoing operations. These challenges underscored the need for a balanced approach to IT leadership and management—where both strategic innovation and operational excellence were prioritized.

Task:
Microsoft's IT leadership had a twofold task: drive innovation and strategic growth through visionary leadership while ensuring that day-to-day IT operations were managed efficiently and reliably. This required a clear delineation between IT leadership, which focused on setting a strategic direction and driving innovation, and IT management, which concentrated on executing these strategies and maintaining operational stability.

Action:
Under the leadership of Satya Nadella, who became CEO in 2014, Microsoft implemented a dual approach to IT leadership and management:

1. **Visionary Leadership:** Nadella emphasized the importance of innovation and strategic vision, steering Microsoft towards cloud computing and AI as key areas for growth. He articulated a clear vision for the company's future, moving away from its reliance on the Windows operating system and toward a cloud-first, mobile-first strategy. This strategic shift was pivotal in transforming Microsoft's business model and positioning it as a leader in cloud services with platforms like Azure.

2. **Operational Management:** Simultaneously, Microsoft's IT management focused on executing the strategic vision set by leadership. This included optimizing the company's existing IT infrastructure to support new cloud-based services and ensuring the reliability and security of its products. IT managers were responsible for managing resources, controlling budgets, and maintaining the stability of Microsoft's extensive global IT operations.

3. **Leadership Development Programs:** Microsoft invested in leadership development programs to cultivate both visionary leaders and effective managers within its IT teams. These programs focused on building strategic thinking, innovation, and management skills, ensuring the company could sustain its dual approach to leadership and management.

4. **Enhancing Collaboration:** Microsoft fostered close collaboration between its IT leaders and managers. Regular alignment meetings and communication channels were established to ensure that the strategic goals set by leadership were effectively translated into actionable plans and efficiently executed by management.

Mastering IT Leadership and Management, Strategies for Success in the Digital Age

Result:
As a result of these actions, Microsoft successfully navigated one of the most significant transformations in its history. The clear distinction and collaboration between IT leadership and IT management allowed the company to innovate rapidly while maintaining operational excellence. Under Nadella's leadership, Microsoft's market value soared, and the company reclaimed its position as a leading technology giant. The strategic shift towards cloud computing and AI not only revitalized Microsoft's product offerings but also drove substantial revenue growth. Meanwhile, strong operational management ensured that these new services were reliable, secure, and scalable, further solidifying Microsoft's competitive advantage.

This case study illustrates the importance of balancing IT leadership and management. By clearly defining and differentiating these roles, organizations like Microsoft can achieve both innovation and stability, driving long-term success in a rapidly changing technological landscape.

Mastering IT Leadership and Management, Strategies for Success in the Digital Age

Best Practices

1. **Balance Vision with Execution:** Effective IT leadership requires balancing visionary leadership and operational management. IT leaders should set a clear strategic direction, while IT managers focus on executing that vision through careful planning, resource allocation, and performance monitoring. Leaders should communicate the big picture, and managers should ensure that day-to-day activities align with this vision.

2. **Cultivate Collaborative Leadership and Management:** The most successful IT initiatives often involve close collaboration between leaders and managers. IT leaders should foster a collaborative environment where managers feel empowered to contribute their expertise in project execution and resource management. Regular alignment meetings between leaders and managers can ensure that strategic goals are effectively translated into actionable plans.

3. **Adapt Leadership Style to Situations:** IT professionals must be flexible in their approach, understanding when to lead with a visionary mindset and when to manage with a focus on stability and execution. For example, during times of transformation, a visionary approach may be needed, while during steady-state operations, a focus on efficiency and stability is crucial.

4. **Leverage Data for Decision-Making:** Both IT leadership and management should utilize data-driven decision-making processes. Leaders can use data to inform strategic decisions and anticipate future trends, while managers can apply data to optimize operations, monitor progress, and adjust tactics as needed. This ensures that decisions at both levels are based on solid evidence rather than intuition alone.

5. **Develop Leadership and Management Skills Equally:** IT professionals should aim to develop both leadership and management skills, understanding that these roles are complementary. Leaders should be capable of managing when needed, and managers should be able to step into leadership roles as required. Investing in training and development programs that build both sets of skills will prepare IT professionals to handle diverse challenges.

Mastering IT Leadership and Management, Strategies for Success in the Digital Age

Lessons Learned

1. **Distinction Between Leadership and Management:** Understanding the differences between leadership and management is crucial for the success of IT initiatives. Leadership involves setting a vision and inspiring teams, while management focuses on executing strategies and maintaining operational efficiency. This distinction allows organizations to effectively allocate responsibilities and ensure that both strategic direction and day-to-day operations are handled appropriately.

2. **Importance of Clear Communication:** The success of IT initiatives often hinges on clear communication between leaders and managers. Leaders must clearly articulate the vision, goals, and strategic priorities, while managers need to communicate progress, challenges, and resource needs. Misalignment in communication can lead to confusion, delays, and suboptimal outcomes.

3. **Value of Leadership in Driving Innovation:** Visionary leadership is essential for driving innovation and guiding organizations through change. Leaders who focus on long-term goals and encourage creativity within their teams are more likely to identify new opportunities and spearhead transformative projects. As seen in Microsoft's dual approach under Satya Nadella, visionary leadership can significantly impact an organization's ability to innovate and grow.

4. **Management's Role in Ensuring Stability:** While leadership drives change, management ensures that the organization remains stable during transitions. Effective management involves maintaining the reliability and security of IT systems, managing budgets, and ensuring that projects are completed on time and within scope. This balance between change and continuity is key to sustaining long-term success.

5. **The Need for Continuous Learning:** Both IT leaders and managers must commit to continuous learning and adaptation. The rapidly changing technology landscape means that strategies and tactics that worked in the past may not be effective in the future. Leaders and managers must stay updated on industry trends, emerging technologies, and best practices to ensure that their skills remain relevant and their approaches effective.

By integrating these best practices and lessons learned, IT leaders and managers can effectively navigate their respective roles, ensuring that their organizations achieve both immediate operational goals and long-term strategic success.

Mastering IT Leadership and Management, Strategies for Success in the Digital Age

Conclusion

In the realm of Information Technology, understanding the distinction and interplay between leadership and management is crucial for the success of any organization. As explored in this chapter, while IT leadership and IT management serve different functions, they are both essential and complementary roles within the IT ecosystem.

Leadership in IT is about setting a vision, inspiring and motivating teams, and driving innovation and change. IT leaders are tasked with aligning technology strategies with broader business goals, fostering a culture of creativity, and steering the organization toward a future where technology acts as a key enabler of success.

Management, on the other hand, focuses on the execution of strategies, ensuring that day-to-day operations run smoothly and that projects are completed efficiently and effectively. IT managers are responsible for organizing resources, controlling budgets, and maintaining the stability and reliability of IT systems that support the organization's operations.

The differences between leadership and management—vision vs. execution, innovation vs. stability, and inspiration vs. supervision—highlight the unique value each role brings to an organization. However, the most effective IT professionals are those who can skillfully balance both leadership and management responsibilities. By blending strategic vision with operational excellence, IT leaders and managers can work together to achieve both immediate and long-term objectives.

As we conclude Chapter 2, it is evident that mastering the balance between IT leadership and management is key to navigating the complexities of the IT landscape. By understanding the distinctions and overlaps between these roles, IT professionals can better position themselves to drive their organizations forward, ensuring both the successful implementation of technology initiatives and the achievement of strategic business goals. The insights gained in this chapter lay the groundwork for further exploration of how IT leaders can build a vision, manage change, and lead their teams through the challenges of the digital age.

Mastering IT Leadership and Management, Strategies for Success in the Digital Age

Quizzes

I. Multiple Choice Questions:

1. **Which of the following best describes the primary focus of IT leadership?**

    A. Managing day-to-day IT operations
    B. Executing strategies and maintaining systems
    C. Setting a vision and driving innovation
    D. Ensuring projects are completed on time

2. **IT management is primarily concerned with:**

    A. Anticipating future technology trends
    B. Motivating and inspiring teams
    C. The execution of strategies and maintaining stability
    D. Aligning IT goals with broader business objectives

3. **Which of the following is a key difference between IT leadership and IT management?**

    A. Leadership focuses on vision; management focuses on execution.
    B. Leadership is about stability; management is about change.
    C. Leadership is tactical; management is strategic.
    D. Leadership manages resources; management inspires teams.

4. **The dual approach to IT leadership and management at Microsoft under Satya Nadella emphasized:**

    A. Exclusive focus on hardware management
    B. Outsourcing IT operations to external vendors
    C. Balancing visionary leadership with operational management
    D. Limiting innovation to maintain stability

II. True/False Questions:
1. IT leaders are primarily responsible for managing day-to-day IT operations. (True/False)
2. Effective IT leadership requires the ability to set a strategic direction for the future. (True/False)
3. IT management focuses on change and innovation within an organization. (True/False)
4. IT leaders and IT managers must work together to ensure both vision and execution are achieved. (True/False)

Mastering IT Leadership and Management, Strategies for Success in the Digital Age

Exercises

I. Case Study Reflection:
   - **Objective:** Analyze the dual approach to IT leadership and management at Microsoft.
   - **Instructions:**
     1. Summarize the actions taken by Satya Nadella to balance leadership and management within Microsoft.
     2. Identify the key outcomes of this balanced approach and how it contributed to Microsoft's success.
     3. Reflect on how a similar approach could be applied in your own organization, particularly in balancing strategic vision with operational efficiency.

II. Leadership vs. Management Role-Playing:
   - **Objective:** Understand the differences between IT leadership and IT management through role-playing.
   - **Instructions:**
     1. Split into pairs, with one person taking on the role of an IT leader and the other as an IT manager.
     2. The IT leader will present a strategic vision for a new technology initiative, while the IT manager will outline how to implement this vision practically, addressing potential challenges.
     3. After the role-play, discuss how the roles complemented each other and what challenges arose during the collaboration.

III. Vision and Execution Planning:
   - **Objective:** Develop a plan that incorporates both IT leadership and management aspects.
   - **Instructions:**
     1. Choose a hypothetical IT project that requires both strategic leadership and detailed management.
     2. As an IT leader, outline the strategic goals and vision for this project.
     3. As an IT manager, create a detailed execution plan that includes timelines, resource allocation, and risk management strategies.
     4. Present your plan, highlighting how both leadership and management perspectives are essential for the project's success.

IV. Self-Assessment:
   - **Objective:** Reflect on your own strengths and areas for improvement in IT leadership and management.
   - **Instructions:**

Mastering IT Leadership and Management, Strategies for Success in the Digital Age

1. Assess your current role: Are your responsibilities more aligned with IT leadership or IT management?
2. Identify three strengths you possess in your current role and three areas where you can improve.
3. Develop an action plan to enhance your skills in either leadership, management, or both, depending on your career goals.

V. Group Discussion:
- **Objective:** Explore the interplay between IT leadership and management.
- **Instructions:**
    1. In a group setting, discuss real-world scenarios where the balance between leadership and management was critical to success.
    2. Each participant should share an example from their experience or research, focusing on how the roles of IT leader and IT manager complemented each other.
    3. Conclude the discussion by identifying best practices for balancing these roles in different organizational contexts.

These quizzes and exercises are designed to help readers of Chapter 2 better understand the distinct but complementary roles of IT leadership and management, and to apply these concepts in practical scenarios.

Mastering IT Leadership and Management, Strategies for Success in the Digital Age

Chapter 3: Building a Vision for IT

"THE BEST WAY TO PREDICT THE FUTURE IS TO CREATE IT."
— **Peter Drucker**

Creating a Strategic IT Vision

A strategic IT vision is not just about the direction of the technology department but how it aligns with and drives the overall goals of the organization. As an IT leader, one of your most critical responsibilities is to create and articulate a clear, compelling vision that inspires your team and guides decision-making. A well-crafted IT vision serves as a roadmap for the future, helping the organization navigate the rapidly changing technological landscape and remain competitive.

1. **Understanding the Business Objectives:** The foundation of any IT vision is a deep understanding of the organization's business objectives. What are the company's long-term goals? What challenges does it face? How can IT support these objectives? Whether the goal is to enter new markets, enhance customer experience, improve operational efficiency, or innovate with new products, the IT vision must be directly linked to these overarching business goals.

2. **Engaging Stakeholders:** Building a strategic IT vision is not a solitary task. It requires input and buy-in from key stakeholders across the organization. Engage with executives, department heads, and other key figures to understand their needs, concerns, and expectations. This collaborative approach ensures that the IT vision is not only aligned with business objectives but is also supported by those who will help bring it to life.

3. **Assessing the Current State of IT:** Before planning for the future, it's essential to have a clear picture of where the organization currently stands in terms of IT capabilities. Conduct a thorough assessment of your current IT infrastructure, systems, and processes. Identify strengths, weaknesses, opportunities, and threats (SWOT analysis). This assessment provides a baseline from which to build your vision, highlighting areas that need improvement and those that can be leveraged for future growth.

4. **Identifying Emerging Technologies:** A forward-looking IT vision must consider the potential impact of emerging technologies. Stay informed about trends in AI, cloud computing, cybersecurity, data analytics, and other relevant fields. Determine how these technologies could be harnessed to support the organization's goals. While innovation is important, it's equally crucial to remain realistic—focus on technologies that are not only cutting-edge but also applicable and beneficial to your specific business context.

5. **Articulating the Vision:** Once you have a clear understanding of the business objectives, stakeholder needs, current IT capabilities, and emerging technologies, it's time to articulate your vision. Your IT vision should be clear, concise, and inspiring. It

Mastering IT Leadership and Management, Strategies for Success in the Digital Age

should outline where you want the IT function to be in the next 3 to 5 years and how it will support the business in achieving its goals. The vision statement should be easy to understand and communicate, resonating with both IT professionals and business leaders.

6. **Setting Strategic Objectives:** To turn the IT vision into reality, you need to set clear, measurable strategic objectives. These objectives should align with the broader business strategy and serve as milestones on the path to achieving the vision. Examples might include modernizing the IT infrastructure, improving cybersecurity posture, enabling digital transformation, or enhancing data analytics capabilities. Each objective should be accompanied by specific, measurable, achievable, relevant, and time-bound (SMART) goals.

Mastering IT Leadership and Management, Strategies for Success in the Digital Age

Aligning IT Strategy with Business Objectives

The success of your IT vision hinges on its alignment with the organization's broader business strategy. IT cannot operate in isolation—its initiatives must support and enhance the company's overall goals. This alignment ensures that IT investments provide tangible value to the organization and that technology is leveraged strategically to drive growth and innovation.

1. **Communicating with Business Leaders:** Effective communication with business leaders is essential for aligning IT strategy with business objectives. Regularly engage with the CEO, CFO, and other key executives to understand the company's strategic priorities. Share your IT vision with them and seek their feedback to ensure it aligns with the organization's direction. This ongoing dialogue builds trust and ensures that IT initiatives are seen as integral to the company's success.

2. **Translating Business Goals into IT Initiatives:** Once you understand the business objectives, translate them into specific IT initiatives. For example, if the business goal is to improve customer experience, the IT strategy might include initiatives such as implementing a new CRM system, enhancing mobile app functionality, or utilizing data analytics to personalize customer interactions. Each IT initiative should have a clear connection to the business goal it supports, demonstrating how technology will enable the organization to achieve its objectives.

3. **Prioritizing IT Investments:** Not all IT initiatives can be pursued simultaneously, so it's crucial to prioritize them based on their strategic value. Collaborate with business leaders to identify which initiatives will have the greatest impact on the organization's goals. Consider factors such as ROI, risk, resource availability, and alignment with the business strategy. By prioritizing initiatives that deliver the most value, you can ensure that IT resources are allocated effectively and that the IT function is recognized as a key driver of business success.

4. **Monitoring and Adjusting the Strategy:** Business strategies evolve, and so must the IT strategy. Establish mechanisms for regularly reviewing and adjusting your IT strategy to ensure it remains aligned with the company's changing needs. This could involve quarterly strategy reviews, regular meetings with business leaders, or continuous monitoring of key performance indicators (KPIs). By staying agile and responsive, you can ensure that your IT strategy continues to deliver value as the business environment changes.

Mastering IT Leadership and Management, Strategies for Success in the Digital Age

Communicating the Vision to Stakeholders

A vision, no matter how well-crafted, is only effective if it is communicated clearly and embraced by those responsible for executing it. As an IT leader, it's your responsibility to ensure that the IT vision is understood and supported by everyone in the organization—from the C-suite to front-line IT staff.

1. **Tailoring the Message:** Different stakeholders have different concerns and priorities, so it's important to customize your communication for each audience. For executives, emphasize how the IT vision supports business goals and delivers ROI. For IT staff, focus on how the vision will improve efficiency, enhance their work experience, and create opportunities for professional growth. For end-users, highlight how IT initiatives will make their jobs easier and more productive.

2. **Building a Narrative:** People are more likely to embrace a vision if it's presented as part of a compelling narrative. Create a story around your IT vision—why it's important, how it will benefit the organization, and the role each individual plays in bringing it to life. Use industry insights and case studies to illustrate how the vision will address current challenges and capitalize on opportunities.

3. **Engaging Stakeholders Early:** Involve key stakeholders in the development of the IT vision from the outset. This ensures the vision aligns with their needs and fosters a sense of ownership and commitment. Hold workshops, brainstorming sessions, and one-on-one meetings to gather input and feedback. By engaging stakeholders early, you can build a coalition of support to help drive the vision forward.

4. **Using Multiple Channels:** Effective communication requires reaching your audience through multiple channels. In addition to formal presentations and meetings, use emails, newsletters, intranet posts, and social media to share the IT vision. Visual aids such as infographics and videos can make the vision more accessible and engaging.

5. **Reinforcing the Message:** Communicating the IT vision is not a one-time event—it requires continuous reinforcement. Regularly update stakeholders on the progress of IT initiatives, celebrate successes, and address challenges openly. Use every opportunity to connect ongoing work to the broader vision, reminding everyone of the ultimate goal and maintaining momentum.

Mastering IT Leadership and Management, Strategies for Success in the Digital Age

Industry Case Study: IBM's Strategic Vision for IT Transformation

Situation:
In the early 2010s, IBM faced significant challenges as it sought to transition from a traditional hardware and software company to a leader in cloud computing, AI, and data analytics. The rapid pace of technological change and the emergence of new competitors required IBM to rethink its IT strategy and align its technology initiatives with its broader business objectives. While the company's existing IT infrastructure and strategy were robust, they were not fully optimized to support the new direction IBM needed to take to remain competitive in a rapidly evolving market.

Task:
IBM's IT leadership was tasked with developing and articulating a clear, strategic vision for IT that would guide the company through this transformation. This vision needed to align with IBM's goal of becoming a leader in cloud computing, AI, and data analytics while ensuring that its IT initiatives supported business growth, operational efficiency, and innovation.

Action:
To build a strategic IT vision, IBM's leadership undertook the following steps:

1. **Conducting a Thorough Assessment:** IBM began by assessing its current IT landscape, identifying areas that required modernization and those that could be leveraged for growth. This involved evaluating existing infrastructure, processes, and capabilities while considering the organization's strategic goals and market trends.

2. **Engaging Stakeholders:** IBM involved key stakeholders from across the organization, including executives, business unit leaders, and IT team members, in the vision-building process. This collaborative approach ensured that the IT vision was comprehensive, relevant, and aligned with the business's needs.

3. **Defining Clear Objectives:** Based on the assessment and stakeholder input, IBM defined clear strategic objectives for its IT function. These objectives focused on areas such as digital transformation, enhancing operational efficiency, and leveraging emerging technologies like AI and cloud computing to drive innovation.

4. **Communicating the Vision:** IBM's leadership effectively communicated the IT vision across the organization, ensuring that all employees understood its importance and how it would be achieved. This ongoing communication helped maintain momentum and align all team members with the company's strategic direction.

5. **Implementing and Monitoring Progress:** IBM developed a strategic plan outlining the key initiatives, timelines, and resources required to achieve the IT vision. Regular monitoring and adjustments ensured that the company stayed on track and could address any challenges that arose during the transformation process.

Mastering IT Leadership and Management, Strategies for Success in the Digital Age

Result:
As a result of these efforts, IBM successfully transitioned into a leader in cloud computing, AI, and data analytics. The clear and strategic IT vision served as a roadmap for all technology-related initiatives, ensuring alignment with IBM's broader business goals. This alignment fostered greater innovation, operational efficiency, and competitive advantage. IBM's ability to communicate and execute its IT vision across the organization cultivated a sense of shared purpose and direction, motivating IT teams to contribute meaningfully to the company's objectives. The successful implementation of this strategic IT vision positioned IBM for sustained growth and success in the digital age, allowing it to remain a key player in the technology industry.

Mastering IT Leadership and Management, Strategies for Success in the Digital Age

Best Practices

1. **Align IT Vision with Business Objectives:** The foundation of any successful IT vision is its alignment with the organization's broader business goals. IT leaders should collaborate with business executives to understand the company's long-term objectives and ensure that the IT vision directly supports these goals. This alignment guarantees that IT initiatives add tangible value to the business and contribute to its overall success.

2. **Engage Stakeholders Early and Often:** Building an IT vision is a collaborative effort that requires input from key stakeholders across the organization. IT leaders should involve executives, department heads, and end-users in the vision-building process to ensure that the vision addresses their needs and has their support. Engaging stakeholders early helps build consensus and fosters a sense of ownership and commitment to the IT vision.

3. **Conduct a Thorough Assessment of Current IT Capabilities:** Before crafting a vision for the future, IT leaders must clearly understand the current state of their organization's IT infrastructure, systems, and processes. A thorough assessment, including a SWOT analysis, helps identify strengths to leverage, weaknesses to address, and opportunities for improvement. This assessment provides a realistic foundation for building a vision that is both ambitious and achievable.

4. **Incorporate Emerging Technologies Thoughtfully:** A forward-looking IT vision should consider the potential impact of emerging technologies. IT leaders should stay informed about trends in AI, cloud computing, cybersecurity, and other relevant fields, evaluating how these technologies can be leveraged to support the organization's goals. However, it's important to focus on technologies that are not only cutting-edge but also practical and beneficial within the specific business context.

5. **Communicate the Vision Clearly and Compellingly:** Once the IT vision is developed, it must be communicated effectively to all stakeholders. IT leaders should articulate the vision in clear, concise, and inspiring language that resonates with both technical and non-technical audiences. Using multiple communication channels and regularly reinforcing the message ensures that the vision is understood and embraced throughout the organization.

6. **Set Strategic Objectives with SMART Goals:** Turning an IT vision into reality requires setting clear, measurable strategic objectives. These objectives should align with the broader business strategy and be broken down into specific, measurable, achievable, relevant, and time-bound (SMART) goals. This approach provides a roadmap for achieving the vision and allows progress to be tracked and adjusted as needed.

Mastering IT Leadership and Management, Strategies for Success in the Digital Age

Lessons Learned

1. **Importance of Strategic Alignment:** IT initiatives are most successful when they are directly aligned with the organization's strategic objectives. Without this alignment, IT efforts may be perceived as disconnected from the business, leading to a lack of support and suboptimal results. The process of aligning the IT vision with business goals should be ongoing, with regular reviews and adjustments as business priorities evolve.

2. **The Power of Stakeholder Involvement:** Engaging stakeholders in the vision-building process not only ensures that their needs are addressed but also builds a coalition of support for the vision. As demonstrated in IBM's strategic IT transformation, involving stakeholders early on can result in a more comprehensive and widely accepted vision, increasing the likelihood of successful implementation.

3. **The Need for Realistic Planning:** While it's important to be visionary, the IT vision must also be grounded in the reality of the organization's current capabilities and resources. Overly ambitious visions that do not account for existing limitations can lead to frustration, delays, and failure. A realistic assessment of the current state of IT, combined with thoughtful planning, ensures that the vision is achievable.

4. **Adapting to Technological Advances:** The technology landscape is constantly evolving, and IT leaders must be prepared to adapt their vision as new technologies emerge. However, not all emerging technologies will be relevant or beneficial to every organization. IT leaders must critically assess which technologies are likely to deliver the most value and focus their efforts on those that align with the business's strategic goals.

5. **Continuous Communication is Key:** Even the most well-crafted IT vision can fail if it is not effectively communicated. Continuous communication, using a variety of channels and tailored messages for different audiences, is essential to ensure that the vision is understood, embraced, and acted upon by all stakeholders. Regular updates on progress and achievements help maintain momentum and keep the vision at the forefront of the organization's efforts.

By following these best practices and learning from past experiences, IT leaders can build and implement a strategic vision that drives their organizations forward in the ever-changing digital landscape.

Mastering IT Leadership and Management, Strategies for Success in the Digital Age

Conclusion

Building a strategic vision for IT is one of the most critical responsibilities of an IT leader. A well-crafted IT vision not only sets the direction for the technology function but also ensures that IT initiatives are aligned with the organization's broader business objectives. As discussed in this chapter, creating and executing a vision for IT involves understanding the business's goals, engaging stakeholders, assessing the current state of IT, and identifying emerging technologies that can drive future success.

A strategic IT vision serves as a roadmap that guides decision-making, prioritizes investments, and inspires the IT team to achieve excellence. By aligning IT strategy with business objectives, IT leaders can ensure that technology is leveraged as a powerful enabler of business growth, innovation, and competitive advantage.

Effective communication is key to the success of any IT vision. IT leaders must articulate the vision clearly and compellingly, ensuring that all stakeholders—from executives to front-line IT staff—understand and are committed to the goals set forth. Engaging stakeholders early and often, building a compelling narrative, and using multiple communication channels are essential strategies for gaining buy-in and driving the vision forward.

As we conclude Chapter 3, it's evident that building a vision for IT is not a one-time task but an ongoing process requiring continuous alignment with the organization's evolving needs and the ever-changing technological landscape. IT leaders who master the art of vision-building and execution will be well-equipped to lead their organizations through the complexities and opportunities of the digital age. The insights and strategies discussed in this chapter provide a strong foundation for navigating the challenges of strategic IT management and ensuring that IT remains a vital contributor to the organization's success.

Mastering IT Leadership and Management, Strategies for Success in the Digital Age

Quizzes

I. Multiple Choice Questions:

1. What is the first step in creating a strategic IT vision?

    A. Communicating the vision to stakeholders
    B. Conducting a SWOT analysis
    C. Understanding the organization's business objectives
    D. Identifying emerging technologies

2. Which of the following best describes the role of stakeholders in building an IT vision?

    A. Stakeholders should be informed after the vision is finalized.
    B. Stakeholders should be involved early and throughout the vision-building process.
    C. Stakeholders are not necessary for the vision-building process.
    D. Stakeholders should only be involved if there are budget considerations.

3. Which of the following is NOT a recommended practice when articulating an IT vision?

    A. Using technical jargon to ensure accuracy
    B. Tailoring the message to different audiences
    C. Building a compelling narrative around the vision
    D. Using multiple communication channels to share the vision

4. What is the importance of setting strategic objectives with SMART goals in the context of an IT vision?

    A. To make the vision more aspirational
    B. To provide a clear roadmap for achieving the vision
    C. To focus on immediate, short-term wins
    D. To avoid involving stakeholders

II. True/False Questions:
1. A strategic IT vision should only focus on emerging technologies. (True/False)
2. Engaging stakeholders early in the process of building an IT vision increases the likelihood of successful implementation. (True/False)
3. A well-crafted IT vision does not need to be communicated beyond the IT department. (True/False)
4. Continuous communication and reinforcement are key to ensuring the IT vision is embraced throughout the organization. (True/False)

Mastering IT Leadership and Management, Strategies for Success in the Digital Age

Exercises

I. SWOT Analysis Exercise:
- **Objective:** Conduct a SWOT analysis to assess the current state of IT within your organization.
- **Instructions:**
    1. Identify the strengths, weaknesses, opportunities, and threats related to your organization's IT capabilities.
    2. Based on this analysis, propose one strategic initiative that could be included in your IT vision.
    3. Present your SWOT analysis and proposed initiative to a peer or mentor for feedback.

II. Vision Statement Workshop:
- **Objective:** Develop a clear and compelling vision statement for your IT department.
- **Instructions:**
    1. Draft a vision statement that aligns with your organization's broader business objectives.
    2. Ensure the vision statement is concise, inspiring, and understandable by both technical and non-technical stakeholders.
    3. Share the vision statement with your team and gather their feedback to refine it further.

III. Stakeholder Engagement Plan:
- **Objective:** Create a plan for engaging stakeholders in the IT vision-building process.
- **Instructions:**
    1. Identify the key stakeholders who should be involved in developing your IT vision.
    2. Outline the steps you will take to involve these stakeholders, including meetings, workshops, and feedback sessions.
    3. Develop a timeline for stakeholder engagement, ensuring their input is incorporated at critical points in the vision-building process.

IV. IT Vision Communication Strategy:
- **Objective:** Develop a communication strategy to effectively share your IT vision across the organization.
- **Instructions:**
    1. Identify the different audiences (e.g., executives, IT staff, end-users) that need to understand the IT vision.

Mastering IT Leadership and Management, Strategies for Success in the Digital Age

   2. Tailor the messaging for each audience, focusing on how the vision aligns with their needs and concerns.
   3. Choose multiple communication channels (e.g., emails, presentations, intranet postings) to disseminate the vision.
   4. Plan for ongoing communication to reinforce the vision and provide updates on progress.

V. Case Study Analysis:
   - **Objective:** Analyze the case study of IBM's Strategic Vision for IT Transformation provided in the chapter.
   - **Instructions:**
      1. Summarize the key steps IBM took to develop and implement its IT vision.
      2. Identify the challenges IBM faced and how they were addressed.
      3. Reflect on how the lessons from IBM's experience could be applied to your organization's IT vision development.

These exercises are designed to reinforce the key concepts discussed in Chapter 3, encouraging readers to apply these ideas in practical, reflective, and collaborative ways.

Mastering IT Leadership and Management, Strategies for Success in the Digital Age

Conclusion of Part 1: Foundations of IT Leadership

The foundation of IT leadership is rooted in the understanding that technology is no longer just a support function but a strategic driver of business success. Throughout Part 1 of this book, we have explored the evolving role of IT leaders, the distinctions between leadership and management, and the critical importance of building a strategic vision for IT. These foundational elements are essential for any IT leader aspiring to guide their organization through the complexities of the digital age.

The journey began with an examination of how the role of IT leaders has transformed over time. No longer confined to the back office, modern IT leaders are expected to be strategic thinkers, innovators, and change agents who can align technology initiatives with broader business goals. This evolution demands a diverse set of competencies, including strategic vision, communication skills, and the ability to lead through change.

We then explored the crucial distinction between IT leadership and IT management. While leadership is about setting direction, inspiring teams, and driving innovation, management focuses on executing strategies, ensuring operational efficiency, and maintaining stability. Both roles are vital, and the most effective IT professionals are those who can seamlessly integrate leadership and management to achieve organizational success.

Finally, we examined the process of building a strategic vision for IT—an essential task for any IT leader. A well-crafted vision provides a roadmap for the future, aligns IT initiatives with business objectives, and inspires the entire organization to pursue excellence. Communication and stakeholder engagement are key to turning this vision into reality, ensuring that all parts of the organization are aligned and committed to the shared goals.

As we conclude Part 1, it is clear that a strong foundation in IT leadership is the cornerstone of any successful IT strategy. By mastering the principles discussed in these chapters, IT leaders can position themselves and their organizations for long-term success in an increasingly complex and competitive environment. The insights gained here set the stage for further exploration into the essential skills, strategic management practices, and future trends that will shape the next generation of IT leadership.

Mastering IT Leadership and Management, Strategies for Success in the Digital Age

Part 2: Essential Skills for IT Leaders

"THE SINGLE BIGGEST WAY TO IMPACT AN ORGANIZATION IS TO FOCUS ON LEADERSHIP DEVELOPMENT. THERE IS ALMOST NO LIMIT TO THE POTENTIAL OF AN ORGANIZATION THAT RECRUITS GOOD PEOPLE, RAISES THEM UP AS LEADERS, AND CONTINUALLY DEVELOPS THEM."

— **John C. Maxwell**

Mastering IT Leadership and Management, Strategies for Success in the Digital Age

Chapter 4: Leading IT Teams

"THE STRENGTH OF THE TEAM IS EACH INDIVIDUAL MEMBER. THE STRENGTH OF EACH MEMBER IS THE TEAM."
— Phil Jackson

Building and Nurturing High-Performance IT Teams

Leading an IT team requires more than just technical expertise; it demands the ability to build and nurture a high-performance team that consistently delivers results. A successful IT leader must be skilled in identifying and developing talent, fostering collaboration, and creating an environment where team members feel motivated, valued, and empowered to contribute their best work.

1. **Identifying and Attracting Top Talent:** The foundation of a high-performance IT team lies in its people. As an IT leader, one of your primary responsibilities is to attract and hire top talent. This involves not only finding individuals with the right technical skills but also identifying those who have the potential to grow, adapt, and thrive in your organization's culture. When recruiting, look for candidates who demonstrate not just technical proficiency but also problem-solving abilities, a willingness to learn, and strong communication skills. Building a diverse team with a range of experiences and perspectives can also lead to more innovative solutions and better decision-making.

2. **Fostering Collaboration and Teamwork:** In today's IT environment, collaboration is key to success. The complexity of modern IT projects often requires input from multiple disciplines, including software development, network engineering, cybersecurity, and data analysis. As an IT leader, it's your role to foster a culture of collaboration where team members feel comfortable sharing ideas, asking for help, and working together to solve problems. Encourage open communication and ensure that team members have the tools and resources needed to collaborate effectively, whether they are in the same office or working remotely.

3. **Empowering and Motivating IT Professionals:** Empowering your team members means giving them the autonomy to make decisions and take ownership of their work. When individuals feel that they have control over their tasks and the ability to influence outcomes, they are more likely to be motivated and engaged. Provide clear goals and expectations, but allow your team the flexibility to determine how best to achieve them. Additionally, recognize and reward achievements, both big and small. Positive reinforcement can go a long way in maintaining motivation and fostering a culture of excellence.

4. **Developing Leadership Skills Within the Team:** Building a high-performance team also involves developing the next generation of leaders. Identify individuals within your team who show leadership potential and provide them with opportunities to grow their skills. This could include assigning them to lead projects, mentoring them, or

Mastering IT Leadership and Management, Strategies for Success in the Digital Age

offering access to leadership training and development programs. By nurturing leadership skills within your team, you create a pipeline of future leaders who can take on more responsibilities and contribute to the long-term success of the organization.

5. **Managing Team Dynamics:** High-performance teams are not without challenges. Conflicts can arise, especially in high-pressure environments where deadlines are tight and stakes are high. As an IT leader, it's important to proactively manage team dynamics. Address conflicts early and facilitate constructive discussions that focus on finding solutions rather than assigning blame. Promote a culture of respect and inclusion, ensuring that all team members feel valued and heard. By effectively managing team dynamics, you can maintain a positive and productive work environment.

Mastering IT Leadership and Management, Strategies for Success in the Digital Age

Leadership Styles in IT

Effective IT leadership requires a flexible approach to leadership styles, as different situations and team members may require different approaches. Understanding and adapting your leadership style to the needs of your team is crucial for driving performance and achieving organizational goals.

1. **Identifying and Attracting Top Talent:** The foundation of a high-performance IT team lies in its people. As an IT leader, one of your primary responsibilities is to attract and hire top talent. This involves not only finding individuals with the right technical skills but also identifying those who have the potential to grow, adapt, and thrive in your organization's culture. When recruiting, look for candidates who demonstrate not just technical proficiency but also problem-solving abilities, a willingness to learn, and strong communication skills. Building a diverse team with a range of experiences and perspectives can also lead to more innovative solutions and better decision-making.

2. **Fostering Collaboration and Teamwork:** In today's IT environment, collaboration is key to success. The complexity of modern IT projects often requires input from multiple disciplines, including software development, network engineering, cybersecurity, and data analysis. As an IT leader, it's your role to foster a culture of collaboration where team members feel comfortable sharing ideas, asking for help, and working together to solve problems. Encourage open communication and ensure that team members have the tools and resources needed to collaborate effectively, whether they are in the same office or working remotely.

3. **Empowering and Motivating IT Professionals:** Empowering your team members means giving them the autonomy to make decisions and take ownership of their work. When individuals feel that they have control over their tasks and the ability to influence outcomes, they are more likely to be motivated and engaged. Provide clear goals and expectations, but allow your team the flexibility to determine how best to achieve them. Additionally, recognize and reward achievements, both big and small. Positive reinforcement can go a long way in maintaining motivation and fostering a culture of excellence.

4. **Developing Leadership Skills Within the Team:** Building a high-performance team also involves developing the next generation of leaders. Identify individuals within your team who show leadership potential and provide them with opportunities to grow their skills. This could include assigning them to lead projects, mentoring them, or offering access to leadership training and development programs. By nurturing leadership skills within your team, you create a pipeline of future leaders who can take on more responsibilities and contribute to the long-term success of the organization.

5. **Managing Team Dynamics:** High-performance teams are not without challenges. Conflicts can arise, especially in high-pressure environments where deadlines are tight and stakes are high. As an IT leader, it's important to proactively manage team dynamics. Address conflicts early and facilitate constructive discussions that focus on finding solutions rather than assigning blame. Promote a culture of respect and

Mastering IT Leadership and Management, Strategies for Success in the Digital Age

inclusion, ensuring that all team members feel valued and heard. By effectively managing team dynamics, you can maintain a positive and productive work environment.

Mastering IT Leadership and Management, Strategies for Success in the Digital Age

Empowering and Motivating IT Professionals

A motivated and empowered team is essential for achieving high performance in IT. As an IT leader, your ability to inspire and motivate your team can significantly impact their productivity, job satisfaction, and overall success.

1. **Providing Clear Goals and Expectations:** Clarity is key to motivating your team. Ensure that team members understand what is expected of them and how their work contributes to the organization's overall goals. Set clear, achievable goals and provide regular feedback on their progress. When team members have a clear sense of purpose and direction, they are more likely to be motivated to achieve their best.

2. **Encouraging Autonomy:** Empower your team by giving them the autonomy to make decisions and take ownership of their work. When team members feel trusted and have control over how they complete their tasks, they are more likely to be engaged and motivated. Encourage a culture of accountability, where team members take responsibility for their results and are recognized for their achievements.

3. **Fostering a Positive Work Environment:** A positive work environment is crucial for motivation. Create a culture where team members feel valued, respected, and supported. Recognize and celebrate successes, both big and small. Encourage work-life balance and provide opportunities for professional development and growth. A positive work environment not only boosts motivation but also improves retention and job satisfaction.

4. **Providing Opportunities for Growth and Development:** IT professionals are often driven by a desire to learn and grow. Offer opportunities for your team members to develop their skills through training, mentoring, or new challenges. Encourage continuous learning and create a culture where professional development is valued and supported. When team members see opportunities for advancement and growth, they are more likely to be motivated to excel in their roles.

5. **Recognizing and Rewarding Contributions:** Recognition and rewards are powerful motivators. Regularly acknowledge the contributions of your team members and offer rewards that are meaningful to them. This could include formal recognition programs, financial incentives, or simple gestures of appreciation. By recognizing and rewarding hard work and achievements, you reinforce positive behavior and motivate your team to continue performing at a high level.

Mastering IT Leadership and Management, Strategies for Success in the Digital Age

Industry Case Study: Leading High-Performance IT Teams at Google

Situation:
Google, a global leader in technology, has consistently been recognized for its ability to innovate and maintain high levels of performance across its IT teams. The company's success is largely attributed to its unique approach to team leadership and management, where fostering collaboration, empowering employees, and encouraging a culture of continuous learning and innovation are central tenets. However, leading diverse, high-performance teams in such a fast-paced environment is challenging. Google's IT leaders must balance the need for creativity with operational efficiency, ensuring that their teams are both innovative and productive.

Task:
Google's IT leaders were tasked with building and nurturing high-performance IT teams capable of driving innovation while maintaining operational excellence. This required identifying top talent, fostering a collaborative environment, and implementing leadership strategies that empower and motivate IT professionals to achieve their best work. The challenge was to maintain high levels of engagement and creativity within teams while also ensuring that projects were delivered on time and met the organization's strategic goals.

Action:
To achieve these objectives, Google's IT leadership implemented several key strategies:

1. **Hiring and Developing Top Talent:** Google focused on recruiting individuals with strong technical skills, as well as creativity, problem-solving abilities, and a talent for teamwork. The company invested heavily in training and development programs to continuously upskill employees, ensuring they remained at the forefront of technological advancements.

2. **Fostering a Collaborative Culture:** Google encouraged a culture of collaboration by designing open office spaces, utilizing collaborative tools, and promoting cross-functional teams. This environment allowed IT professionals from different disciplines to work together, share ideas, and develop innovative solutions to complex problems.

3. **Empowering and Motivating Employees:** Google's leadership empowered IT teams by providing them with autonomy in their work. Employees were encouraged to explore new ideas and approaches, with the support and resources needed to experiment and innovate. This empowerment was complemented by a system of recognition and rewards that celebrated both individual and team achievements.

4. **Adapting Leadership Styles:** Recognizing that different situations and team dynamics require different leadership approaches, Google's IT leaders were trained to be flexible in their management styles. For instance, they employed a more directive approach during critical project phases while adopting a coaching style to support ongoing professional development and team growth.

Mastering IT Leadership and Management, Strategies for Success in the Digital Age

Result:
As a result of these actions, Google's IT teams consistently delivered high-quality, innovative solutions that drove the company's success in the competitive tech industry. The emphasis on collaboration and empowerment led to increased employee satisfaction, higher retention rates, and a strong sense of ownership among team members. By adapting their leadership styles to meet the needs of their teams, Google's IT leaders were able to maintain a balance between creativity and operational efficiency, ensuring that projects were not only innovative but also aligned with the company's strategic goals. The overall impact was a series of groundbreaking products and services that solidified Google's position as a leader in technology, while also creating a work environment that attracted and retained top IT talent.

This case study illustrates the importance of effective IT leadership in building and nurturing high-performance teams. By focusing on collaboration, empowerment, and continuous development, IT leaders can foster an environment where innovation thrives and organizational goals are consistently met.

Mastering IT Leadership and Management, Strategies for Success in the Digital Age

Best Practices

1. **Focus on Building a High-Performance Team:** The foundation of a successful IT initiative is a high-performance team. IT leaders should prioritize hiring individuals who not only possess strong technical skills but also align with the organization's culture and values. Building a diverse team with a range of experiences and perspectives can lead to more innovative solutions and better decision-making.

2. **Foster a Collaborative Environment:** Collaboration is key to the success of IT teams. IT leaders should create an environment where team members feel comfortable sharing ideas, asking for help, and working together to solve problems. Open communication and the use of collaborative tools are essential in fostering a culture of teamwork, especially in complex, multidisciplinary IT projects.

3. **Empower and Motivate Team Members:** Empowering team members by giving them autonomy and ownership of their work leads to higher engagement and motivation. IT leaders should provide clear goals and expectations while allowing flexibility in how these goals are achieved. Recognizing and rewarding achievements, both big and small, is crucial for maintaining motivation and fostering a culture of excellence.

4. **Adapt Leadership Style to Team Needs:** Effective IT leadership requires flexibility in leadership style. IT leaders should assess the needs of their team and the demands of the situation, adjusting their approach accordingly. Whether adopting a transformational, servant, situational, or democratic leadership style, the key is to be responsive to the team's dynamics and the specific challenges they face.

5. **Invest in Continuous Development:** Ongoing training and professional development are vital for maintaining a high-performance IT team. IT leaders should invest in opportunities for team members to develop their skills, whether through formal training programs, mentoring, or hands-on experience with new technologies. This commitment to growth ensures that the team remains at the forefront of industry advancements.

6. **Manage Team Dynamics Effectively:** IT leaders must be proactive in managing team dynamics to prevent conflicts from derailing projects. Addressing issues early, facilitating constructive discussions, and promoting a culture of respect and inclusion are critical to maintaining a positive and productive work environment.

Mastering IT Leadership and Management, Strategies for Success in the Digital Age

Lessons Learned

1. **The Importance of Identifying and Attracting the Right Talent:** The success of IT initiatives often hinges on having the right people in place. Leaders at companies like Google have demonstrated the value of not only hiring for technical skills but also for cultural fit and growth potential. Focusing on attracting top talent aligned with the company's values and goals is essential for building a strong, cohesive team.

2. **The Power of Collaboration:** Successful IT initiatives are often the result of effective collaboration among team members with diverse skill sets. Encouraging collaboration and cross-functional teamwork leads to more innovative solutions and better problem-solving. Google's emphasis on open office spaces and collaborative tools has shown how fostering a collaborative culture can drive IT success.

3. **Empowerment Drives Innovation and Performance:** Teams that are empowered to make decisions and take ownership of their work are more likely to be innovative and perform at a high level. Google's approach to giving IT teams autonomy and recognizing their contributions highlights the importance of empowerment in driving both individual and team success.

4. **Leadership Flexibility is Key:** Different situations and team dynamics require different leadership approaches. The ability to adapt leadership styles—whether being more directive during critical phases or adopting a coaching approach for ongoing development—can make the difference between a team that struggles and one that excels. Flexibility in leadership ensures that the team receives the support and guidance it needs at the right time.

5. **Continuous Development Fuels Long-Term Success:** Continuous learning and development are critical for keeping IT teams competitive and capable of tackling new challenges. Companies like Google invest heavily in upskilling their teams, recognizing that a commitment to growth is key to sustaining long-term success. This underscores the importance of prioritizing professional development in IT leadership.

6. **Effective Conflict Resolution Strengthens Teams:** Conflicts are inevitable in any high-performance team, especially in high-pressure IT environments. Successful IT leaders are those who address conflicts head-on and use them as opportunities to strengthen team dynamics. By fostering a culture of respect and inclusion and facilitating constructive dialogue, leaders can turn potential disruptions into opportunities for growth.

By applying these best practices and learning from successful IT initiatives, IT leaders can effectively guide their teams to achieve outstanding results, driving innovation and success in their organizations.

Mastering IT Leadership and Management, Strategies for Success in the Digital Age

Conclusion

Leading IT teams is a multifaceted responsibility that goes beyond managing technology and projects; it's about fostering an environment where innovation, collaboration, and high performance can thrive. Throughout this chapter, we have explored the key elements of building and nurturing high-performance IT teams, various leadership styles, and strategies for empowering and motivating IT professionals.

Building a successful IT team starts with attracting and retaining top talent. As an IT leader, your ability to identify individuals who not only possess the necessary technical skills but also align with the organization's culture and values is critical. Once the team is assembled, fostering collaboration and teamwork becomes essential, driving the synergy needed to tackle complex IT challenges and achieve outstanding results.

Leadership styles play a significant role in how IT teams function. Whether you adopt a transformational, servant, situational, democratic, or laissez-faire leadership style, the key is to adapt your approach to the needs of your team and the demands of the situation. Effective IT leaders are flexible, understanding that different scenarios require different leadership techniques to bring out the best in their teams.

Empowering and motivating IT professionals is perhaps one of the most important aspects of leading a successful IT team. By providing clear goals, encouraging autonomy, fostering a positive work environment, and offering opportunities for growth and development, IT leaders can create a culture of engagement and excellence. Recognizing and rewarding contributions further reinforces this culture, driving continued high performance and innovation.

As we conclude Chapter 4, it is evident that leading IT teams is both an art and a science. It requires a deep understanding of people, processes, and the unique dynamics of the IT landscape. By mastering the principles and strategies discussed in this chapter, IT leaders can cultivate teams that not only meet the demands of today's fast-paced, technology-driven world but also drive their organizations toward future success. The insights gained here provide a strong foundation for the continued exploration of essential skills and strategies vital for effective IT leadership.

Mastering IT Leadership and Management, Strategies for Success in the Digital Age

Quizzes

I. Multiple Choice Questions:
   1. Which of the following is a key responsibility of an IT leader when building a high-performance team?

      A. Micromanaging daily tasks
      B. Attracting and retaining top talent
      C. Limiting communication to email
      D. Delegating all leadership tasks to team members

   2. What is the most important factor in fostering collaboration within IT teams?

      A. Encouraging competition among team members
      B. Setting individual goals that do not overlap
      C. Creating a culture of open communication and teamwork
      D. Ensuring team members work independently

   3. Empowering IT professionals primarily involves:

      A. Allowing them to make decisions and take ownership of their work
      B. Assigning them more work without additional resources
      C. Providing them with rigid instructions on how to complete tasks
      D. Limiting their involvement in strategic decisions

   4. Leadership flexibility is important because:

      A. It allows leaders to enforce the same strategy in all situations
      B. Different situations and team dynamics require different leadership approaches
      C. It helps leaders avoid making tough decisions
      D. It minimizes the need for communication with the team

II. True/False Questions:
   1. Effective IT leadership requires the ability to adapt leadership styles based on team needs and situations. (True/False)
   2. Empowerment in IT teams is best achieved by giving clear, non-negotiable instructions for all tasks. (True/False)
   3. A positive and collaborative work environment is essential for building a high-performance IT team. (True/False)
   4. The only focus of IT leaders should be on the technical skills of the team, rather than their motivation or engagement. (True/False)

Mastering IT Leadership and Management, Strategies for Success in the Digital Age

Exercises

I. Team Dynamics Analysis:
- **Objective:** Analyze the dynamics within your current IT team and identify areas for improvement.
- **Instructions:**
    1. Conduct an assessment of your team's current dynamics, focusing on communication, collaboration, and empowerment.
    2. Identify any barriers to effective teamwork and propose strategies to overcome them.
    3. Share your findings and proposed strategies with your team or a mentor to gather feedback.

II. Leadership Style Reflection:
- **Objective:** Reflect on your leadership style and how it aligns with the needs of your IT team.
- **Instructions:**
    1. Reflect on your approach to leadership within your IT team. Consider whether you tend to be more directive, coaching, or hands-off.
    2. Identify specific situations where a different leadership style might have been more effective.
    3. Develop a plan to adapt your leadership style to better meet the needs of your team in various scenarios.

III. High-Performance Team Workshop:
- **Objective:** Develop a plan to build or enhance a high-performance IT team.
- **Instructions:**
    1. Identify the key characteristics of a high-performance IT team as outlined in the chapter.
    2. Develop a workshop plan to address the current strengths and weaknesses of your team, focusing on talent development, collaboration, and empowerment.
    3. Present the workshop plan to your team or colleagues, and implement the strategies to foster a high-performance environment.

IV. Conflict Resolution Simulation:
- **Objective:** Practice managing conflicts within an IT team to maintain productivity and morale.
- **Instructions:**
    1. Identify a potential or real conflict scenario that could occur within your IT team.

Mastering IT Leadership and Management, Strategies for Success in the Digital Age

    2. Role-play the scenario with a colleague, taking turns as the IT leader and the team members involved in the conflict.
    3. After the role-play, discuss the effectiveness of the conflict resolution strategies used and how they could be improved.

V. Continuous Development Plan:
- **Objective:** Create a continuous development plan for your IT team to ensure ongoing skill enhancement and innovation.
- **Instructions:**
    1. Identify the current skill levels and development needs of each team member.
    2. Develop a plan that includes training opportunities, mentoring, and hands-on experiences to address these needs.
    3. Implement the development plan and monitor progress, making adjustments as necessary to keep the team at the forefront of technological advancements.

These quizzes and exercises are designed to help readers of Chapter 4 better understand and apply the concepts of leading high-performance IT teams, with a focus on practical, real-world scenarios.

Mastering IT Leadership and Management, Strategies for Success in the Digital Age

Chapter 5: Effective Communication

"THE ART OF COMMUNICATION IS THE LANGUAGE OF LEADERSHIP."

— **James Humes**

Bridging the Gap Between IT and Non-IT Stakeholders

One of the most critical aspects of IT leadership is the ability to bridge the gap between IT and non-IT stakeholders. This involves translating technical concepts into language that non-technical colleagues can understand and appreciate, ensuring that the IT function is fully integrated into the broader business strategy. Effective communication is key to breaking down the silos that often exist between IT and other departments and fostering a collaborative environment where technology and business goals are aligned.

1. **Understanding the Audience:** The first step in effective communication is understanding your audience. Non-IT stakeholders—whether they are executives, managers, or employees in other departments—may not have the same level of technical expertise as your IT team. As an IT leader, it's important to gauge the technical knowledge of your audience and adjust your communication style accordingly. This may involve simplifying complex concepts, using analogies, or focusing on the business implications of technology decisions rather than the technical details.

2. **Translating Technical Concepts:** IT leaders must be adept at translating technical jargon into clear, concise language that non-technical stakeholders can easily grasp. This involves focusing on the "why" rather than the "how." For example, instead of explaining the intricacies of a new database system, emphasize how it will improve data accessibility, speed up decision-making, or reduce costs. By framing technology in terms of its business impact, you can ensure that non-IT stakeholders understand the value that IT brings to the organization.

3. **Building Relationships with Business Leaders:** To effectively bridge the gap between IT and non-IT stakeholders, it's essential to build strong relationships with business leaders. This involves more than just attending meetings or sending reports; it requires active engagement and collaboration. Take the time to understand the goals, challenges, and priorities of other departments, and demonstrate how IT can support and enhance their efforts. By positioning yourself as a partner rather than just a service provider, you can build trust and ensure that IT is seen as an integral part of the business.

4. **Facilitating Cross-Functional Collaboration:** Bridging the gap between IT and non-IT stakeholders also involves facilitating cross-functional collaboration. This means creating opportunities for IT professionals to work alongside colleagues from other departments on projects, initiatives, and problem-solving efforts. Cross-functional teams can help break down barriers, foster mutual understanding, and ensure that IT

Mastering IT Leadership and Management, Strategies for Success in the Digital Age

solutions are developed with input from all relevant stakeholders. As an IT leader, you can champion these collaborative efforts by encouraging open communication, providing the necessary tools and resources, and recognizing the contributions of all team members.

5. **Addressing Concerns and Misconceptions:** Non-IT stakeholders may have concerns or misconceptions about technology and its role in the organization. These could include fears about job displacement due to automation, skepticism about the ROI of IT investments, or misunderstandings about cybersecurity risks. It's important to address these concerns head-on and provide clear, evidence-based explanations. By being transparent and proactive in your communication, you can alleviate fears, build confidence in IT initiatives, and foster a positive perception of the IT function.

Mastering IT Leadership and Management, Strategies for Success in the Digital Age

Presenting Technical Concepts to Executive Leadership

Presenting technical concepts to executive leadership is a critical skill for IT leaders. Executives are focused on the big picture—how technology initiatives align with the organization's strategic goals, impact the bottom line, and drive business success. To effectively communicate with executives, IT leaders must present technical concepts in a way that resonates with their concerns and priorities.

1. **Aligning with Business Goals:** When presenting to executive leadership, it's essential to align your message with the organization's business goals. Start by clearly articulating how the technical initiative or project supports the company's strategic objectives. Whether it's improving customer experience, increasing operational efficiency, or enabling innovation, the connection between the technical concept and business outcomes should be front and center in your presentation.

2. **Focusing on Value and ROI:** Executives are primarily concerned with the value that IT initiatives bring to the organization. When presenting technical concepts, focus on the return on investment (ROI) and the potential benefits to the business. This could include cost savings, revenue growth, risk mitigation, or competitive advantage. Use data and metrics to support your claims and provide a clear picture of the financial and strategic impact of the initiative.

3. **Simplifying Complex Concepts:** Technical concepts can be complex, but your presentation to executives should be as simple and straightforward as possible. Avoid technical jargon and focus on the key points that matter most to the leadership team. Use visuals, such as charts, graphs, and diagrams, to illustrate your points and make the information more accessible. Remember, your goal is to convey the essence of the technical concept, not to dive into the technical details.

4. **Anticipating Questions and Concerns:** Executives are likely to have questions and concerns about the technical initiatives you present. Anticipate these questions and prepare clear, concise answers. Be ready to address potential risks, challenges, and uncertainties, and provide reassurance that these issues have been considered and mitigated. By demonstrating that you have thoroughly thought through the initiative, you can build confidence in your leadership and in the IT function.

5. **Engaging the Audience:** Effective presentations are not just about delivering information—they are about engaging the audience. Encourage interaction by asking questions, soliciting feedback, and inviting discussion. This not only helps clarify points but also fosters a sense of collaboration and shared ownership of the initiative. Be responsive to the needs and concerns of the leadership team, and be open to adjusting your approach based on their input.

Mastering IT Leadership and Management, Strategies for Success in the Digital Age

Negotiation and Conflict Resolution in IT

Negotiation and conflict resolution are essential skills for IT leaders. The complexity of IT projects, coupled with the need to balance competing priorities and interests, often leads to situations where these skills are necessary. Effective IT leaders must be able to navigate these challenges and find solutions that are acceptable to all parties involved.

1. **Understanding the Interests of Stakeholders:** Successful negotiation starts with understanding the interests and priorities of all stakeholders involved. This means taking the time to listen to their concerns, goals, and constraints. By understanding what each party values most, you can identify areas of common ground and potential trade-offs. This understanding forms the basis for a collaborative and constructive negotiation process.

2. **Developing a Win-Win Mindset:** Effective negotiation is not about winning at the expense of others; it's about finding solutions that benefit all parties. Adopting a win-win mindset means focusing on shared goals and working towards outcomes that satisfy the interests of everyone involved. This approach not only resolves conflicts but also strengthens relationships and fosters a spirit of collaboration and mutual respect.

3. **Managing Emotions and Tensions:** Conflicts can sometimes lead to heightened emotions and tensions. As an IT leader, it's important to manage these emotions and keep the discussion focused on the issues at hand. Stay calm, remain objective, and avoid personalizing the conflict. Encourage a respectful and constructive dialogue, where all parties feel heard and valued. By maintaining a positive and solution-oriented atmosphere, you can prevent conflicts from escalating and reach a resolution more effectively.

4. **Finding Creative Solutions:** Negotiation and conflict resolution often require creative problem-solving. Be open to exploring alternative solutions that may not have been initially considered. This could involve compromising on certain aspects of the project, finding new ways to allocate resources, or redefining the scope of the initiative. By being flexible and innovative, you can find solutions that address the concerns of all stakeholders and move the project forward.

5. **Closing the Deal:** Once a resolution has been reached, it's important to close the deal by clearly defining the agreed-upon terms and next steps. Document the decisions made, outline the responsibilities of each party, and set a timeline for implementation. By formalizing the agreement, you ensure that everyone is on the same page and that the resolution is carried out as planned.

Mastering IT Leadership and Management, Strategies for Success in the Digital Age

Industry Case Study: Effective Communication at Amazon Web Services (AWS)

Situation:
In the early 2010s, Amazon Web Services (AWS) was rapidly growing as a cloud computing provider. As AWS expanded, the company faced the challenge of ensuring that its highly technical services and offerings were well understood by non-technical stakeholders, including business leaders, customers, and partners. The complex nature of cloud technology often led to communication gaps, where the value and potential of AWS's services were not fully appreciated by decision-makers in client organizations. This situation underscored the need for effective communication strategies that could bridge the gap between AWS's technical expertise and the business goals of its customers.

Task:
AWS leadership needed to develop and implement a communication strategy that could clearly and effectively convey the benefits of cloud technology to a diverse audience. This strategy needed to translate complex technical concepts into language that non-technical stakeholders could easily understand and relate to their business needs. AWS also needed to position itself as a trusted advisor and partner, helping businesses leverage cloud technology to drive innovation and achieve their goals.

Action:
To address these challenges, AWS implemented several key communication strategies:

1. **Simplifying Technical Concepts:** AWS invested in training its sales and technical teams to simplify complex cloud computing concepts. They developed analogies and industry case studies to explain the value of cloud services, such as comparing traditional IT infrastructure to renting versus buying a house. These simplified explanations helped non-technical stakeholders understand how cloud services could benefit their organizations.

2. **Building Strong Relationships:** AWS focused on building strong relationships with business leaders in client organizations. Through regular meetings, workshops, and strategy sessions, AWS teams worked closely with clients to understand their business objectives and challenges. This allowed AWS to tailor its communication and service offerings to meet the specific needs of each client.

3. **Developing Customized Presentations:** AWS created customized presentations and reports that highlighted the business impact of cloud adoption. These presentations focused on metrics that mattered most to business leaders, such as cost savings, scalability, and time-to-market. By aligning the technical benefits of cloud computing with the strategic goals of the organization, AWS was able to secure buy-in from key decision-makers.

4. **Fostering a Culture of Open Communication:** Within AWS, a culture of open communication was encouraged, fostering collaboration between technical and non-technical teams. This approach ensured that all employees were aligned in their messaging and could effectively communicate the value of AWS services to clients.

Mastering IT Leadership and Management, Strategies for Success in the Digital Age

Result:
As a result of these efforts, AWS successfully bridged the communication gap between its technical offerings and the business needs of its clients. The ability to simplify complex concepts and align them with business goals enabled AWS to gain the trust and support of key decision-makers, leading to the rapid adoption of its cloud services across various industries. AWS's strong communication strategies contributed to its position as the leading cloud service provider globally, with a broad and diverse customer base. The focus on effective communication also helped AWS build long-term partnerships with clients, driving sustained growth and innovation.

This case study illustrates the critical role of effective communication in IT leadership, particularly in translating technical concepts into business value and fostering strong relationships with stakeholders. By mastering these communication strategies, IT leaders can ensure that their initiatives are well understood, supported, and aligned with organizational goals.

Mastering IT Leadership and Management, Strategies for Success in the Digital Age

Best Practices

1. **Tailor Communication to Your Audience:** Understanding your audience is the first step in effective communication. IT leaders should tailor their messaging to the technical knowledge and interests of their audience, whether communicating with executive leadership, technical teams, or non-IT stakeholders. Simplifying complex technical concepts and focusing on the business impact rather than technical details helps ensure that your message resonates with the audience.

2. **Bridge the Gap Between IT and Non-IT Stakeholders:** One of the critical roles of an IT leader is to bridge the gap between IT and non-IT stakeholders. This involves translating technical jargon into clear, business-oriented language that non-technical colleagues can understand. By focusing on how IT initiatives support business objectives, IT leaders can foster a more collaborative environment and ensure that IT is seen as a strategic partner, not just a service provider.

3. **Use Multiple Channels for Communication:** Effective communication requires using multiple channels to reach different audiences. IT leaders should employ a mix of formal presentations, emails, reports, meetings, and informal conversations to ensure their message is heard. Visual aids, such as infographics and diagrams, can also help convey complex information more effectively.

4. **Engage in Active Listening:** Communication is not just about delivering a message; it's also about listening. IT leaders should practice active listening to understand the concerns, needs, and perspectives of their stakeholders. By showing that they value input from others, IT leaders can build stronger relationships and foster a more collaborative atmosphere.

5. **Communicate Regularly and Transparently:** Regular and transparent communication is key to maintaining trust and alignment within the organization. IT leaders should keep stakeholders informed of progress, challenges, and changes related to IT initiatives. Transparency in communication helps manage expectations and build confidence in the IT team's ability to deliver results.

6. **Develop Storytelling Skills:** Storytelling is a powerful tool for IT leaders to make their messages more relatable and memorable. By framing technical information within a compelling narrative, IT leaders can engage their audience more effectively and make complex ideas easier to understand. Industry examples and case studies can also help illustrate the practical impact of IT initiatives.

Mastering IT Leadership and Management, Strategies for Success in the Digital Age

Lessons Learned

1. **The Impact of Effective Communication on Project Success:** Successful IT initiatives often hinge on the quality of communication between IT leaders and their stakeholders. Clear, consistent communication ensures that everyone involved understands the goals, challenges, and progress of the project, reducing the risk of misunderstandings and misalignment.

2. **Building Trust Through Transparent Communication:** Trust is a critical component of any successful IT initiative. IT leaders who communicate transparently about both successes and setbacks are more likely to build trust with their stakeholders. This trust is essential for gaining support and buy-in for IT initiatives, especially during challenging times.

3. **The Role of Active Listening in Stakeholder Engagement:** Engaging stakeholders effectively requires more than just delivering information; it requires understanding their perspectives. Active listening allows IT leaders to gather valuable insights, address concerns proactively, and build stronger relationships. This approach fosters a sense of partnership and collaboration, which is crucial for the success of IT projects.

4. **The Power of Visual Communication:** Visual aids can significantly enhance the understanding and retention of complex information. Successful IT leaders use diagrams, charts, and infographics to simplify and clarify technical concepts, making it easier for non-technical stakeholders to grasp the significance of IT initiatives.

5. **Storytelling as a Tool for Influence:** IT leaders who master the art of storytelling can more effectively influence and engage their audience. By presenting technical information within the context of a story, leaders can make their messages more relatable and impactful. This approach helps connect with the audience on an emotional level, making the message more memorable.

6. **The Importance of Consistency in Communication:** Consistency in messaging is crucial for maintaining clarity and alignment. IT leaders should ensure that their communications are consistent across different channels and audiences. This consistency helps to reinforce key messages and ensures that all stakeholders are on the same page regarding the objectives and progress of IT initiatives.

By applying these best practices and lessons learned, IT leaders can enhance their communication effectiveness, build stronger relationships with stakeholders, and drive the success of their IT initiatives.

Mastering IT Leadership and Management, Strategies for Success in the Digital Age

Conclusion

Effective communication is the linchpin of successful IT leadership, bridging the gap between technical expertise and strategic business objectives. Throughout this chapter, we have explored the critical role communication plays in connecting IT with non-IT stakeholders, presenting complex technical concepts to executive leadership, and navigating negotiation and conflict resolution in the dynamic world of IT.

Bridging the gap between IT and non-IT stakeholders is essential for ensuring that technology initiatives are fully integrated into the broader business strategy. IT leaders must be adept at translating technical jargon into language that resonates with their audience, ensuring that the value of IT is clearly understood across the organization. Building strong relationships with business leaders and fostering cross-functional collaboration are key strategies for achieving this alignment.

Presenting technical concepts to executive leadership requires a focus on the big picture—how technology initiatives support the organization's strategic goals, impact the bottom line, and drive competitive advantage. Simplifying complex ideas, aligning with business objectives, and engaging the leadership team are critical skills that enable IT leaders to secure buy-in and support for their initiatives.

Negotiation and conflict resolution are inevitable aspects of IT leadership, where competing priorities and diverse perspectives often collide. Effective IT leaders must approach these challenges with a win-win mindset, manage emotions, and find creative solutions that satisfy all parties involved. By mastering these skills, IT leaders can maintain harmony, build trust, and drive their teams and projects forward.

As we conclude Chapter 5, it's clear that communication is more than just a tool—it is the foundation of effective IT leadership. The ability to communicate clearly, persuasively, and empathetically enables IT leaders to build strong relationships, foster collaboration, and align technology with business success. The insights and strategies discussed in this chapter are essential for any IT leader seeking to navigate the complexities of today's technology landscape and lead with confidence and impact. As we move forward, these communication skills will continue to be a cornerstone of the leadership strategies explored in the subsequent chapters.

Mastering IT Leadership and Management, Strategies for Success in the Digital Age

Quizzes

I. Multiple Choice Questions:
   1. What is the first step in effective communication for IT leaders?

      A. Sending out regular emails
      B. Understanding the audience
      C. Conducting team meetings
      D. Using technical jargon

   2. Why is it important for IT leaders to bridge the gap between IT and non-IT stakeholders?

      A. To minimize the use of technology in business
      B. To ensure IT is seen as a strategic partner
      C. To avoid technical discussions
      D. To reduce IT spending

   3. Which communication strategy involves tailoring the message to the technical knowledge of the audience?

      A. Active listening
      B. Visual communication
      C. Audience understanding
      D. Storytelling

   4. The ability to simplify complex technical concepts for non-technical stakeholders is an example of:

      A. Technical expertise
      B. Effective communication
      C. Stakeholder disengagement
      D. Project management

II. True/False Questions:
   1. Active listening is less important than delivering a clear message. (True/False)
   2. Regular and transparent communication helps build trust within the organization. (True/False)
   3. Using multiple communication channels can dilute the message. (True/False)
   4. Storytelling is an effective tool for making technical information more relatable. (True/False)

Mastering IT Leadership and Management, Strategies for Success in the Digital Age

Exercises

I. Audience Analysis Exercise:
    - **Objective:** Practice tailoring communication to different audiences.
    - **Instructions:**
        1. Identify a recent IT initiative in your organization.
        2. Create a brief communication plan that explains this initiative to three different audiences: executives, IT staff, and non-IT staff.
        3. For each audience, tailor the message to address their specific concerns, technical knowledge, and interests.

II. Role-Playing: Bridging IT and Non-IT Communication:
    - **Objective:** Enhance skills in translating technical concepts into business language.
    - **Instructions:**
        1. Pair up with a colleague. One person will play the role of an IT leader, and the other will play a non-IT stakeholder (e.g., a business leader).
        2. The IT leader will explain a complex technical project to the stakeholder, focusing on the business impact rather than technical details.
        3. After the role-play, discuss the effectiveness of the communication and identify areas for improvement.

III. Storytelling Workshop:
    - **Objective:** Develop storytelling skills to make IT communication more engaging.
    - **Instructions:**
        1. Choose a technical topic that you need to communicate to a non-technical audience.
        2. Develop a short story or analogy that simplifies the topic and illustrates its impact on the business.
        3. Present your story to a group of colleagues and gather feedback on its clarity and impact.

IV. Active Listening Practice:
    - **Objective:** Improve active listening skills in communication.
    - **Instructions:**
        1. Engage in a conversation with a colleague about a current IT project or challenge.
        2. Focus on listening without interrupting, and take notes on key points raised by your colleague.

Mastering IT Leadership and Management, Strategies for Success in the Digital Age

   3. After the conversation, summarize what you heard and ask your colleague if you captured their concerns accurately.
   4. Reflect on how active listening influenced the quality of the conversation.

V. Visual Communication Design:
- **Objective:** Enhance the ability to use visual aids to simplify complex information.
- **Instructions:**
   1. Select a recent IT project or initiative.
   2. Create an infographic or diagram that visually represents the key aspects of the project, such as its goals, processes, and benefits.
   3. Share the visual aid with your team or stakeholders and assess its effectiveness in conveying the intended message.

These quizzes and exercises are designed to help readers of Chapter 5 better understand and apply the principles of effective communication in IT leadership. The focus is on practical, real-world application and the development of communication skills that bridge the gap between technical and non-technical stakeholders.

Mastering IT Leadership and Management, Strategies for Success in the Digital Age

Chapter 6: Decision-Making and Problem-Solving

"IN THE END, WE ARE OUR CHOICES. BUILD YOURSELF A GREAT STORY."

— **Jeff Bezos**

Strategic Decision-Making in IT

Strategic decision-making is at the core of effective IT leadership. As technology becomes increasingly integral to business operations, IT leaders are often tasked with making decisions that have far-reaching implications for the organization's success. Strategic decisions in IT involve more than just selecting the right technologies—they require a deep understanding of the organization's goals, a forward-looking perspective, and the ability to balance risks and opportunities.

1. **Aligning Decisions with Business Goals:** The most critical aspect of strategic decision-making in IT is ensuring that every decision aligns with the broader business goals. Whether it's investing in new technology, choosing a software vendor, or deciding on a cybersecurity strategy, the decision should support the organization's strategic objectives. This requires IT leaders to have a comprehensive understanding of the business's goals and challenges, and to consider how IT can contribute to achieving those goals.

2. **Evaluating Risks and Benefits:** Strategic decisions in IT often involve weighing potential risks and benefits. IT leaders must be adept at identifying the risks associated with different options, including financial, operational, and security risks. At the same time, they must consider potential benefits, such as cost savings, improved efficiency, enhanced customer experience, or competitive advantage. A thorough risk-benefit analysis ensures that decisions are well-informed and balanced.

3. **Considering Long-Term Implications:** Strategic decision-making in IT requires a long-term perspective. IT leaders must think beyond immediate needs and consider how their decisions will impact the organization in the future. This includes anticipating changes in technology, market trends, and regulatory environments. By considering the long-term implications of their decisions, IT leaders can ensure that their choices are sustainable and position the organization for future success.

4. **Involving Stakeholders in the Decision-Making Process:** Effective strategic decision-making in IT involves collaboration with key stakeholders across the organization. IT leaders should engage with executives, department heads, and end-users to gather input and ensure that decisions reflect the needs and priorities of the entire organization. By involving stakeholders in the decision-making process, IT leaders can build consensus, foster support, and ensure alignment with the broader organizational strategy.

Mastering IT Leadership and Management, Strategies for Success in the Digital Age

5. **Making Data-Driven Decisions:** In today's data-driven world, IT leaders have access to vast amounts of information that can inform their decision-making. By leveraging data analytics, IT leaders can gain insights into trends, performance metrics, and potential risks. Data-driven decision-making allows IT leaders to make more informed choices, reduce uncertainty, and increase the likelihood of successful outcomes. However, it's also important to balance data with intuition and experience, especially when data is incomplete or ambiguous.

Mastering IT Leadership and Management, Strategies for Success in the Digital Age

Data-Driven Decision-Making

The ability to make data-driven decisions is a critical competency for modern IT leaders. In an era where data is abundant and accessible, the challenge lies in effectively harnessing that data to drive strategic decisions. Data-driven decision-making involves using data to inform choices, identify trends, and evaluate outcomes, ultimately leading to more accurate and effective decisions.

1. **Gathering and Analyzing Data:** The first step in data-driven decision-making is gathering relevant data from various sources. This could include performance metrics, financial data, customer feedback, market research, and more. Once the data is collected, it needs to be analyzed to identify patterns, correlations, and insights. IT leaders should ensure they have the tools and skills needed to analyze data effectively, whether through advanced analytics platforms, business intelligence tools, or collaboration with data scientists.

2. **Leveraging Predictive Analytics:** Predictive analytics is a powerful tool for data-driven decision-making. By using historical data to predict future outcomes, IT leaders can anticipate trends, identify potential risks, and make proactive decisions. For example, predictive analytics can help IT leaders forecast demand for IT services, assess the likelihood of cybersecurity threats, or estimate the ROI of a technology investment. By leveraging predictive analytics, IT leaders can make decisions that are not only informed by past data but are also forward-looking.

3. **Ensuring Data Quality and Integrity:** The accuracy and reliability of data are critical to making sound decisions. IT leaders must ensure that the data they use is accurate, up-to-date, and free from biases or errors. This involves implementing data governance practices, such as data validation, data cleansing, and regular audits. By maintaining high data quality, IT leaders can make decisions with confidence, knowing that they are based on reliable information.

4. **Balancing Data with Experience and Intuition:** While data is a valuable tool for decision-making, it's important to balance it with experience and intuition. IT leaders bring a wealth of knowledge and expertise to their roles, and this should not be overlooked in favor of purely data-driven approaches. In situations where data is incomplete or where decisions involve significant uncertainty, intuition and experience can provide valuable guidance. The key is to integrate data with judgment, using both to inform decision-making.

5. **Monitoring and Adjusting Decisions:** Data-driven decision-making is not a one-time process; it requires continuous monitoring and adjustment. IT leaders should regularly review the outcomes of their decisions, using data to assess their effectiveness and make adjustments as needed. By continuously monitoring the impact of decisions, IT leaders can ensure they remain aligned with business goals and can adapt to changing circumstances.

Mastering IT Leadership and Management, Strategies for Success in the Digital Age

Problem-Solving Techniques for IT Leaders

Problem-solving is an essential skill for IT leaders, who are often faced with complex challenges that require creative and effective solutions. Whether resolving technical issues, managing project delays, or addressing security vulnerabilities, IT leaders must be able to diagnose problems, identify root causes, and implement solutions that minimize disruption and maximize outcomes.

1. **Root Cause Analysis:** Effective problem-solving begins with identifying the root cause of the issue. This involves going beyond the symptoms to understand the underlying factors contributing to the problem. Techniques such as the "5 Whys" or Fishbone (Ishikawa) Diagrams can be useful tools for root cause analysis. By identifying the true source of the problem, IT leaders can develop solutions that address the issue at its core, rather than simply treating the symptoms.

2. **Creative Problem-Solving:** Many challenges in IT require creative solutions that go beyond conventional approaches. IT leaders should foster a culture of creativity and innovation within their teams, encouraging members to think outside the box and explore new ideas. Techniques such as brainstorming, mind mapping, and lateral thinking can help generate creative solutions to complex problems. By embracing creativity, IT leaders can find innovative ways to overcome challenges and drive success.

3. **Collaborative Problem-Solving:** Problem-solving in IT often involves collaboration across different teams and departments. IT leaders should facilitate collaborative problem-solving by bringing together diverse perspectives and expertise. This could involve forming cross-functional teams, holding problem-solving workshops, or using collaborative tools to gather input from stakeholders. By working together, teams can leverage their collective knowledge and experience to develop more effective solutions.

4. **Decision-Making Under Pressure:** IT leaders are often required to make decisions quickly, especially in high-pressure situations such as system outages, security breaches, or project crises. In these situations, it's important to remain calm, gather the necessary information, and make decisions based on both data and intuition. IT leaders should also be prepared to make decisions with incomplete information, relying on their experience and judgment to guide them. By maintaining composure and making decisive choices, IT leaders can navigate crises and minimize the impact on the organization.

5. **Implementing and Evaluating Solutions:** Once a solution has been identified, it's important to implement it effectively and evaluate its success. IT leaders should develop a clear plan for implementation, including timelines, resources, and responsibilities. After implementation, the solution should be monitored to ensure that it resolves the problem and achieves the desired outcomes. If the solution is not effective, IT leaders should be prepared to revisit the problem and explore alternative approaches.

Mastering IT Leadership and Management, Strategies for Success in the Digital Age

Industry Case Study: Decision-Making and Problem-Solving at Netflix

Situation:
In the early 2010s, Netflix faced a critical decision that would ultimately shape the future of the company. Originally a DVD rental service, Netflix saw the rapid rise of digital streaming as both a challenge and an opportunity. The company needed to decide whether to focus on its existing DVD business or pivot to a streaming-first model—a move that could potentially alienate its current customer base and disrupt its business model. Additionally, Netflix faced the challenge of entering the competitive streaming market, where it would compete against established players like HBO and emerging digital platforms.

Task:
Netflix's leadership had to make a strategic decision that aligned with the company's long-term vision while managing the risks associated with transitioning to a new business model. This decision required a deep understanding of market trends, customer behavior, and technological advancements. Netflix needed to determine the best path forward, balancing the potential benefits of entering the streaming market with the risks of disrupting its existing business.

Action:
To address this challenge, Netflix's leadership took several key actions:

1. **Data-Driven Decision-Making:** Netflix leveraged its vast trove of customer data to understand viewing habits and preferences. By analyzing this data, the company identified a growing trend toward digital consumption and a decline in DVD rentals. This data-driven approach allowed Netflix to make an informed decision about the future of its business, with a strong focus on customer behavior and market trends.

2. **Strategic Vision:** Netflix's leadership, led by CEO Reed Hastings, articulated a clear vision for the future of the company: to become the leading global provider of streaming entertainment. This vision guided the company's decision-making process, ensuring that all strategic choices aligned with this long-term goal. Hastings and his team recognized the potential of streaming technology to revolutionize the entertainment industry and were willing to take calculated risks to achieve this vision.

3. **Incremental Rollout and Testing:** Instead of making a sudden and complete shift to streaming, Netflix gradually introduced its streaming service while continuing to offer DVD rentals. This approach allowed the company to test the market, gather feedback, and make adjustments before fully committing to the new model. By carefully managing the transition, Netflix was able to mitigate risks and ensure a smoother shift to streaming.

4. **Continuous Evaluation and Adaptation:** Netflix's leadership regularly reviewed the performance of its streaming service and made adjustments as needed. This included expanding its content library, improving streaming technology, and

entering new markets. The company's ability to adapt to changing circumstances and customer needs was critical to its success in the streaming industry.

Result:
As a result of these strategic decisions, Netflix successfully transitioned from a DVD rental service to a global leader in streaming entertainment. The company's data-driven approach, combined with a clear strategic vision and careful risk management, enabled Netflix to navigate the challenges of entering a new market and disrupting its own business model. Today, Netflix is one of the most recognized brands in the world, with over 200 million subscribers and a reputation for innovation and excellence in digital entertainment. The company's success illustrates the importance of effective decision-making and problem-solving in navigating complex challenges and achieving long-term business goals.

This case study demonstrates how Netflix's leadership effectively used data, strategic vision, and careful risk management to make critical decisions that shaped the future of the company. By aligning decision-making with long-term goals and continuously adapting to changing circumstances, Netflix was able to achieve success in a highly competitive and rapidly evolving industry.

Mastering IT Leadership and Management, Strategies for Success in the Digital Age

Best Practices

1. **Leverage Data-Driven Decision-Making:** Successful IT leaders rely on data to inform their decisions. By utilizing data analytics, metrics, and KPIs, leaders can gain valuable insights into trends, performance, and potential risks. This data-driven approach ensures that decisions are based on objective evidence rather than intuition alone, leading to more accurate and effective outcomes.

2. **Adopt a Systematic Problem-Solving Approach:** Effective problem-solving in IT requires a systematic approach. IT leaders should break down complex problems into smaller, manageable components and analyze them step by step. Techniques such as root cause analysis, the "5 Whys," and SWOT analysis can help identify the underlying causes of problems and develop targeted solutions.

3. **Involve Key Stakeholders in Decision-Making:** Involving stakeholders in the decision-making process is crucial for gaining buy-in and ensuring that decisions align with the organization's goals. IT leaders should actively engage with business leaders, team members, and other relevant parties to gather input, assess risks, and explore different perspectives. This collaborative approach leads to more informed and widely supported decisions.

4. **Prioritize Decisions Based on Impact and Urgency:** Not all decisions are of equal importance. IT leaders should prioritize decisions based on their potential impact and urgency. By focusing on high-impact, high-priority issues first, leaders can ensure that their efforts are directed toward areas that will deliver the most significant benefits to the organization.

5. **Embrace Agile Decision-Making:** In today's fast-paced business environment, agility is key. IT leaders should be prepared to make decisions quickly and adapt to changing circumstances. Agile decision-making involves iterating on decisions as new information becomes available, allowing leaders to pivot and adjust strategies as needed to stay aligned with business goals.

6. **Cultivate a Culture of Continuous Learning:** Decision-making and problem-solving skills can be continuously improved through learning and reflection. IT leaders should encourage a culture where team members are not afraid to experiment, learn from failures, and share insights. Regularly reviewing past decisions and outcomes can provide valuable lessons that inform future decision-making.

Mastering IT Leadership and Management, Strategies for Success in the Digital Age

Lessons Learned

1. **The Power of Data in Decision-Making:** Data-driven decision-making has proven to be a game-changer in successful IT initiatives. Organizations that effectively leverage data are better equipped to anticipate challenges, seize opportunities, and make decisions that drive positive outcomes. The lesson here is that access to accurate, relevant data is crucial for informed decision-making.

2. **The Value of a Structured Problem-Solving Process:** A structured approach to problem-solving enables IT leaders to tackle complex challenges more effectively. Techniques like root cause analysis and the "5 Whys" help leaders get to the heart of issues, ensuring that solutions address the root causes rather than just the symptoms. This approach leads to more sustainable and impactful solutions.

3. **Stakeholder Engagement Enhances Decision Quality:** Involving stakeholders in the decision-making process results in better decisions and stronger support for implementation. Stakeholder engagement ensures that decisions are well-rounded, taking into account various perspectives and potential impacts. This inclusiveness fosters collaboration and reduces resistance to change.

4. **The Need for Prioritization in Decision-Making:** Not every problem or decision requires immediate attention. Successful IT leaders learn to prioritize based on impact and urgency, focusing their resources on the most critical issues first. This prioritization ensures that high-stakes decisions receive the attention and resources needed to be successful.

5. **Agility is Essential in Modern IT Leadership:** The ability to make quick, informed decisions and adapt to new information is essential in the ever-changing landscape of IT. Agile decision-making practices, which allow for rapid iterations and adjustments, help IT leaders navigate uncertainty and respond effectively to evolving business needs.

6. **Learning from Past Decisions Improves Future Outcomes:** Reflecting on past decisions—both successful and unsuccessful—provides valuable insights that can improve future decision-making. Organizations that cultivate a culture of continuous learning, where team members are encouraged to learn from their experiences, are better positioned to make smarter, more effective decisions over time.

By adopting these best practices and learning from successful IT initiatives, IT leaders can enhance their decision-making and problem-solving capabilities, driving their organizations toward greater success in the digital age.

Mastering IT Leadership and Management, Strategies for Success in the Digital Age

Conclusion

Decision-making and problem-solving are at the heart of effective IT leadership. As IT leaders navigate the complexities of today's fast-paced, technology-driven environment, their ability to make informed decisions and solve complex problems becomes a critical determinant of their organization's success. Throughout this chapter, we have explored the essential skills and strategies that IT leaders must develop to excel in these areas.

Strategic decision-making in IT is about more than just selecting the right technologies; it requires aligning decisions with the organization's broader business goals, evaluating risks and benefits, and considering the long-term implications of each choice. By involving stakeholders in the decision-making process and leveraging data-driven insights, IT leaders can make decisions that not only address immediate needs but also position the organization for future success.

Data-driven decision-making has emerged as a powerful tool for IT leaders. With the ability to gather, analyze, and interpret data, IT leaders can make more accurate and effective decisions. However, it's important to balance data with experience and intuition, especially in situations where data may be incomplete or ambiguous. The integration of data with sound judgment ensures that decisions are both informed and contextually relevant.

Problem-solving, an equally crucial skill, requires a methodical approach that starts with identifying the root cause of an issue and involves creative and collaborative solutions. IT leaders must be prepared to lead their teams through challenging situations, make decisions under pressure, and implement solutions that minimize disruption and maximize outcomes. The ability to adapt and remain resilient in the face of challenges is what separates successful IT leaders from the rest.

As we conclude Chapter 6, it's clear that decision-making and problem-solving are more than just technical skills—they are essential leadership competencies that enable IT leaders to drive their organizations forward. By mastering these skills, IT leaders can navigate the uncertainties of the digital landscape with confidence, ensuring that their teams and projects are always moving in the right direction. The principles and strategies discussed in this chapter provide a strong foundation for the continued exploration of leadership excellence as we move into the next areas of IT management and beyond.

Mastering IT Leadership and Management, Strategies for Success in the Digital Age

Quizzes

I. Multiple Choice Questions:

1. What is the most critical aspect of strategic decision-making in IT?

    A. Selecting the latest technology
    B. Aligning decisions with business goals
    C. Ensuring minimal risk
    D. Implementing decisions quickly

2. Which of the following techniques is used for root cause analysis?

    A. Brainstorming
    B. SWOT Analysis
    C. The "5 Whys"
    D. Mind Mapping

3. When making decisions under pressure, IT leaders should prioritize:

    A. Gathering all possible data before acting
    B. Maintaining composure and making decisive choices
    C. Delaying decisions until more information is available
    D. Consulting with every team member involved

4. Which of the following is NOT a best practice for effective problem-solving in IT?

    A. Fostering a culture of creativity
    B. Involving stakeholders in the decision-making process
    C. Ignoring past experiences to avoid bias
    D. Using a systematic approach to problem-solving

II. True/False Questions:

1. Data-driven decision-making should be balanced with experience and intuition. (True/False)
2. The primary focus of decision-making in IT should always be on immediate, short-term gains. (True/False)
3. Collaborative problem-solving can lead to more effective solutions by leveraging diverse perspectives. (True/False)
4. Continuous monitoring and adjusting decisions are unnecessary once an IT project is in motion. (True/False)

Mastering IT Leadership and Management, Strategies for Success in the Digital Age

Exercises

I. Root Cause Analysis Exercise:
   - **Objective:** Apply root cause analysis techniques to identify the underlying cause of a recent IT issue.
   - **Instructions:**
     1. Select a recent IT problem or incident within your organization.
     2. Use the "5 Whys" technique or a Fishbone (Ishikawa) Diagram to trace the root cause of the issue.
     3. Document the steps taken and the conclusions drawn from the analysis.
     4. Present your findings to your team and propose a solution that addresses the root cause, not just the symptoms.

II. Data-Driven Decision-Making Workshop:
   - **Objective:** Practice making decisions based on data analysis.
   - **Instructions:**
     1. Gather relevant data related to a strategic decision your IT department needs to make (e.g., adopting a new technology, optimizing a process).
     2. Analyze the data to identify trends, risks, and potential outcomes.
     3. Develop a decision-making plan that incorporates this data, balancing it with your intuition and experience.
     4. Discuss the plan with your team, emphasizing the rationale behind the decision and the data supporting it.

III. Creative Problem-Solving Session:
   - **Objective:** Encourage creative thinking in addressing a complex IT challenge.
   - **Instructions:**
     1. Identify a complex problem that requires a novel solution (e.g., improving system performance, enhancing cybersecurity).
     2. Organize a brainstorming session with your team, encouraging them to think outside the box.
     3. Use techniques like mind mapping or lateral thinking to explore unconventional solutions.
     4. Evaluate the proposed ideas and select the most viable solution for implementation.

IV. Decision-Making Under Pressure Simulation:
   - **Objective:** Develop the ability to make effective decisions in high-pressure situations.
   - **Instructions:**

Mastering IT Leadership and Management, Strategies for Success in the Digital Age

1. Create a scenario where your IT team faces a critical issue that requires immediate action (e.g., a system outage, a security breach).
2. Role-play the situation, with team members acting out their roles under the pressure of time constraints and incomplete information.
3. After the simulation, debrief with the team, discussing the decisions made, the rationale behind them, and any lessons learned.

V. Stakeholder Engagement Plan:
- **Objective:** Improve the quality of decision-making through stakeholder involvement.
- **Instructions:**
  1. Identify a strategic IT decision that requires broad support across the organization.
  2. Develop a stakeholder engagement plan that outlines how you will involve key stakeholders in the decision-making process.
  3. Include strategies for gathering input, addressing concerns, and building consensus.
  4. Implement the plan and evaluate its effectiveness in improving the decision's quality and acceptance.

These quizzes and exercises are designed to help readers of Chapter 6 better understand and apply the principles of effective decision-making and problem-solving in IT leadership, focusing on real-world scenarios and strategic thinking.

Mastering IT Leadership and Management, Strategies for Success in the Digital Age

Chapter 7: Managing Change in IT

"CHANGE IS THE LAW OF LIFE. AND THOSE WHO LOOK ONLY TO THE PAST OR PRESENT ARE CERTAIN TO MISS THE FUTURE."

— **John F. Kennedy**

Leading IT Change Initiatives

Change is a constant in the world of IT. Whether it's the implementation of new technologies, the adoption of new processes, or the reorganization of teams, IT leaders are often at the forefront of driving change within their organizations. Leading IT change initiatives requires not only technical expertise but also strong leadership skills, strategic thinking, and the ability to manage the human side of change.

1. **Understanding the Need for Change:** The first step in leading a successful IT change initiative is understanding the underlying reasons for the change. What are the business drivers behind the change? Is it to improve efficiency, reduce costs, enhance customer service, or gain a competitive advantage? By clearly articulating the rationale for the change, IT leaders can ensure that the initiative aligns with the organization's strategic goals and addresses real business needs.

2. **Developing a Clear Change Strategy:** Once the need for change has been identified, IT leaders must develop a clear strategy for implementing it. This involves setting clear objectives, defining the scope of the change, and outlining the steps needed to achieve the desired outcomes. A well-defined change strategy provides a roadmap for the initiative and helps ensure that all stakeholders are aligned and working toward the same goals.

3. **Building a Change Management Team:** Leading a successful IT change initiative often requires the support of a dedicated change management team. This team should include individuals with the skills and expertise needed to drive the change, as well as representatives from different parts of the organization who can provide insights and help build buy-in. The change management team is responsible for planning, coordinating, and executing the initiative, as well as managing any risks or challenges that arise along the way.

4. **Communicating the Change:** Effective communication is critical to the success of any change initiative. IT leaders must clearly communicate the goals, benefits, and impact of the change to all stakeholders, including executives, managers, employees, and customers. This involves not only explaining the technical aspects of the change but also addressing any concerns or fears stakeholders may have. Regular updates and open communication channels help build trust and keep everyone informed and engaged throughout the change process.

Mastering IT Leadership and Management, Strategies for Success in the Digital Age

5. **Engaging Stakeholders and Building Buy-In:** Successful change initiatives require the active engagement and support of all stakeholders. IT leaders must work to build buy-in from executives, managers, and employees by involving them in the change process, addressing their concerns, and demonstrating how the change will benefit both them and the organization. This can be achieved through workshops, meetings, and other forms of collaboration, as well as by recognizing and rewarding individuals who contribute to the success of the change initiative.

Mastering IT Leadership and Management, Strategies for Success in the Digital Age

Overcoming Resistance to Change

Resistance to change is a common challenge in any organization, and IT initiatives are no exception. Whether due to fear of the unknown, concerns about job security, or simply a preference for the status quo, employees and stakeholders may resist changes to the way they work. IT leaders must be prepared to identify and address resistance in order to successfully implement change.

1. **Identifying Sources of Resistance:** The first step in overcoming resistance to change is identifying where and why it exists. Resistance can take many forms, from overt opposition to passive non-compliance. It can stem from various sources, including a lack of understanding, fear of job loss, concerns about increased workload, or skepticism about the benefits of the change. IT leaders should take the time to listen to employees and stakeholders, understand their concerns, and identify the root causes of resistance.

2. **Addressing Concerns and Fears:** Once the sources of resistance have been identified, IT leaders must address them head-on. This involves providing clear, accurate information about the change, dispelling myths or misconceptions, and addressing any fears or concerns stakeholders may have. For example, if employees are worried about job loss due to automation, IT leaders can reassure them by explaining how the new technology will enhance their roles rather than replace them. By addressing concerns directly, IT leaders can reduce resistance and build support for the change initiative.

3. **Involving Employees in the Change Process:** One of the most effective ways to overcome resistance to change is to involve employees in the change process. When employees feel they have a voice in the change and that their input is valued, they are more likely to support the initiative. IT leaders can involve employees by seeking their feedback, including them in decision-making, and providing opportunities for them to contribute to the success of the change. This approach not only reduces resistance but also fosters a sense of ownership and commitment to the change.

4. **Providing Training and Support:** Resistance to change often arises from a lack of understanding or confidence in new technology or processes. IT leaders can address this by providing comprehensive training and support to help employees develop the skills and knowledge they need to succeed in the new environment. This could include formal training programs, one-on-one coaching, or online resources. By investing in employee development, IT leaders can reduce resistance and ensure a smoother transition.

5. **Celebrating Successes:** Recognizing and celebrating successes is an important part of overcoming resistance to change. By highlighting the positive outcomes of the change and acknowledging the contributions of those who have embraced it, IT leaders can reinforce the benefits of the change and encourage others to get on board. Celebrating successes also helps build momentum and keep the change initiative moving forward.

Mastering IT Leadership and Management, Strategies for Success in the Digital Age

Change Management Frameworks and Models

Effective change management requires a structured approach, and several frameworks and models are available to guide IT leaders in their change initiatives. These frameworks provide a systematic way to plan, implement, and monitor change, ensuring that all aspects of the process are addressed and that the initiative is successful.

1. **The ADKAR Model:** The ADKAR model is a goal-oriented change management framework that focuses on the individual stages of change. ADKAR stands for Awareness, Desire, Knowledge, Ability, and Reinforcement. According to this model, successful change requires individuals to be aware of the need for change, have the desire to support it, possess the knowledge and ability to implement it, and receive reinforcement to sustain the change. IT leaders can use the ADKAR model to identify where individuals are in the change process and provide targeted support to help them move forward.

2. **Kotter's 8-Step Change Model:** John Kotter's 8-step change model is one of the most widely recognized change management frameworks. It outlines a series of steps that organizations can take to successfully implement change, including creating a sense of urgency, building a guiding coalition, developing a vision and strategy, communicating the change, empowering employees, generating short-term wins, consolidating gains, and anchoring the change in the organization's culture. IT leaders can use Kotter's model as a roadmap for planning and executing change initiatives, ensuring that all critical steps are addressed.

3. **Lewin's Change Management Model:** Kurt Lewin's change management model is based on the concept of unfreezing, changing, and refreezing. According to this model, successful change requires first unfreezing the existing state, implementing the change, and then refreezing the new state to make it permanent. IT leaders can use Lewin's model to guide the process of transitioning from the old way of doing things to the new way, ensuring that the change is fully integrated and sustainable.

4. **The McKinsey 7-S Model:** The McKinsey 7-S model is a holistic framework that examines seven key elements of an organization: strategy, structure, systems, shared values, style, staff, and skills. According to this model, successful change requires alignment and coordination across all seven elements. IT leaders can use the McKinsey 7-S model to assess the organization's readiness for change, identify areas that need adjustment, and ensure that all aspects of the organization are aligned with the change initiative.

5. **The Prosci Change Management Framework:** The Prosci change management framework combines individual change management with organizational change management. It emphasizes the importance of managing change at both the individual and organizational levels, using tools such as the ADKAR model, change management assessments, and change management plans. IT leaders can use the Prosci framework to ensure that change initiatives are supported by both the organization and its people.

Mastering IT Leadership and Management, Strategies for Success in the Digital Age

Industry Case Study: Managing Change at Procter & Gamble (P&G) through IT Leadership

Situation:
In the early 2000s, Procter & Gamble (P&G), one of the world's largest consumer goods companies, faced the challenge of modernizing its IT systems to keep pace with rapid global expansion and streamline operations. The company's existing IT infrastructure was fragmented, with numerous legacy systems that were difficult to integrate and maintain. This created inefficiencies and impeded P&G's ability to innovate and respond quickly to market changes. The company needed to undergo a significant IT transformation to remain competitive and continue its growth trajectory.

Task:
The task for P&G's IT leadership was to manage a large-scale IT change initiative that would standardize and integrate the company's global IT systems. This involved not only updating technology but also addressing the organizational and cultural challenges associated with such a major transformation. IT leaders needed to ensure that the new systems were adopted smoothly across the organization, with minimal disruption to ongoing operations.

Action:
To effectively manage this change, P&G's IT leadership implemented several strategic actions:

1. **Developing a Clear Change Management Strategy:** P&G's IT leaders began by formulating a comprehensive change management plan. This plan included a clear vision for the IT transformation, specific goals and timelines, and a detailed roadmap for how the change would be implemented across the organization. They also identified potential risks and developed strategies to mitigate them.

2. **Engaging Stakeholders Early:** Understanding that successful change requires buy-in from all levels of the organization, P&G's IT leaders engaged stakeholders early in the process. They communicated the benefits of the new IT systems to both senior executives and front-line employees, highlighting how these changes would support P&G's overall business strategy. Regular updates and open communication channels helped maintain transparency and build trust throughout the organization.

3. **Investing in Training and Support:** To ensure a smooth transition, P&G provided extensive training programs for employees at all levels. This training was designed to help employees understand the new systems and processes and equip them with the skills needed to adapt to the changes. P&G also established support systems, such as help desks and peer mentoring, to assist employees as they navigated the new IT environment.

4. **Managing Resistance to Change:** P&G's IT leaders anticipated resistance and addressed it proactively. They created a network of change champions within the organization who could advocate for the new systems and help address concerns

among their peers. By involving employees in the change process and giving them a sense of ownership, P&G was able to reduce resistance and foster a more positive attitude toward the transformation.

Result:
As a result of these actions, P&G successfully implemented one of the largest and most complex IT transformations in its history. The new, integrated IT systems significantly improved operational efficiency, enabling P&G to streamline its supply chain, reduce costs, and respond more quickly to market demands. The company's ability to manage this change effectively not only minimized disruptions but also set the stage for continued innovation and growth. P&G emerged from the transformation stronger, more agile, and better equipped to compete in the global marketplace.

This case study demonstrates the importance of strategic change management in IT leadership. By developing a clear plan, engaging stakeholders, investing in training, and proactively managing resistance, P&G's IT leaders successfully guided the organization through a complex transformation, delivering lasting benefits that aligned with the company's strategic objectives.

Mastering IT Leadership and Management, Strategies for Success in the Digital Age

Best Practices

1. **Develop a Clear Change Management Strategy:** Successful IT change initiatives begin with a well-defined change management strategy. IT leaders should outline the goals, scope, timeline, and resources needed for the change. This strategy should include a detailed plan for communication, training, and stakeholder engagement to ensure that all aspects of the change are managed effectively.

2. **Engage Stakeholders Early and Often:** Early and continuous engagement with stakeholders is crucial for managing change successfully. IT leaders should involve stakeholders in the planning process to understand their concerns, gather input, and build support for the change. Regular updates and open communication throughout the change process help to maintain trust and alignment.

3. **Communicate the Vision and Benefits of Change:** Clear communication of the vision and benefits of the change is essential for gaining buy-in from all levels of the organization. IT leaders should articulate how the change aligns with the organization's strategic goals and how it will benefit stakeholders. This messaging should be consistent and reinforced through various communication channels.

4. **Provide Comprehensive Training and Support:** Training is a critical component of successful change management. IT leaders should ensure that all affected employees receive the necessary training to adapt to new systems, processes, or technologies. Ongoing support, such as help desks, user manuals, and peer mentoring, can help ease the transition and address any issues that arise.

5. **Address Resistance Proactively:** Resistance to change is natural and should be anticipated. IT leaders should proactively address resistance by understanding the root causes, listening to concerns, and providing reassurance. Involving change champions—trusted individuals within the organization who advocate for the change—can help to mitigate resistance and encourage others to embrace the new direction.

6. **Monitor Progress and Adjust as Needed:** Continuous monitoring of the change process is essential for identifying challenges and making necessary adjustments. IT leaders should establish key performance indicators (KPIs) to track progress and gather feedback regularly. This allows for timely interventions if the change initiative is not progressing as planned.

7. **Celebrate Successes and Learn from Challenges:** Recognizing and celebrating milestones and successes during the change process helps to maintain momentum and morale. Additionally, reflecting on challenges and lessons learned can provide valuable insights for future change initiatives. IT leaders should foster a culture of continuous improvement where feedback is valued and applied.

Mastering IT Leadership and Management, Strategies for Success in the Digital Age

Lessons Learned

1. **The Importance of a Structured Approach:** A structured approach to change management is essential for navigating the complexities of IT initiatives. Organizations that succeed in managing change often have a clear strategy, detailed plans, and well-defined roles and responsibilities. This structure ensures that all aspects of the change are addressed, reducing the likelihood of disruptions or setbacks.

2. **Stakeholder Involvement is Key to Success:** Involving stakeholders early in the change process increases the chances of success. When stakeholders feel heard and included, they are more likely to support the change. As seen in successful IT initiatives, stakeholder engagement helps build trust, reduce resistance, and ensure that the change meets the needs of the organization.

3. **Effective Communication Drives Buy-In:** Clear and consistent communication is a cornerstone of successful change management. IT leaders who effectively communicate the vision, purpose, and benefits of the change are more likely to gain buy-in from employees and other stakeholders. This communication helps align everyone with the change objectives and reduces uncertainty.

4. **Training and Support are Essential for Adoption:** Comprehensive training and ongoing support are critical for ensuring that employees can successfully adopt new systems or processes. In successful IT change initiatives, organizations invest in training programs that not only teach the technical aspects of the change but also address the cultural and behavioral adjustments needed.

5. **Proactive Resistance Management Prevents Disruption:** Anticipating and managing resistance proactively can prevent it from becoming a major obstacle. By addressing concerns early and involving change champions, IT leaders can turn potential resistance into an opportunity for engagement and improvement. This proactive approach helps maintain the momentum of the change initiative.

6. **Continuous Monitoring Ensures Success:** Regularly monitoring the progress of the change initiative allows IT leaders to identify and address issues before they escalate. Successful organizations use KPIs and feedback mechanisms to track the effectiveness of the change and make necessary adjustments. This ongoing oversight ensures that the change stays on course and achieves its intended outcomes.

7. **Learning from Each Change Initiative Builds Future Success:** Every change initiative offers lessons that can be applied to future efforts. Successful IT leaders take the time to reflect on what worked well and what didn't, using these insights to refine their approach to change management. This commitment to continuous improvement helps build organizational resilience and adaptability.

By applying these best practices and learning from successful IT change initiatives, IT leaders can navigate the challenges of change more effectively, ensuring that their

Mastering IT Leadership and Management, Strategies for Success in the Digital Age

organizations are well-positioned to thrive in a dynamic and evolving technological landscape.

Mastering IT Leadership and Management, Strategies for Success in the Digital Age

Conclusion

Managing change in IT is a critical leadership competency in today's rapidly evolving technological landscape. As explored in this chapter, IT leaders are often at the forefront of driving change within their organizations, whether through the adoption of new technologies, the implementation of new processes, or the reorganization of teams. Successfully leading these change initiatives requires a blend of strategic thinking, strong communication skills, and an understanding of the human side of change.

Leading IT change initiatives begins with a clear understanding of the need for change and the development of a well-defined strategy. By articulating the business drivers behind the change and setting clear objectives, IT leaders can align their teams and stakeholders around a common vision. Building a dedicated change management team and engaging stakeholders early in the process are essential steps in ensuring that the change is embraced and executed effectively.

Overcoming resistance to change is one of the most significant challenges IT leaders face. Whether due to fear of the unknown, concerns about job security, or a preference for the status quo, resistance can hinder the success of any change initiative. IT leaders must proactively address these concerns, involve employees in the change process, and provide the necessary training and support to ease the transition.

Utilizing established change management frameworks and models, such as the ADKAR Model, Kotter's 8-Step Change Model, and Lewin's Change Management Model, provides a structured approach to navigating the complexities of change. These frameworks help IT leaders manage both the technical and human aspects of change, ensuring that the change is not only implemented but also sustained over the long term.

As we conclude Chapter 7, it is clear that managing change in IT is not just about implementing new technologies or processes—it is about guiding people through the transition and ensuring that the organization emerges stronger and more resilient. IT leaders who master the art of change management will be well-equipped to lead their organizations through the inevitable shifts and transformations that define the digital age. The insights and strategies discussed in this chapter provide a solid foundation for approaching change with confidence and driving successful outcomes in any IT initiative. As we move forward, these principles will continue to inform our exploration of strategic IT management and leadership.

Mastering IT Leadership and Management, Strategies for Success in the Digital Age

Quizzes

I. Multiple Choice Questions:

1. What is the first step in leading a successful IT change initiative?

    A. Developing a training program
    B. Understanding the business drivers behind the change
    C. Announcing the change to all employees
    D. Forming a change management team

2. Why is stakeholder engagement crucial in managing IT change initiatives?

    A. It allows for faster decision-making
    B. It ensures compliance with industry regulations
    C. It builds trust and reduces resistance to change
    D. It simplifies the technical aspects of the change

3. Which of the following is NOT a best practice for managing resistance to change?

    A. Identifying sources of resistance early
    B. Ignoring resistance in hopes it will dissipate
    C. Involving employees in the change process
    D. Addressing concerns and fears directly

4. According to Kotter's 8-Step Change Model, what is the purpose of generating short-term wins?

    A. To complete the change process quickly
    B. To maintain momentum and validate the change effort
    C. To satisfy executive demands
    D. To avoid the need for further change

II. True/False Questions:

1. Effective communication is only necessary during the initial stages of an IT change initiative. (True/False)
2. Proactively managing resistance can prevent disruptions during the change process. (True/False)
3. Comprehensive training is essential for helping employees adapt to new systems or processes. (True/False)
4. Once a change is implemented, there is no need to monitor its progress or impact. (True/False)

Mastering IT Leadership and Management, Strategies for Success in the Digital Age

Exercises

I. Change Management Strategy Development:
   - **Objective:** Develop a comprehensive change management strategy for a hypothetical IT initiative.
   - **Instructions:**
     1. Identify a significant change that your IT department might face, such as adopting a new technology or restructuring the team.
     2. Develop a change management strategy that includes the following:
        - A clear vision and objectives for the change
        - A detailed plan for stakeholder engagement
        - Communication strategies to ensure transparency
        - Methods for addressing resistance and fostering buy-in
        - Training and support plans for employees
     3. Present your strategy to a peer or mentor for feedback.

II. Case Study Analysis:
   - **Objective:** Analyze the case study of Procter & Gamble's IT transformation as described in the chapter.
   - **Instructions:**
     1. Summarize the key actions taken by P&G's IT leadership to manage the change process.
     2. Identify the challenges faced and how they were addressed.
     3. Reflect on how the lessons learned from P&G's experience could be applied to your organization.

III. Resistance Management Role-Play:
   - **Objective:** Practice managing resistance to change in a controlled environment.
   - **Instructions:**
     1. Create a scenario where an IT change initiative is met with resistance from a group of employees.
     2. Role-play the situation with a colleague, taking turns as the IT leader and the resistant employees.
     3. After the role-play, discuss the effectiveness of the strategies used to address resistance and consider alternative approaches.

IV. Stakeholder Communication Plan:
   - **Objective:** Develop a communication plan to engage stakeholders throughout the change process.
   - **Instructions:**
     1. Identify the key stakeholders for a specific IT change initiative.

Mastering IT Leadership and Management, Strategies for Success in the Digital Age

    2. Create a communication plan that outlines how you will keep stakeholders informed and engaged at each stage of the change process.
    3. Include different communication channels, frequency of updates, and key messages tailored to each stakeholder group.
    4. Implement the plan in a simulated environment and evaluate its effectiveness.

V. Continuous Monitoring and Adjustment:
- **Objective:** Learn how to continuously monitor and adjust change initiatives to ensure success.
- **Instructions:**
    1. Select a change initiative that is currently underway or was recently completed in your organization.
    2. Develop a set of key performance indicators (KPIs) to monitor the progress and impact of the change.
    3. Create a feedback mechanism to gather input from employees and stakeholders regularly.
    4. Use the collected data to make adjustments to the change initiative as needed to ensure its continued success.

These quizzes and exercises are designed to help readers of Chapter 7 better understand and apply the principles of managing change in IT, focusing on real-world scenarios, strategic planning, and effective communication.

Mastering IT Leadership and Management, Strategies for Success in the Digital Age

Conclusion of Part 2: Essential Skills for IT Leaders

Part 2 of this book has explored the essential skills that every IT leader must master to thrive in today's complex and fast-paced digital environment. As we've seen, effective leadership in IT is not solely about technical expertise; it requires a blend of strategic thinking, people management, communication, and decision-making capabilities that collectively drive organizational success.

Leading IT teams demands more than just overseeing projects and technology; it involves building and nurturing high-performance teams, adapting leadership styles to diverse situations, and empowering and motivating professionals to reach their full potential. The ability to foster collaboration and create a positive, innovative work culture is key to achieving sustained success.

Communication stands out as a critical skill that bridges the gap between IT and the broader business. Whether it's presenting technical concepts to executives, translating IT strategies for non-technical stakeholders, or resolving conflicts, IT leaders must communicate clearly, persuasively, and empathetically to align technology initiatives with business goals and foster collaboration across the organization.

Decision-making and problem-solving are at the core of IT leadership. The ability to make informed, strategic decisions and tackle complex problems head-on ensures that IT leaders can navigate challenges, mitigate risks, and capitalize on opportunities. Balancing data-driven insights with experience and intuition, and leading teams through high-pressure situations, are essential to maintaining momentum and achieving desired outcomes.

As we conclude Part 2, it's clear that mastering these essential skills is fundamental for any IT leader aiming to guide their organization through the uncertainties and opportunities of the digital age. The competencies discussed in these chapters form the backbone of effective IT leadership, equipping leaders to not only manage today's challenges but also to anticipate and prepare for the demands of the future.

With a strong foundation in these essential skills, IT leaders are better positioned to engage in strategic management practices, navigate digital transformations, and drive their organizations toward long-term success. As we move into the next sections of the book, these skills will continue to play a pivotal role in the broader context of strategic IT management and leadership.

Mastering IT Leadership and Management, Strategies for Success in the Digital Age

Part 3: Strategic IT Management

"STRATEGY IS NOT THE CONSEQUENCE OF PLANNING, BUT THE OPPOSITE: ITS STARTING POINT."

— Henry Mintzberg

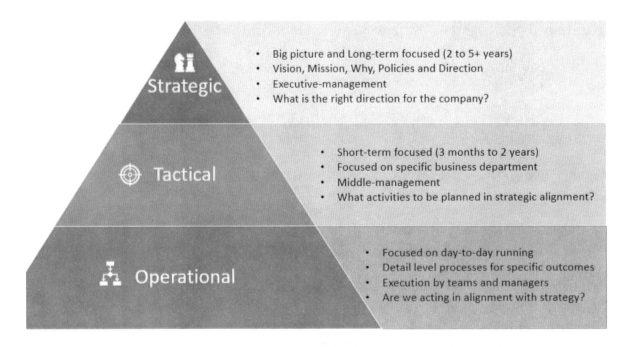

Mastering IT Leadership and Management, Strategies for Success in the Digital Age

Chapter 8: IT Governance and Compliance

"GOOD GOVERNANCE IS THE ART OF PUTTING WISE THOUGHT INTO PRUDENT ACTION IN A WAY THAT ADVANCES THE WELL-BEING OF THOSE GOVERNED."
— **Diane Kalen-Sukra**

Implementing IT Governance Frameworks

Effective IT governance is essential for aligning IT strategy with business objectives, ensuring accountability, and managing risks. It provides a structured framework that guides decision-making, prioritizes IT investments, and ensures that IT delivers value to the organization. Implementing an IT governance framework involves defining roles and responsibilities, establishing policies and procedures, and ensuring that IT activities are aligned with the organization's goals.

1. **Understanding IT Governance:**
   IT governance is the framework that ensures IT supports and enhances the overall goals of the organization. It involves processes, structures, and mechanisms that direct and control IT decision-making, resource allocation, and performance management. IT governance is not just about compliance with regulations; it's about optimizing IT's contribution to the business and ensuring that IT investments deliver value.

2. **Choosing the Right IT Governance Framework:**
   There are several IT governance frameworks that organizations can adopt, each with its own strengths and focus areas. The choice of framework depends on the organization's size, industry, regulatory environment, and specific needs. Some of the most widely used IT governance frameworks include:

   - **COBIT (Control Objectives for Information and Related Technologies):**
     COBIT is a comprehensive framework providing best practices for IT governance and management. It focuses on aligning IT with business goals, managing IT risks, and ensuring that IT resources are used effectively and efficiently. COBIT is widely used in organizations that require a high level of control and accountability in their IT operations.

   - **ITIL (Information Technology Infrastructure Library):**
     ITIL is a framework for IT service management that focuses on delivering high-quality IT services to meet business needs. It provides best practices for managing IT services, including service strategy, design, transition, operation, and continual service improvement. ITIL is particularly useful for organizations aiming to improve IT service delivery and customer satisfaction.

   - **ISO/IEC 38500:**
     ISO/IEC 38500 is an international standard for IT governance that provides

Mastering IT Leadership and Management, Strategies for Success in the Digital Age

principles and guidelines for governing IT within organizations. It emphasizes aligning IT with business objectives, managing it effectively, and ensuring it delivers value to stakeholders. ISO/IEC 38500 is often used by organizations aiming to ensure their IT governance practices meet global standards.

3. **Defining Roles and Responsibilities:**
   A key component of IT governance is defining the roles and responsibilities of those involved in IT decision-making. This includes establishing clear lines of accountability, ensuring a distinction between governance and management, and defining the responsibilities of IT leaders, business leaders, and other stakeholders. For example, the board of directors may be responsible for setting overall IT strategy, while the CIO is responsible for implementing that strategy and managing IT operations.

4. **Establishing Policies and Procedures:**
   IT governance requires a set of policies and procedures to guide IT activities and ensure alignment with business objectives. These policies should cover areas such as IT risk management, resource management, performance management, and compliance. They should be regularly reviewed and updated to remain relevant and effective. IT leaders must also communicate these policies to all relevant stakeholders, ensuring a clear understanding of their importance and impact.

5. **Monitoring and Reporting:**
   Effective IT governance requires ongoing monitoring and reporting to ensure IT activities are delivering desired outcomes. This includes tracking key performance indicators (KPIs), monitoring IT risks, and regularly reporting on IT performance to the board of directors and other stakeholders. IT leaders should establish a governance dashboard to provide a clear view of IT performance and allow for timely decision-making and corrective actions when necessary.

Mastering IT Leadership and Management, Strategies for Success in the Digital Age

Ensuring Compliance with Industry Regulations

Compliance with industry regulations is a critical aspect of IT governance. Organizations must ensure that their IT activities comply with a wide range of laws, regulations, and standards governing the use of technology, data, and information systems. Non-compliance can result in significant legal, financial, and reputational risks, making it essential for IT leaders to implement robust compliance programs.

1. **Understanding Regulatory Requirements:**
   The first step in ensuring compliance is understanding the regulatory requirements that apply to the organization. This includes identifying the relevant laws, regulations, and standards that govern IT activities, such as data protection laws (e.g., GDPR, CCPA), industry-specific regulations (e.g., HIPAA for healthcare, PCI DSS for payment card processing), and cybersecurity standards (e.g., NIST, ISO 27001). IT leaders should work closely with legal and compliance teams to ensure a comprehensive understanding of these requirements.

2. **Implementing Compliance Controls:**
   Once the regulatory requirements have been identified, IT leaders must implement the necessary controls to ensure compliance. This includes establishing policies and procedures for data protection, access control, incident response, and other key areas of IT operations. IT leaders should also ensure that these controls are integrated into the organization's overall IT governance framework and are regularly tested and audited for effectiveness.

3. **Conducting Compliance Audits:**
   Regular compliance audits are essential for ensuring that the organization's IT activities align with regulatory requirements. These audits should be conducted by independent auditors with the expertise to assess the organization's compliance with relevant laws and standards. The findings should be reported to the board of directors and used to inform any necessary corrective actions.

4. **Training and Awareness:**
   Compliance with industry regulations requires a high level of awareness and understanding among all employees, not just those in the IT department. IT leaders should implement training programs that educate employees on the importance of compliance, the specific regulations applicable to their roles, and the policies and procedures they must follow. Regular training and awareness programs help create a culture of compliance within the organization and reduce the risk of non-compliance.

5. **Staying Up-to-Date with Regulatory Changes:**
   The regulatory landscape is constantly evolving, with new laws and standards being introduced regularly. IT leaders must stay current with these changes and ensure that their compliance programs are updated accordingly. This may involve collaborating with legal and compliance teams, attending industry conferences, and subscribing to regulatory updates. By staying informed, IT leaders can ensure their organization remains compliant with the latest regulatory requirements.

Mastering IT Leadership and Management, Strategies for Success in the Digital Age

Ensuring Compliance with Industry Regulations

In today's rapidly evolving digital landscape, compliance with industry regulations is not only a legal requirement but also a critical component of an organization's overall risk management strategy. IT leaders must ensure that their organization's IT systems, processes, and practices align with relevant regulations to protect sensitive data, avoid legal penalties, and maintain stakeholder trust. This chapter explores the importance of compliance, strategies for achieving it, and the role of IT governance in sustaining long-term compliance.

Understanding Regulatory Requirements
The first step in ensuring compliance is thoroughly understanding the specific regulations that apply to your organization. These regulations often vary based on industry, geographic location, and the type of data handled by the organization. Common regulatory frameworks include:

- **General Data Protection Regulation (GDPR):** A comprehensive data protection regulation that applies to organizations operating within the European Union (EU) or handling the data of EU residents. GDPR mandates stringent data protection measures and grants individuals significant rights over their personal data.

- **Health Insurance Portability and Accountability Act (HIPAA):** U.S. regulations focused on protecting sensitive patient health information. HIPAA requires covered entities and their business associates to implement robust security measures to safeguard Protected Health Information (PHI).

- **Sarbanes-Oxley Act (SOX):** U.S. legislation that establishes requirements for financial reporting and corporate governance. IT systems involved in financial reporting must comply with SOX to ensure the integrity and accuracy of financial data.

- **Payment Card Industry Data Security Standard (PCI DSS):** A set of security standards designed to protect credit card information during processing, storage, and transmission. Organizations that handle cardholder data must adhere to PCI DSS requirements to ensure data security.

Developing a Compliance Strategy
A proactive compliance strategy is essential for managing the complexities of regulatory requirements. This strategy should be integrated into the broader IT governance framework and include the following key elements:

1. **Compliance Assessment:** Conduct regular assessments to identify which regulations apply to your organization and evaluate the current state of compliance. This involves auditing existing IT systems, processes, and policies to determine gaps and areas for improvement.

Mastering IT Leadership and Management, Strategies for Success in the Digital Age

2. **Policy Development:** Develop and document clear policies and procedures that align with regulatory requirements. These policies should cover data protection, access control, incident response, and other critical areas. Ensure that policies are regularly reviewed and updated to reflect regulatory changes.

3. **Employee Training and Awareness:** Compliance is not just an IT responsibility; it requires commitment from the entire organization. Implement ongoing training programs to educate employees about regulatory requirements and their role in maintaining compliance. This includes understanding data privacy principles, recognizing phishing attempts, and adhering to security protocols.

4. **Technology Implementation:** Leverage technology to support compliance efforts. This includes deploying encryption, access management tools, and monitoring systems to protect sensitive data and ensure that only authorized personnel have access to critical systems. Regularly update and patch systems to address vulnerabilities.

5. **Third-Party Management:** Many organizations rely on third-party vendors for services like cloud storage or payment processing. Ensure that these vendors comply with relevant regulations by conducting due diligence, reviewing their security practices, and obtaining assurances of compliance.

6. **Continuous Monitoring and Reporting:** Establish mechanisms for continuous compliance monitoring. This includes tracking regulatory changes, auditing IT systems, and generating compliance reports for internal stakeholders and regulatory bodies. Regular reporting helps demonstrate compliance and identifies areas for improvement.

Integrating Compliance into IT Governance
Compliance should be an integral part of your IT governance framework. This integration ensures that compliance is not treated as a one-time project but as an ongoing process embedded in the organization's IT strategy. Key steps include:

1. **Aligning IT Goals with Regulatory Requirements:**
   Ensure that IT goals and projects are aligned with regulatory requirements from the outset. This involves incorporating compliance considerations into IT project planning, system design, and risk management processes.

2. **Establishing Accountability:**
   Assign clear responsibilities for compliance within the IT leadership team. This includes designating a Chief Compliance Officer or a similar role to oversee compliance efforts and report to senior management and the board of directors.

3. **Regular Review and Adaptation:**
   The regulatory landscape is constantly evolving. Regularly review and update your IT governance framework to adapt to new regulations and emerging compliance

challenges. This proactive approach helps the organization stay ahead of potential risks and avoid costly penalties.

4. **Embedding Compliance in the Organizational Culture:**
   Promote a culture of compliance across the organization. This involves reinforcing the importance of compliance in all IT activities and encouraging employees to prioritize regulatory requirements in their daily work.

Conclusion

Ensuring compliance with industry regulations is a critical aspect of IT governance that safeguards the organization's assets, reputation, and legal standing. By developing a robust compliance strategy, leveraging technology, and integrating compliance into the broader IT governance framework, IT leaders can effectively manage regulatory risks and support the organization's long-term success. As regulations continue to evolve, maintaining compliance will require ongoing vigilance, adaptability, and a commitment to excellence in IT management.

Mastering IT Leadership and Management, Strategies for Success in the Digital Age

2. **Policy Development:** Develop and document clear policies and procedures that align with regulatory requirements. These policies should cover data protection, access control, incident response, and other critical areas. Ensure that policies are regularly reviewed and updated to reflect regulatory changes.

3. **Employee Training and Awareness:** Compliance is not just an IT responsibility; it requires commitment from the entire organization. Implement ongoing training programs to educate employees about regulatory requirements and their role in maintaining compliance. This includes understanding data privacy principles, recognizing phishing attempts, and adhering to security protocols.

4. **Technology Implementation:** Leverage technology to support compliance efforts. This includes deploying encryption, access management tools, and monitoring systems to protect sensitive data and ensure that only authorized personnel have access to critical systems. Regularly update and patch systems to address vulnerabilities.

5. **Third-Party Management:** Many organizations rely on third-party vendors for services like cloud storage or payment processing. Ensure that these vendors comply with relevant regulations by conducting due diligence, reviewing their security practices, and obtaining assurances of compliance.

6. **Continuous Monitoring and Reporting:** Establish mechanisms for continuous compliance monitoring. This includes tracking regulatory changes, auditing IT systems, and generating compliance reports for internal stakeholders and regulatory bodies. Regular reporting helps demonstrate compliance and identifies areas for improvement.

Integrating Compliance into IT Governance

Compliance should be an integral part of your IT governance framework. This integration ensures that compliance is not treated as a one-time project but as an ongoing process embedded in the organization's IT strategy. Key steps include:

1. **Aligning IT Goals with Regulatory Requirements:**
   Ensure that IT goals and projects are aligned with regulatory requirements from the outset. This involves incorporating compliance considerations into IT project planning, system design, and risk management processes.

2. **Establishing Accountability:**
   Assign clear responsibilities for compliance within the IT leadership team. This includes designating a Chief Compliance Officer or a similar role to oversee compliance efforts and report to senior management and the board of directors.

3. **Regular Review and Adaptation:**
   The regulatory landscape is constantly evolving. Regularly review and update your IT governance framework to adapt to new regulations and emerging compliance

challenges. This proactive approach helps the organization stay ahead of potential risks and avoid costly penalties.

4. **Embedding Compliance in the Organizational Culture:**
   Promote a culture of compliance across the organization. This involves reinforcing the importance of compliance in all IT activities and encouraging employees to prioritize regulatory requirements in their daily work.

Conclusion

Ensuring compliance with industry regulations is a critical aspect of IT governance that safeguards the organization's assets, reputation, and legal standing. By developing a robust compliance strategy, leveraging technology, and integrating compliance into the broader IT governance framework, IT leaders can effectively manage regulatory risks and support the organization's long-term success. As regulations continue to evolve, maintaining compliance will require ongoing vigilance, adaptability, and a commitment to excellence in IT management.

Mastering IT Leadership and Management, Strategies for Success in the Digital Age

Risk Management in IT

Risk management is a key component of IT governance and compliance. IT leaders must proactively identify, assess, and mitigate risks that could impact the organization's IT operations and overall business objectives. Effective risk management helps protect the organization from potential threats, minimize the impact of incidents, and ensure the continuity of IT services.

1. **Identifying IT Risks:**
   The first step in IT risk management is identifying risks that could impact the organization's IT operations. These risks may come from various sources, including cyber threats, hardware and software failures, human error, and natural disasters. IT leaders should conduct a thorough risk assessment to identify potential risks, assess their likelihood and impact, and prioritize them based on severity.

2. **Implementing Risk Mitigation Controls:**
   Once risks are identified, IT leaders must implement controls to mitigate them. This includes deploying technical controls such as firewalls, encryption, and access controls, along with administrative controls like policies, procedures, and training programs. IT leaders should also consider redundancy and backup solutions to ensure the continuity of IT services in the event of a failure or incident.

3. **Developing an Incident Response Plan:**
   An effective incident response plan is essential for managing IT risks and minimizing the impact of incidents. The plan should outline the steps to be taken in the event of an incident, including how the incident will be detected, reported, and managed. It should also define the roles and responsibilities of the incident response team and provide guidelines for communicating with stakeholders, including customers, employees, and regulators.

4. **Monitoring and Reviewing Risks:**
   IT risk management is an ongoing process that requires continuous monitoring and review. IT leaders should regularly assess the organization's risk landscape, evaluate the effectiveness of existing controls, and make adjustments as needed. This may involve conducting regular risk assessments, reviewing incident reports, and staying informed about emerging threats and vulnerabilities.

5. **Reporting on IT Risks:**
   IT leaders must ensure there is a clear and effective process for reporting on IT risks to the board of directors and other stakeholders. This includes providing regular updates on the organization's risk profile, highlighting key risks and mitigation efforts, and making recommendations for necessary actions. By delivering timely and accurate information, IT leaders can ensure that decision-makers have the insights they need to manage IT risks effectively.

Mastering IT Leadership and Management, Strategies for Success in the Digital Age

Industry Case Study: IT Governance and Compliance at JPMorgan Chase

Situation:
In the wake of the 2008 financial crisis, financial institutions faced heightened scrutiny and regulatory pressure to ensure robust governance and compliance practices. JPMorgan Chase, one of the largest banks in the United States, recognized the need to strengthen its IT governance and compliance frameworks to mitigate risks, protect customer data, and comply with increasingly stringent regulations such as the Dodd-Frank Act and the Gramm-Leach-Bliley Act (GLBA). The bank's existing governance structures required enhancement to address the growing complexity of its operations and the rapid pace of technological change.

Task:
JPMorgan Chase's IT leadership was tasked with implementing a comprehensive IT governance framework to ensure compliance with industry regulations, enhance risk management, and align IT initiatives with the bank's strategic objectives. This involved not only adhering to regulatory requirements but also creating a resilient IT infrastructure capable of supporting the bank's global operations while safeguarding against potential threats.

Action:
To achieve these goals, JPMorgan Chase undertook several key initiatives:

1. **Establishing a Robust IT Governance Framework:**
   The bank implemented a governance framework based on best practices from frameworks like COBIT and ISO/IEC 38500. This framework provided clear guidelines for IT decision-making, resource allocation, and performance management, ensuring that IT initiatives aligned with the bank's business goals and regulatory requirements.

2. **Enhancing Compliance Monitoring and Reporting:**
   JPMorgan Chase developed sophisticated monitoring and reporting mechanisms to ensure ongoing compliance with relevant regulations. This included automated compliance checks, regular audits, and detailed reporting to senior management and regulatory bodies. The bank also integrated compliance into its broader IT governance framework, ensuring compliance considerations were embedded in all IT projects and processes.

3. **Fostering a Culture of Compliance:**
   Recognizing that effective compliance requires more than just policies and procedures, JPMorgan Chase focused on fostering a culture of compliance across the organization. This involved comprehensive training programs for employees, ongoing communication about the importance of compliance, and the establishment of accountability structures to ensure adherence to governance standards.

4. **Continuous Risk Management:**
   The bank strengthened its risk management practices by conducting regular risk

assessments and implementing controls to mitigate identified risks. This proactive approach allowed JPMorgan Chase to stay ahead of potential threats and maintain the resilience of its IT infrastructure.

Result:
As a result of these efforts, JPMorgan Chase achieved a higher level of IT governance and compliance, significantly reducing the risks associated with regulatory breaches and misaligned IT initiatives. The enhanced governance framework ensured that IT investments were strategically aligned with the bank's business goals, maximizing value and supporting long-term success. The bank's ability to integrate compliance into its IT governance framework not only helped meet regulatory requirements but also built trust with stakeholders and enhanced its reputation in the financial industry.

This case study demonstrates the importance of robust IT governance and compliance practices in the financial sector. By adopting a proactive and comprehensive approach, JPMorgan Chase was able to navigate the complex regulatory landscape, safeguard its operations, and position itself for continued growth in a competitive environment.

Mastering IT Leadership and Management, Strategies for Success in the Digital Age

Best Practices

1. **Implement a Robust IT Governance Framework:**
   Establishing a strong IT governance framework is crucial for ensuring that IT activities align with the organization's goals and comply with relevant regulations. Frameworks like COBIT, ITIL, or ISO 27001 provide structured approaches to governance, helping organizations manage IT resources effectively and ensure IT supports business objectives.

2. **Align IT Governance with Business Strategy:**
   IT governance should not operate in a silo; it must be closely aligned with the organization's overall business strategy. IT leaders should ensure that governance practices support strategic goals and drive value. This alignment ensures that IT investments, risk management, and resource allocation contribute to the organization's long-term success.

3. **Ensure Comprehensive Compliance Management:**
   Compliance with industry regulations and standards is a key component of IT governance. IT leaders should establish processes for monitoring and ensuring compliance with relevant laws, regulations, and standards. Regular audits, continuous monitoring, and clear documentation are essential for maintaining compliance and avoiding legal or financial penalties.

4. **Establish Clear Roles and Responsibilities:**
   Clear roles and responsibilities are essential for effective IT governance and compliance. IT leaders should define who is responsible for governance tasks, such as policy creation, risk management, and compliance monitoring. This clarity ensures accountability and prevents gaps in governance.

5. **Integrate Risk Management into Governance:**
   Risk management should be an integral part of IT governance. IT leaders should develop a risk management strategy that identifies, assesses, and mitigates risks related to IT operations. This proactive approach helps organizations avoid potential issues and ensures risks are managed in alignment with the organization's risk appetite.

6. **Foster a Culture of Compliance:**
   A strong culture of compliance is necessary for the success of IT governance initiatives. IT leaders should promote awareness and understanding of governance and compliance requirements across the organization. Training programs, regular communication, and leadership by example are effective ways to build and maintain this culture.

7. **Leverage Technology for Governance and Compliance:**
   Technology can be a powerful enabler of effective governance and compliance. IT leaders should leverage tools and platforms that automate compliance tracking, risk

Mastering IT Leadership and Management, Strategies for Success in the Digital Age

management, and governance reporting. Automation reduces the burden on staff, increases accuracy, and ensures governance processes are consistently applied.

Mastering IT Leadership and Management, Strategies for Success in the Digital Age

Lessons Learned

1. **The Importance of a Structured Governance Framework:**
Successful IT governance requires a structured framework that provides clear guidelines and best practices. Organizations that implement frameworks like COBIT or ITIL benefit from a standardized approach to managing IT resources, ensuring that governance practices are consistent and aligned with industry standards.

2. **Alignment with Business Objectives Drives Value:**
IT governance is most effective when closely aligned with the organization's strategic goals. By ensuring that IT activities support business objectives, IT leaders can demonstrate the value of IT investments and ensure that governance practices contribute to the organization's overall success.

3. **Compliance is an Ongoing Process:**
Compliance is not a one-time effort but an ongoing process requiring continuous monitoring and updating. Successful organizations recognize the need for regular audits, real-time compliance tracking, and proactive management of regulatory changes. This approach helps maintain compliance and reduces the risk of penalties.

4. **Clear Accountability Enhances Governance:**
Defining clear roles and responsibilities within the IT governance framework is crucial for effective management. When accountability is clearly established, it ensures that governance tasks are completed efficiently and that there are no gaps in oversight. This clarity also helps prevent conflicts and confusion among team members.

5. **Risk Management is Central to Governance:**
Integrating risk management into IT governance ensures that potential issues are identified and addressed before they can impact the organization. Successful IT initiatives incorporate risk assessments into their governance processes, allowing organizations to manage risks proactively and avoid costly disruptions.

6. **Building a Compliance Culture is Key to Sustainability:**
A strong culture of compliance is essential for sustaining effective governance practices. Organizations that prioritize compliance through training, communication, and leadership engagement are more likely to maintain adherence to regulations and standards. This culture also supports long-term success by embedding governance and compliance into the organization's DNA.

7. **Technology Enhances Governance Efficiency:**
Leveraging technology to support governance and compliance processes can significantly enhance efficiency and accuracy. Automation tools that handle compliance tracking, risk assessments, and reporting reduce manual workloads and ensure governance processes are applied consistently across the organization. Successful IT leaders use these tools to streamline governance and improve outcomes.

Mastering IT Leadership and Management, Strategies for Success in the Digital Age

By implementing these best practices and learning from successful IT governance and compliance initiatives, IT leaders can ensure their organizations not only meet regulatory requirements but also derive strategic value from their IT investments.

Mastering IT Leadership and Management, Strategies for Success in the Digital Age

Conclusion

IT governance and compliance are critical components of an organization's strategic framework, serving as the pillars that ensure technology aligns with business objectives and operates within the bounds of legal and regulatory requirements. Throughout this chapter, we have explored the essential elements of implementing effective IT governance frameworks, ensuring compliance with industry regulations, and managing risks within the IT landscape.

Effective IT governance provides the structure and processes necessary for decision-making, resource allocation, and performance management, all of which are crucial for maximizing the value of IT investments. By establishing clear roles, responsibilities, and accountability, organizations can ensure their IT functions are not only efficient but also strategically aligned with broader business goals.

Compliance, meanwhile, is an ongoing responsibility that requires vigilance, adaptability, and a proactive approach. Navigating the complex regulatory landscape is no small task, but it is essential for protecting the organization from legal penalties, reputational damage, and operational risks. By integrating compliance into the broader IT governance framework, organizations can maintain stakeholder trust and ensure long-term success.

As we conclude Chapter 8, it's clear that IT governance and compliance are not just about adhering to rules and regulations; they are about enabling the organization to thrive in a competitive and constantly changing environment. IT leaders who prioritize governance and compliance will not only safeguard their organizations but also create a resilient, adaptable IT infrastructure that supports innovation and growth.

The principles and practices discussed in this chapter provide a foundation for effective IT leadership, empowering leaders to make informed decisions, manage risks, and steer their organizations toward sustainable success. As we continue our exploration of strategic IT management, these foundational concepts will remain central to navigating the complexities of the digital age.

Mastering IT Leadership and Management, Strategies for Success in the Digital Age

Quizzes

I. Multiple Choice Questions:

1. Which framework is commonly used to establish a robust IT governance structure?

    A. Agile
    B. Lean
    C. COBIT
    D. Six Sigma

2. What is the primary goal of aligning IT governance with business strategy?

    A. To reduce IT costs
    B. To ensure compliance with industry standards
    C. To support business objectives and drive value
    D. To enhance technical capabilities

3. Which of the following is a key element of effective IT compliance management?

    A. Ignoring regulatory updates until absolutely necessary
    B. Conducting regular compliance audits
    C. Implementing ad-hoc policies
    D. Relying solely on manual processes

4. What role does technology play in IT governance and compliance?

    A. It complicates governance processes
    B. It automates and streamlines compliance tracking and reporting
    C. It replaces the need for governance frameworks
    D. It eliminates the need for human oversight

II. True/False Questions:
  1. IT governance is only about compliance with regulatory requirements. (True/False)
  2. A structured governance framework helps ensure that IT investments deliver value to the organization. (True/False)
  3. Compliance is a one-time effort that requires no ongoing management. (True/False)
  4. Embedding compliance into the organizational culture is crucial for sustained adherence to regulations. (True/False)

Mastering IT Leadership and Management, Strategies for Success in the Digital Age

Exercises

I. Governance Framework Selection:
   - **Objective:** Evaluate and select an appropriate IT governance framework for your organization.
   - **Instructions:**
     1. Research three different IT governance frameworks (e.g., COBIT, ITIL, ISO/IEC 38500).
     2. Compare the strengths and weaknesses of each framework in relation to your organization's size, industry, and strategic goals.
     3. Recommend the framework that best aligns with your organization's needs and justify your choice.

II. Compliance Audit Simulation:
   - **Objective:** Conduct a simulated compliance audit to assess your organization's adherence to relevant regulations.
   - **Instructions:**
     1. Identify a specific regulatory requirement (e.g., GDPR, HIPAA) applicable to your organization.
     2. Create an audit checklist based on this requirement, including areas such as data protection, access control, and incident response.
     3. Perform a mock audit, assessing your organization's compliance in these areas.
     4. Document any gaps or issues found during the audit and propose corrective actions.

III. Risk Management Integration:
   - **Objective:** Integrate risk management into the IT governance framework.
   - **Instructions:**
     1. Identify the top three IT risks facing your organization.
     2. Develop a risk management plan that includes risk identification, assessment, mitigation strategies, and monitoring processes.
     3. Ensure that this risk management plan is integrated into your existing IT governance framework, aligning it with business objectives.

IV. Compliance Culture Assessment:
   - **Objective:** Evaluate and improve the culture of compliance within your organization.
   - **Instructions:**
     1. Conduct a survey among employees to assess their understanding of and adherence to compliance requirements.

Mastering IT Leadership and Management, Strategies for Success in the Digital Age

2. Analyze the results to identify areas where the culture of compliance may be lacking.
3. Develop a plan to strengthen compliance culture through training, communication, and leadership engagement.
4. Implement the plan and track its effectiveness over time.

V. Technology in Governance and Compliance:
- **Objective:** Leverage technology to enhance governance and compliance efforts.
- **Instructions:**
    1. Identify technology tools (e.g., compliance tracking software, risk management platforms) that could improve your organization's governance and compliance processes.
    2. Evaluate the potential benefits and challenges of implementing these tools.
    3. Develop a proposal for integrating one or more of these tools into your IT governance framework, including a timeline and budget considerations.

These quizzes and exercises are designed to help readers of Chapter 8 better understand and apply the principles of IT governance and compliance, with a focus on practical application and strategic alignment.

Mastering IT Leadership and Management, Strategies for Success in the Digital Age

Chapter 9: IT Project and Portfolio Management

"A PROJECT IS COMPLETE WHEN IT STARTS WORKING FOR YOU, RATHER THAN YOU WORKING FOR IT."
— **Scott Allen**

Principles of IT Project Management

Effective IT project management is crucial for delivering technology solutions that meet organizational needs on time, within budget, and to the required quality standards. IT projects are often complex, involving multiple stakeholders, technical challenges, and tight deadlines. As an IT leader, mastering the principles of project management is key to ensuring successful outcomes and maximizing the value delivered to the organization.

1. **Defining Project Scope and Objectives:** The foundation of any successful IT project is a clear definition of its scope and objectives. The project scope outlines what the project will deliver, including specific features, functions, and outcomes. It also defines what is out of scope, helping to manage expectations and prevent scope creep. The project objectives should align with the organization's strategic goals and provide clear, measurable targets for success. IT leaders must ensure the scope and objectives are well-defined, agreed upon by all stakeholders, and documented at the outset of the project.

2. **Planning and Scheduling:** Once the scope and objectives are defined, the next step is to create a detailed project plan and schedule. The project plan outlines the tasks and activities required to achieve the objectives, including task sequences, dependencies, resource allocation, and timelines. The project schedule specifies when each task will be completed and establishes key milestones and deadlines. Effective planning and scheduling require a thorough understanding of the project's requirements, risks, and constraints. IT leaders should involve the project team and stakeholders in the planning process to ensure the plan is realistic, achievable, and aligned with business priorities.

3. **Resource Management:** IT projects often require significant resources, including people, technology, and budget. Effective resource management involves identifying the resources needed, allocating them efficiently, and managing them throughout the project lifecycle. IT leaders must ensure the project has the right mix of skills and expertise, that resources are available when needed, and that the project remains within budget. This may involve negotiating with other departments for resources, managing conflicts over allocation, and adjusting the project plan to accommodate resource constraints.

4. **Risk Management:** Risk is inherent in IT project management, and successful projects require proactive risk management. This involves identifying potential risks that could impact success, assessing their likelihood and impact, and developing strategies to mitigate them. IT leaders should conduct a thorough risk assessment at the

Mastering IT Leadership and Management, Strategies for Success in the Digital Age

project's start and continuously monitor risks throughout its lifecycle. By managing risks proactively, IT leaders can reduce the likelihood of delays, cost overruns, and failures, ensuring the project delivers its intended value.

5. **Communication and Stakeholder Engagement:** Clear and consistent communication is critical to the success of any IT project. IT leaders must ensure that all stakeholders are informed about the project's progress, challenges, and any changes. This involves regular meetings, status reports, and updates, along with informal communication channels for addressing issues as they arise. Effective communication also requires engaging stakeholders throughout the project, ensuring their needs and expectations are understood and addressed. By keeping stakeholders informed and involved, IT leaders can build support for the project, manage expectations, and address concerns before they escalate.

6. **Quality Assurance and Testing:** Delivering a high-quality product is a key objective of IT project management. Quality assurance involves implementing processes and standards to ensure that deliverables meet the required criteria. This includes regular testing and validation of the product or system, as well as continuous monitoring and improvement of processes. IT leaders should establish a quality management plan that outlines quality standards, testing and validation procedures, and responsibilities for quality assurance. Prioritizing quality ensures that the project meets the organization's needs and delivers long-term value.

7. **Change Management:** IT projects are often subject to changes in scope, requirements, or priorities. Effective change management involves controlling and managing these changes to minimize disruption and keep the project on track. IT leaders should establish a change management process that includes evaluating the impact of proposed changes, obtaining stakeholder approval, and updating the project plan accordingly. By managing changes effectively, IT leaders can ensure the project adapts to evolving needs while maintaining its objectives and timelines.

8. **Project Closure and Evaluation:** The final stage of IT project management is project closure and evaluation. This involves completing all activities, delivering the final product or system, and obtaining formal acceptance from stakeholders. IT leaders should conduct a post-project review to evaluate success, identify lessons learned, and document best practices for future projects. This review should assess the project's performance against its objectives, scope, schedule, and budget, as well as the effectiveness of the management processes. By conducting a thorough evaluation, IT leaders can ensure that future projects benefit from the knowledge and experience gained.

Mastering IT Leadership and Management, Strategies for Success in the Digital Age

Managing IT Portfolios for Strategic Alignment

IT portfolio management is a critical component of IT governance, involving the oversight of the organization's entire set of IT projects, programs, and initiatives. The goal of IT portfolio management is to ensure that the organization's IT investments align with its strategic objectives, resources are allocated efficiently, and risks are managed effectively. By taking a portfolio-based approach, IT leaders can prioritize projects, balance short-term and long-term goals, and maximize the overall value delivered by IT.

1. **Understanding IT Portfolio Management:** IT portfolio management involves overseeing and coordinating the organization's IT projects, programs, and initiatives as a cohesive portfolio. This approach enables IT leaders to assess the collective impact of IT investments, identify interdependencies and synergies, and make informed decisions about resource allocation. IT portfolio management is not just about managing individual projects; it's about optimizing the entire portfolio to achieve the organization's strategic objectives.

2. **Aligning the IT Portfolio with Business Strategy:** The most important aspect of IT portfolio management is ensuring that the portfolio is aligned with the organization's business strategy. This involves evaluating each project or program in terms of its strategic value, risk, and return on investment (ROI). IT leaders should prioritize projects that support the organization's key goals, such as revenue growth, cost reduction, customer satisfaction, or innovation. By aligning the IT portfolio with business strategy, IT leaders can ensure that IT investments deliver maximum value to the organization.

3. **Balancing the IT Portfolio:** A well-managed IT portfolio includes a balanced mix of projects, programs, and initiatives that address both short-term and long-term needs. IT leaders must balance investments in new and innovative projects with the maintenance and enhancement of existing systems. This may involve allocating resources between projects that deliver immediate benefits and those that position the organization for future success. Balancing the portfolio also involves managing risk by diversifying investments across different areas, technologies, and time horizons.

4. **Resource Allocation and Prioritization:** Resource allocation is a key challenge in IT portfolio management. IT leaders must ensure that resources are allocated to the most strategically important projects while managing constraints such as budget, personnel, and technology. Prioritization is essential to ensure that limited resources are used effectively. IT leaders should establish criteria for prioritizing projects based on factors such as strategic alignment, ROI, risk, and urgency. By prioritizing projects, IT leaders can ensure that resources are focused on the initiatives that deliver the greatest value to the organization.

5. **Monitoring and Adjusting the IT Portfolio:** The IT portfolio is dynamic, and IT leaders must continuously monitor and adjust it to respond to changes in the business environment, technology landscape, and organizational priorities. This involves regularly reviewing the performance of the portfolio, assessing the progress of

Mastering IT Leadership and Management, Strategies for Success in the Digital Age

individual projects, and making adjustments as needed. IT leaders should be prepared to reallocate resources, adjust priorities, or even terminate projects that are no longer aligned with strategic goals. By taking a proactive approach to portfolio management, IT leaders can ensure that the portfolio remains aligned with the organization's objectives and delivers the desired outcomes.

6. **Measuring Portfolio Performance:** Measuring the performance of the IT portfolio is essential for ensuring that it delivers value to the organization. IT leaders should establish key performance indicators (KPIs) for the portfolio, such as ROI, cost savings, project success rates, and alignment with business goals. Regularly monitoring these KPIs allows IT leaders to assess the effectiveness of the portfolio management process, identify areas for improvement, and make data-driven decisions about future investments. By measuring portfolio performance, IT leaders can demonstrate the value of IT to the organization and ensure that IT continues to play a strategic role in the business.

Mastering IT Leadership and Management, Strategies for Success in the Digital Age

Best Practices in IT Project Delivery

Successful IT project delivery is the result of a combination of disciplined project management, effective governance, and a commitment to continuous improvement. By adhering to best practices, IT leaders can increase the likelihood of project success, mitigate risks, and deliver significant value to their organizations. Below are some best practices that should be incorporated into every IT project.

1. **Establishing Clear Goals and Requirements**

One of the most critical factors in successful IT project delivery is the establishment of clear, well-defined goals and requirements from the outset. This clarity ensures that all stakeholders have a shared understanding of the project's objectives and what constitutes success.

- **Engage Stakeholders Early:** Involve all key stakeholders, including business leaders, end-users, and technical teams, in the requirements-gathering process. This collaboration helps identify and document the needs, expectations, and constraints of the project, ensuring that the final product meets the business's needs.

- **Define Scope Clearly:** Clearly define the scope of the project, including the boundaries of what will and will not be delivered. This helps prevent scope creep, where additional features or functions are added without corresponding increases in time, budget, or resources.

- **Document Requirements Thoroughly:** All requirements should be documented in a detailed, accessible format. This documentation serves as the foundation for project planning, development, and testing. It also acts as a reference point for managing changes throughout the project lifecycle.

2. **Implementing Agile Methodologies**

Agile methodologies have become a cornerstone of modern IT project management, particularly for projects that require flexibility and iterative development. Agile promotes a dynamic approach that allows teams to respond quickly to changes, improve collaboration, and deliver incremental value.

- **Adopt Iterative Development:** Agile methodologies, such as Scrum or Kanban, focus on iterative development, where projects are broken down into smaller, manageable components. These components are developed, tested, and delivered in cycles (sprints), allowing for continuous improvement and adaptation.

- **Emphasize Collaboration:** Agile practices emphasize close collaboration among team members and stakeholders. Daily stand-up meetings, sprint reviews, and retrospectives foster open communication, quick decision-making, and continuous feedback, leading to better project outcomes.

- **Deliver Incremental Value:** Instead of waiting until the end of the project to deliver the final product, Agile encourages the delivery of incremental value throughout the project. This approach allows stakeholders to see progress early and often, providing opportunities to refine and adjust the product based on feedback.

Mastering IT Leadership and Management, Strategies for Success in the Digital Age

3. Focusing on Quality Assurance

Quality assurance (QA) is an integral part of IT project delivery. Ensuring that the project's deliverables meet the required quality standards is critical for achieving business objectives and maintaining stakeholder satisfaction.

- **Integrate QA Throughout the Project:** Quality assurance should not be an afterthought; it should be integrated into every phase of the project lifecycle. This includes continuous testing during development, validation of requirements, and regular code reviews to identify and address issues early.

- **Adopt Automated Testing:** Where possible, implement automated testing to increase efficiency and consistency in QA processes. Automated tests can quickly identify defects, ensure that new changes do not introduce errors, and free up QA resources to focus on more complex testing scenarios.

- **Conduct Regular Peer Reviews:** Regular peer reviews of code, designs, and documentation help maintain high standards of quality. These reviews provide opportunities for team members to catch errors, share knowledge, and improve overall project quality.

4. Managing Risks Proactively

Risk management is a critical aspect of IT project delivery. Proactively identifying, assessing, and mitigating risks helps prevent potential issues from derailing the project and ensures effective risk management.

- **Conduct a Thorough Risk Assessment:** At the start of the project, conduct a comprehensive risk assessment to identify potential risks that could impact the project. This assessment should consider technical, financial, operational, and regulatory risks.

- **Develop Risk Mitigation Plans:** For each identified risk, develop a mitigation plan that outlines how the risk will be managed if it materializes. This plan should include specific actions, assigned responsibilities, and contingency measures.

- **Monitor Risks Continuously:** Risk management is an ongoing process that requires continuous monitoring throughout the project. Regularly review and update the risk register, assess the effectiveness of mitigation strategies, and adjust plans as necessary to address emerging risks.

5. Effective Change Management

Changes in project scope, requirements, or priorities are inevitable in IT projects. Effective change management ensures that these changes are controlled and managed in a way that minimizes disruption and keeps the project on track.

- **Establish a Change Control Process:** Implement a formal change control process that defines how changes will be requested, evaluated, and approved. This process should include criteria for assessing the impact of changes on scope, budget, schedule, and quality.

Mastering IT Leadership and Management, Strategies for Success in the Digital Age

- **Communicate Changes Clearly:** Any changes to the project should be communicated clearly to all stakeholders. This includes explaining the reasons for the change, how it will affect the project, and what steps will be taken to implement it.

- **Manage Stakeholder Expectations:** Changes can impact stakeholder expectations, so it's important to manage these carefully. Keep stakeholders informed of any changes and ensure they understand the implications for the project's outcomes and timelines.

6. **Ensuring Stakeholder Engagement**

Active stakeholder engagement is crucial to the success of IT projects. Engaged stakeholders provide valuable insights, help align the project with business needs, and support the project through to completion.

- **Identify Key Stakeholders:** Early in the project, identify all key stakeholders, including those who will be affected by the project and those who have decision-making authority. Understand their interests, expectations, and concerns.

- **Maintain Regular Communication:** Keep stakeholders informed through regular updates, meetings, and reports. Provide opportunities for them to give feedback, ask questions, and express concerns. This continuous communication helps build trust and ensures that stakeholders remain supportive of the project.

- **Involve Stakeholders in Decision-Making:** Whenever possible, involve stakeholders in key project decisions, such as changes to scope, timelines, or deliverables. Their input can provide valuable perspectives and increase their commitment to the project's success.

7. **Continuous Improvement**

Continuous improvement is a best practice that involves regularly reviewing and refining project management processes, tools, and methodologies to enhance efficiency, quality, and outcomes.

- **Conduct Post-Project Reviews:** After project completion, conduct a post-project review to evaluate what went well, what could have been done better, and what lessons were learned. Document these insights and apply them to future projects to improve performance.

- **Encourage Feedback and Innovation:** Foster a culture where team members are encouraged to provide feedback on processes and suggest innovations. Continuous improvement thrives in an environment where ideas are welcomed and tested.

- **Adapt to New Trends and Technologies:** The IT landscape is constantly evolving, so it's important to stay informed about new trends, tools, and methodologies that can enhance project delivery. Be open to adopting new approaches that can improve project outcomes.

Mastering IT Leadership and Management, Strategies for Success in the Digital Age

Industry Case Study: IT Project and Portfolio Management at Cisco Systems

Situation:
In the late 2000s, Cisco Systems, a global leader in networking technology, recognized the need to better manage its IT projects and portfolios to align with its rapidly evolving business strategies. With the increasing complexity of its operations and the growing need to maintain a competitive edge in the technology industry, Cisco faced challenges in delivering IT projects on time and within budget. Additionally, the company needed to ensure that its IT investments were strategically aligned with its business objectives, maximizing value and minimizing risk.

Task:
Cisco's IT leadership was tasked with implementing a robust IT project and portfolio management framework that would enable the company to prioritize projects based on their strategic importance, manage resources effectively, and ensure that all IT initiatives were aligned with business goals. This effort required improving not only the management of individual projects but also overseeing the entire IT portfolio to support long-term growth and innovation.

Action:
To achieve these goals, Cisco undertook several key initiatives:

1. **Adopting Agile Methodologies:** Cisco transitioned to Agile project management methodologies, particularly Scrum, to enhance the flexibility and responsiveness of its IT projects. This shift allowed teams to deliver value incrementally, adjust to changing requirements, and reduce the risk of project failure.

2. **Implementing Portfolio Management Tools:** Cisco introduced advanced portfolio management tools to track and manage its IT projects more effectively. These tools provided real-time visibility into project performance, resource allocation, and financials, enabling IT leaders to make informed decisions and prioritize initiatives that aligned with Cisco's strategic goals.

3. **Enhancing Stakeholder Engagement:** Cisco's IT leadership emphasized the importance of engaging stakeholders throughout the project lifecycle. By involving key business leaders in the decision-making process, Cisco ensured that IT projects were closely aligned with business needs, and stakeholders were fully committed to the success of these initiatives.

4. **Continuous Improvement and Post-Project Reviews:** Cisco established a culture of continuous improvement by conducting post-project reviews to identify lessons learned and best practices. These insights were then applied to future projects, leading to improved performance and higher success rates.

Result:
As a result of these actions, Cisco achieved significant improvements in IT project delivery and portfolio management. The adoption of Agile methodologies led to faster project completion times and greater adaptability to changing business needs. The implementation

Mastering IT Leadership and Management, Strategies for Success in the Digital Age

of portfolio management tools provided Cisco with better control over its IT investments, ensuring that resources were allocated to the most strategically important projects. Enhanced stakeholder engagement fostered stronger alignment between IT and business objectives, while the focus on continuous improvement ensured that Cisco's IT projects consistently delivered value to the organization.

This case study highlights the importance of effective IT project and portfolio management in driving organizational success. By adopting best practices such as Agile methodologies, robust portfolio management tools, and continuous improvement processes, Cisco was able to align its IT initiatives with business goals, optimize resource allocation, and maintain its competitive edge in the technology industry.

Mastering IT Leadership and Management, Strategies for Success in the Digital Age

Best Practices

1. **Align IT Projects with Strategic Business Goals:** Successful IT project and portfolio management begins with ensuring that all projects are closely aligned with the organization's strategic goals. IT leaders should prioritize projects that deliver the most value to the business and support long-term objectives. This alignment ensures that resources are used effectively and that IT initiatives contribute to the overall success of the organization.

2. **Implement a Robust Portfolio Management Process:** Effective portfolio management involves the systematic selection, prioritization, and management of a portfolio of IT projects. IT leaders should establish a governance framework that includes criteria for project selection, risk assessment, and resource allocation. This process ensures that the organization's IT portfolio is balanced and that projects are aligned with business priorities.

3. **Use Agile Methodologies for Project Management:** Agile methodologies, such as Scrum or Kanban, are highly effective for managing IT projects in today's fast-paced environment. These methodologies emphasize flexibility, iterative development, and continuous feedback, allowing teams to respond quickly to changes and deliver value incrementally. IT leaders should encourage the adoption of Agile practices to enhance project efficiency and adaptability.

4. **Establish Clear Project Governance:** Clear governance structures are essential for successful IT project management. IT leaders should define roles, responsibilities, and decision-making processes for project teams. This governance framework ensures accountability, promotes effective communication, and helps manage risks and issues proactively.

5. **Focus on Effective Resource Management:** Managing resources effectively is critical to the success of IT projects. IT leaders should ensure that project teams have the necessary skills, tools, and support to complete their tasks. This includes balancing workloads across the portfolio, optimizing resource allocation, and addressing any constraints that could impact project delivery.

6. **Monitor and Manage Project Risks:** Proactive risk management is key to minimizing the impact of potential issues on IT projects. IT leaders should establish a risk management process that includes regular risk assessments, mitigation planning, and continuous monitoring. This approach helps identify risks early and allows for timely interventions to keep projects on track.

7. **Leverage Project Management Tools and Technology:** Utilizing project management tools and technology can significantly enhance the efficiency and effectiveness of IT project and portfolio management. IT leaders should adopt tools that support project planning, tracking, collaboration, and reporting. These tools provide real-time visibility into project status and help teams stay aligned and on schedule.

Mastering IT Leadership and Management, Strategies for Success in the Digital Age

Lessons Learned

1. **Strategic Alignment Ensures Project Success:** Projects that are closely aligned with an organization's strategic goals are more likely to deliver value and gain executive support. Successful IT initiatives prioritize projects that contribute to business objectives, ensuring that resources are focused on high-impact areas. This alignment helps justify investments and secure the necessary resources.

2. **Portfolio Management Balances Risk and Reward:** Effective portfolio management balances the risks and rewards of various projects. Organizations that manage their IT portfolios well can optimize resource allocation, ensuring that high-priority projects receive the attention they need while managing overall risk exposure. This balanced approach leads to better decision-making and more consistent project outcomes.

3. **Agile Methodologies Enhance Flexibility:** The adoption of Agile methodologies has proven to be transformative for many IT projects. Agile practices enable teams to adapt quickly to changing requirements and deliver incremental value throughout the project lifecycle. Organizations that embrace Agile approaches are better positioned to navigate uncertainty and deliver successful outcomes.

4. **Governance Provides Structure and Accountability:** Clear governance structures are critical to maintaining control over IT projects. Without well-defined roles and processes, projects can easily become disorganized and fall behind schedule. Successful IT projects have strong governance frameworks that ensure accountability, facilitate decision-making, and keep projects on track.

5. **Resource Management is Key to Meeting Deadlines:** Effective resource management is essential for ensuring that projects are completed on time and within budget. Organizations that excel in IT project management are adept at optimizing resources, balancing workloads, and addressing resource constraints proactively. This focus on resource management helps prevent delays and cost overruns.

6. **Proactive Risk Management Prevents Project Failures:** Risks are an inherent part of any IT project, but proactive risk management can significantly reduce their impact. Successful IT leaders implement risk management processes that identify potential issues early, plan mitigation strategies, and monitor risks continuously. This proactive approach helps keep projects on course and avoids costly failures.

7. **Technology Enhances Project Management Efficiency:** The use of project management tools and technology is essential for managing complex IT projects effectively. Tools that provide real-time visibility, facilitate collaboration, and support detailed planning are invaluable for keeping projects on track. Organizations that leverage these tools are better equipped to manage their projects efficiently and achieve their desired outcomes.

Mastering IT Leadership and Management, Strategies for Success in the Digital Age

By adopting these best practices and learning from successful IT project and portfolio management initiatives, IT leaders can drive their organizations toward more effective project execution, better alignment with business goals, and improved overall outcomes.

Mastering IT Leadership and Management, Strategies for Success in the Digital Age

Conclusion

IT Project and Portfolio Management are at the core of delivering value through technology within an organization. In this chapter, we explored the fundamental principles and best practices that enable IT leaders to manage projects effectively and strategically align their IT portfolios with business goals.

Successfully managing IT projects requires a deep understanding of project management principles, including planning, execution, monitoring, and closing. By adhering to these principles, IT leaders can ensure that projects are completed on time, within budget, and to the desired quality standards. However, effective project management also involves being agile and adaptable, ready to respond to the changes and challenges that inevitably arise during the project lifecycle.

Portfolio management, on the other hand, takes a broader, strategic view of all IT initiatives within the organization. It involves prioritizing projects based on their alignment with business objectives, potential return on investment, and ability to mitigate risks. By managing the IT portfolio strategically, IT leaders can ensure that resources are allocated effectively and that the organization focuses on the initiatives that will drive the most value.

Throughout this chapter, we also discussed the importance of best practices in IT project delivery, such as stakeholder engagement, risk management, and continuous improvement. These practices help IT leaders navigate the complexities of project and portfolio management, ensuring that projects not only meet their immediate goals but also contribute to the long-term success of the organization.

As we conclude Chapter 9, it is clear that IT Project and Portfolio Management are essential skills for any IT leader seeking to drive organizational success through technology. By mastering the principles and practices discussed in this chapter, IT leaders can ensure that their projects are not only well-managed but also strategically aligned with the organization's broader goals. This strategic approach to managing IT initiatives sets the stage for sustained success, enabling IT leaders to deliver value consistently and effectively in a rapidly evolving digital landscape.

Moving forward, these skills will remain crucial as we explore other aspects of strategic IT management, such as financial stewardship and navigating digital transformations, in the subsequent chapters of this book.

Mastering IT Leadership and Management, Strategies for Success in the Digital Age

Quizzes

I. Multiple Choice Questions:

1. What is the primary goal of IT portfolio management?

    A. Reducing IT costs
    B. Managing individual IT projects separately
    C. Ensuring IT investments align with strategic business objectives
    D. Increasing the number of IT projects

2. Which of the following best describes the concept of "scope creep" in IT project management?

    A. Deliberate expansion of the project scope to improve outcomes
    B. Uncontrolled changes or continuous growth in a project's scope
    C. A planned extension of project deliverables
    D. The reduction of project scope to meet deadlines

3. Effective resource management in IT projects involves:

    A. Allocating all resources to the most urgent tasks
    B. Ensuring that the project has the right mix of skills and resources available when needed
    C. Focusing only on financial resources
    D. Avoiding the use of external resources at all costs

4. In IT portfolio management, what is the purpose of balancing the portfolio?

    A. To focus only on short-term projects
    B. To ensure that all projects deliver immediate financial returns
    C. To maintain a mix of short-term and long-term projects that align with business goals
    D. To reduce the number of projects to a manageable level

II. True/False Questions:
    1. Agile methodologies are primarily focused on flexibility and iterative development in IT projects. (True/False)
    2. Stakeholder engagement is only necessary during the planning phase of an IT project. (True/False)
    3. Effective IT portfolio management requires continuous monitoring and adjustment based on changing business needs. (True/False)
    4. Proactive risk management in IT projects can prevent potential delays and cost overruns. (True/False)

Mastering IT Leadership and Management, Strategies for Success in the Digital Age

Exercises

I. IT Portfolio Analysis Exercise:
   - **Objective:** Evaluate the current IT portfolio to ensure alignment with business strategy.
   - **Instructions:**
     1. Identify all ongoing IT projects within your organization.
     2. Assess each project's alignment with the organization's strategic objectives, including its potential return on investment (ROI), risk level, and strategic importance.
     3. Develop a plan to balance the portfolio, ensuring a mix of short-term and long-term projects. Consider reallocating resources to projects that deliver the greatest value.

II. Project Risk Management Workshop:
   - **Objective:** Enhance skills in identifying and mitigating risks in IT projects.
   - **Instructions:**
     1. Choose a recent IT project and conduct a thorough risk assessment.
     2. Identify potential risks, assess their likelihood and impact, and develop mitigation strategies for each risk.
     3. Present your findings to your team, and discuss how these risks can be managed throughout the project's lifecycle.

III. Agile Methodology Simulation:
   - **Objective:** Experience the implementation of Agile methodologies in a controlled environment.
   - **Instructions:**
     1. Simulate an Agile project using a short development cycle (e.g., a week-long sprint).
     2. Assign roles (e.g., Scrum Master, Product Owner, Development Team) and conduct daily stand-up meetings, sprint planning, and sprint reviews.
     3. After the simulation, discuss the benefits and challenges of using Agile methodologies, and how they could be applied to actual projects.

IV. Stakeholder Engagement Plan:
   - **Objective:** Develop a comprehensive stakeholder engagement plan for an IT project.
   - **Instructions:**
     1. Identify all key stakeholders for a selected IT project.

Mastering IT Leadership and Management, Strategies for Success in the Digital Age

    2. Create a communication plan that outlines how you will engage with these stakeholders throughout the project's lifecycle, including regular updates, feedback mechanisms, and decision-making involvement.
    3. Implement the plan in a mock project scenario and evaluate its effectiveness in maintaining stakeholder support and managing expectations.

V. Post-Project Review Exercise:
- **Objective:** Learn from completed IT projects to improve future project management practices.
- **Instructions:**
    1. Conduct a post-project review of a recently completed IT project, focusing on what went well and what could have been improved.
    2. Document lessons learned, including challenges faced and how they were addressed.
    3. Develop a set of best practices based on these lessons and share them with your team for application in future projects.

These quizzes and exercises are designed to help readers of Chapter 9 better understand and apply the principles of IT project and portfolio management, focusing on practical application and strategic alignment.

Mastering IT Leadership and Management, Strategies for Success in the Digital Age

Chapter 10: Financial Management for IT Leaders

"FINANCIAL MANAGEMENT IS NOT JUST ABOUT MANAGING MONEY; IT'S ABOUT MANAGING THE BUSINESS THAT CREATES AND USES MONEY."

— **Robert Kiyosaki**

Effective financial management is a critical component of IT leadership. For IT leaders, the ability to manage budgets, control costs, and present a compelling case for IT investments is essential to ensuring that technology initiatives deliver value to the organization. This chapter explores the key principles of financial management in IT, including budgeting, cost management, understanding financial metrics, and making the case for IT investments.

Budgeting and Cost Management in IT

Budgeting and cost management are foundational elements of financial management for IT leaders. A well-managed budget ensures that resources are allocated effectively, projects are funded appropriately, and costs are controlled. This section discusses essential practices for budgeting and cost management in IT.

1. **Developing an IT Budget:**

The IT budget is a financial plan that outlines the expected costs of IT operations, projects, and initiatives for a specific period, typically a fiscal year. Developing an IT budget involves forecasting expenses related to hardware, software, personnel, maintenance, and other IT services.

- **Identify Key Expenditures:** Start by identifying the key expenditures required to support ongoing IT operations and planned projects. This includes costs for infrastructure, software licenses, cloud services, staffing, training, and support.

- **Prioritize Spending:** Prioritize spending based on the organization's strategic goals and the value that each IT initiative will deliver. High-priority projects that align with business objectives should receive necessary funding, while lower-priority initiatives may be deferred or scaled back.

- **Engage Stakeholders:** Collaborate with business leaders and other stakeholders during the budgeting process to ensure that the IT budget aligns with the broader organizational strategy. Stakeholder input is crucial for gaining buy-in and ensuring that the budget reflects the organization's priorities.

- **Monitor and Adjust:** Once the budget is approved, it's important to monitor spending closely throughout the year. Regularly compare actual expenses to budgeted amounts, identify any variances, and make adjustments as needed to stay on track.

Mastering IT Leadership and Management, Strategies for Success in the Digital Age

2. Controlling IT Costs:
Cost control is essential for ensuring that IT operates within its budget and delivers value to the organization. IT leaders must implement strategies to manage and control costs effectively.

- **Optimize Resource Allocation:** Efficiently allocate resources by ensuring that personnel, equipment, and services are used optimally. Avoid over-provisioning or underutilizing resources, and consider options such as virtualization, cloud services, and outsourcing to reduce costs.

- **Implement Cost-Saving Measures:** Look for opportunities to reduce costs without compromising quality or service. This could include negotiating better terms with vendors, consolidating contracts, automating manual processes, and reducing energy consumption through green IT practices.

- **Track and Report Costs:** Maintain detailed records of IT expenditures and regularly report on cost performance to stakeholders. Transparency in cost reporting helps build trust and ensures that IT leaders are accountable for managing the budget effectively.

- **Review Contracts and Vendor Relationships:** Regularly review contracts and vendor relationships to ensure the organization is receiving value for money. Renegotiate contracts, switch vendors if necessary, and explore alternative solutions to achieve cost savings.

Mastering IT Leadership and Management, Strategies for Success in the Digital Age

Understanding IT Financial Metrics

Financial metrics are key performance indicators (KPIs) that help IT leaders assess the financial health of their IT operations and projects. Understanding and effectively using these metrics is essential for making informed decisions and demonstrating the value of IT investments.

1. **Return on Investment (ROI):**

ROI measures the financial return generated by an IT investment relative to its cost. It is calculated as the net benefit (gain) from the investment divided by the cost of the investment. A positive ROI indicates that the investment has generated more value than it cost, making it a key metric for evaluating the success of IT projects.

- **Calculate ROI for Projects:** When proposing or evaluating IT projects, calculate the expected ROI to determine whether the project is financially viable. Consider both tangible benefits, such as cost savings and revenue growth, and intangible benefits, such as improved customer satisfaction or increased agility.

- **Use ROI to Prioritize Investments:** Use ROI as a criterion for prioritizing IT investments. Projects with higher ROI should generally be prioritized, as they are more likely to deliver significant value to the organization.

2. **Total Cost of Ownership (TCO):**

TCO is a comprehensive measure of the total cost of acquiring, operating, and maintaining an IT asset or system over its entire lifecycle. It includes direct costs, such as purchase price and maintenance fees, as well as indirect costs, such as training, downtime, and disposal.

- **Assess TCO for IT Assets:** When evaluating IT assets, such as hardware, software, or cloud services, assess their TCO to understand the full financial impact over time. This helps avoid underestimating costs and ensures that the organization makes informed purchasing decisions.

- **Compare TCO for Different Solutions:** Use TCO to compare different IT solutions and choose the one that offers the best value for money. Consider both short-term and long-term costs, and weigh them against the expected benefits of each solution.

3. **Budget Variance:**

Budget variance is the difference between the budgeted and actual costs of an IT project or operation. A positive variance indicates that the project is under budget, while a negative variance indicates that it is over budget.

- **Monitor Budget Variances Regularly:** Regularly monitor budget variances to identify any deviations from the planned budget. Understanding the reasons for variances helps IT leaders take corrective action and avoid budget overruns.

- **Analyze Variances for Continuous Improvement:** Analyze the causes of budget variances to identify areas for improvement in budgeting and cost management. Use this analysis to refine future budgets and enhance the accuracy of financial forecasting.

Mastering IT Leadership and Management, Strategies for Success in the Digital Age

4. Payback Period:

The payback period is the time it takes for an IT investment to generate enough benefits to cover its initial cost. It is a simple measure of the time required to recoup the investment.

- **Calculate Payback Period for Investments:** Calculate the payback period for IT investments to assess their risk and liquidity. Shorter payback periods are generally preferred, as they indicate that the investment will start delivering value sooner.

- **Use Payback Period for Risk Assessment:** Use the payback period as part of the risk assessment for IT projects. Projects with longer payback periods may carry higher risks, especially in rapidly changing technology environments.

Mastering IT Leadership and Management, Strategies for Success in the Digital Age

Making the Case for IT Investments

Securing funding and support for IT investments is a crucial responsibility for IT leaders. To make a compelling case, it is essential to demonstrate the strategic value, financial benefits, and alignment of the proposed investments with the organization's overarching goals. This section explores the key strategies for effectively advocating for IT investments, ensuring that they are recognized as critical enablers of business success.

1. **Aligning Investments with Business Strategy**

The most important factor in making the case for IT investments is demonstrating their alignment with the organization's strategic objectives. IT investments must not only meet the technological needs of the organization but also support and drive key business goals such as revenue growth, cost reduction, competitive advantage, and enhanced customer satisfaction.

- **Identify Strategic Priorities:** Understanding the organization's strategic priorities is the first step. IT leaders should align proposed investments with these priorities, positioning the investments as essential to achieving the organization's broader objectives. For example, if the organization is focused on improving customer experience, an investment in a new CRM system or customer analytics platform should be directly tied to this goal.

- **Highlight Business Impact:** Clearly articulate the business impact of the IT investment. This involves demonstrating how the investment will improve specific business outcomes, such as increasing operational efficiency, enabling faster decision-making, or enhancing product innovation. Use industry case studies to illustrate the potential benefits and how they will contribute to the organization's success.

- **Communicate in Business Terms:** When presenting IT investments to non-technical stakeholders, it is important to communicate in business terms. Focus on how the investment will solve business problems, create new opportunities, or mitigate risks. Avoid technical jargon and emphasize the value the investment will bring to the organization as a whole.

2. **Demonstrating Financial Value**

To gain approval for IT investments, it is essential to demonstrate their financial value. Decision-makers need to see that the proposed investments will deliver a strong return on investment (ROI), minimize costs over time, and provide clear financial benefits to the organization.

- **Present a Cost-Benefit Analysis:** A detailed cost-benefit analysis is key to making a compelling financial case. This analysis should outline all costs associated with the investment, including initial acquisition costs, implementation expenses, ongoing maintenance, and potential risks. It should also quantify the expected benefits, such as cost savings, increased revenues, or efficiency gains. By presenting both sides of the equation, IT leaders can provide a balanced view of the investment's financial impact.

Mastering IT Leadership and Management, Strategies for Success in the Digital Age

- **Use Financial Metrics:** Financial metrics such as ROI, total cost of ownership (TCO), and payback period are powerful tools for demonstrating the value of IT investments. ROI measures the profitability of the investment, while TCO provides a comprehensive view of the costs involved over the asset's lifecycle. The payback period indicates how quickly the investment will start delivering financial returns. These metrics offer concrete evidence that the investment is financially sound and will contribute positively to the organization's bottom line.

- **Consider Both Tangible and Intangible Benefits:** While financial metrics often focus on tangible benefits, such as cost reductions or revenue increases, it is also important to consider intangible benefits. These may include improved customer satisfaction, enhanced brand reputation, or increased employee productivity. Although harder to quantify, intangible benefits can significantly contribute to the organization's long-term success and should be factored into the overall value proposition.

3. **Addressing Risks and Mitigation Strategies**

Decision-makers often have concerns about the risks associated with IT investments, particularly those involving new technologies or large-scale implementations. To make a convincing case, IT leaders must address these risks directly and provide clear strategies for mitigating them.

- **Identify Key Risks:** Start by identifying the key risks associated with the proposed IT investment. These could include technical challenges, potential disruptions to business operations, regulatory compliance issues, or the risk of not achieving the expected benefits. Being transparent about potential risks demonstrates a thorough understanding of the investment and its implications.

- **Develop Mitigation Plans:** For each identified risk, develop a mitigation plan that outlines how the risk will be managed. This could involve contingency planning, phased implementation approaches, additional training and support, or vendor guarantees. By presenting a well-thought-out risk management plan, IT leaders can reassure decision-makers that the risks are being proactively addressed and that the likelihood of negative outcomes is minimized.

- **Balance Risks and Rewards:** It is important to balance the discussion of risks with the potential rewards of the investment. While acknowledging the risks, emphasize the strategic and financial benefits the investment will bring to the organization. Decision-makers are more likely to support an investment if they see that the potential rewards outweigh the risks.

4. **Engaging Stakeholders**

Successfully advocating for IT investments requires effective engagement with a broad range of stakeholders across the organization. Building support among these stakeholders is essential for gaining approval and ensuring the successful implementation of the investment.

Mastering IT Leadership and Management, Strategies for Success in the Digital Age

- **Identify and Understand Stakeholders:** Begin by identifying all key stakeholders, including business leaders, finance teams, and end-users who will be impacted by the investment. Understand their concerns, interests, and priorities. Different stakeholders may have different perspectives, and addressing these effectively is crucial for gaining their support.

- **Tailor the Message:** Tailor your message to address the specific concerns and priorities of different stakeholders. For example, business leaders may focus on how the investment aligns with strategic objectives and drives growth, while finance teams may be more concerned with cost control and ROI. By customizing the message, IT leaders can make the investment more relevant and compelling to each group.

- **Build Consensus:** Work to build consensus among stakeholders by involving them in the decision-making process and addressing their concerns. Regular communication, collaborative discussions, and transparency are key to building trust and ensuring that stakeholders are aligned with the investment's goals. Engaged and supportive stakeholders are more likely to champion the investment and contribute to its success.

5. **Preparing a Compelling Business Case**

A well-prepared business case is the culmination of the process of advocating for IT investments. The business case should be comprehensive, well-researched, and clearly presented to secure approval from decision-makers.

- **Include All Relevant Information:** The business case should encompass all pertinent details, including the strategic rationale for the investment, a detailed cost-benefit analysis, an assessment of risks and mitigation strategies, and an implementation plan. Providing supporting evidence, such as data, metrics, and case studies, strengthens the argument and enhances credibility.

- **Structure the Business Case Effectively:** Organize the business case in a clear and logical structure. Start with an executive summary that highlights the key points and benefits of the investment. Follow with detailed sections on strategic alignment, financial analysis, risk management, and stakeholder engagement. Conclude with a clear recommendation and a call to action.

- **Present the Business Case Persuasively:** Present the business case to decision-makers in a concise and persuasive manner. Use visuals, such as charts and graphs, to illustrate key points and make the information more accessible. Be prepared to answer questions and address any concerns that may arise during the presentation.

Mastering IT Leadership and Management, Strategies for Success in the Digital Age

Industry Case Study: Financial Management at Intel Corporation

Situation:
In the early 2000s, Intel Corporation, a leading semiconductor manufacturer, faced the challenge of balancing its aggressive investment in research and development (R&D) with the need to maintain strong financial performance. Intel's leadership recognized that to stay competitive in the fast-paced technology industry, significant investments in next-generation technologies were necessary. However, these investments had to be carefully managed to ensure a strong return on investment (ROI) while supporting Intel's long-term strategic objectives.

Task:
Intel's IT leadership was tasked with implementing a robust financial management strategy to fund R&D initiatives while maintaining fiscal discipline. This involved developing accurate budgets, managing costs effectively, and ensuring that all IT investments were aligned with Intel's broader business goals. The challenge was to balance the need for innovation with the imperative to deliver value to shareholders.

Action:
To address this challenge, Intel undertook several key actions:

1. **Strategic Budgeting and Forecasting:** Intel's IT leadership implemented a rigorous budgeting process that involved detailed forecasting of costs associated with R&D and other IT initiatives. This process included close collaboration with finance teams to ensure that IT budgets were aligned with the company's overall financial strategy. By accurately forecasting expenses and planning for contingencies, Intel was able to allocate resources effectively and avoid budget overruns.

2. **Cost Management Initiatives:** Intel introduced several cost management initiatives aimed at optimizing resource allocation and reducing unnecessary expenses. These included negotiating better terms with vendors, consolidating IT services to achieve economies of scale, and adopting more cost-efficient technologies, such as cloud computing. These measures helped Intel control costs without compromising the quality of its IT services.

3. **ROI and Financial Metrics:** Intel's IT leadership focused on demonstrating the financial value of IT investments by calculating ROI, Total Cost of Ownership (TCO), and payback periods for major projects. These financial metrics were used to evaluate the potential benefits of IT initiatives and to prioritize those that offered the greatest value to the company. By presenting these metrics to senior management, Intel was able to secure support for its IT investments and ensure they were strategically aligned with the company's goals.

4. **Aligning IT Investments with Business Strategy:** Intel prioritized aligning all IT investments with its broader business strategy. This involved identifying key strategic priorities, such as the development of new semiconductor technologies, and ensuring that IT spending was directed towards initiatives that supported these

Mastering IT Leadership and Management, Strategies for Success in the Digital Age

goals. Intel's IT leadership worked closely with business units to ensure that IT projects were not only technically sound but also strategically valuable.

Result:
As a result of these actions, Intel maintained a strong financial position while continuing to invest heavily in R&D. The company's disciplined approach to financial management ensured that its IT investments delivered significant value, both in terms of technological innovation and financial performance. Intel's ability to balance cost control with strategic investment allowed it to remain a leader in the semiconductor industry, driving innovation and maintaining a competitive edge.

The success of Intel's financial management strategy highlights the importance of aligning IT spending with business goals, managing costs effectively, and using financial metrics to demonstrate the value of IT initiatives. This case study illustrates how effective financial management practices can enable IT leaders to support innovation while maintaining fiscal responsibility. By mastering the principles of budgeting, cost management, and financial analysis, IT leaders can ensure their departments contribute to the overall success of the organization.

Mastering IT Leadership and Management, Strategies for Success in the Digital Age

Best Practices

1. **Align IT Budgeting with Strategic Business Objectives:**
   Effective financial management begins with aligning the IT budget with the organization's strategic goals. IT leaders should ensure that all expenditures contribute to broader business objectives, whether by driving innovation, enhancing efficiency, or improving customer experience. This alignment helps justify IT investments and ensures that resources are allocated to the most impactful initiatives.

2. **Adopt a Value-Based Approach to IT Spending:**
   Rather than focusing solely on cost control, IT leaders should adopt a value-based approach to spending. This involves evaluating IT investments based on the value they bring to the organization, such as increased revenue, cost savings, or improved operational efficiency. By focusing on value, IT leaders can make more informed decisions about resource allocation.

3. **Implement Rigorous Cost Management Practices:**
   Cost management is a critical component of financial management in IT. IT leaders should establish processes for tracking and controlling costs throughout the project lifecycle. This includes setting clear budget expectations, regularly monitoring expenditures, and implementing cost-saving measures where possible. Effective cost management helps avoid budget overruns and ensures that projects are completed within financial constraints.

4. **Utilize Financial Metrics to Measure IT Performance:**
   IT leaders should leverage financial metrics to assess the performance of IT initiatives. Key metrics such as Return on Investment (ROI), Total Cost of Ownership (TCO), and Cost-Benefit Analysis (CBA) provide valuable insights into the financial impact of IT projects. These metrics help IT leaders make data-driven decisions and demonstrate the financial value of IT to stakeholders.

5. **Engage in Transparent Financial Reporting:**
   Transparency in financial reporting is essential for building trust with stakeholders. IT leaders should ensure that financial reports are accurate, comprehensive, and presented in a way that is understandable to non-technical audiences. Regular financial updates and clear communication of financial performance help maintain stakeholder confidence and support.

6. **Plan for Long-Term Financial Sustainability:**
   Long-term financial planning is crucial for sustaining IT initiatives over time. IT leaders should develop multi-year financial plans that account for future technology needs, potential risks, and changing business conditions. This forward-looking approach ensures that IT investments are sustainable and aligned with the organization's long-term strategy.

Mastering IT Leadership and Management, Strategies for Success in the Digital Age

7. **Leverage Technology for Financial Management:**
    IT leaders can enhance financial management by leveraging technology tools that automate budgeting, forecasting, and financial reporting. These tools provide real-time insights into financial performance, enabling more accurate and efficient management of IT finances. Automation also reduces the risk of errors and frees up time for strategic financial planning.

Mastering IT Leadership and Management, Strategies for Success in the Digital Age

Lessons Learned

1. **Strategic Alignment Maximizes Financial Impact:**
   Aligning IT budgets with the organization's strategic objectives ensures that IT investments deliver maximum value. Successful IT leaders prioritize spending on initiatives that support key business goals, leading to better outcomes and a stronger case for future funding.

2. **Value-Based Spending Enhances Decision-Making:**
   A value-based approach to IT spending allows leaders to focus on the long-term benefits of their investments rather than just the costs. By evaluating projects based on the value they create, IT leaders can make more informed decisions that contribute to the overall success of the organization.

3. **Effective Cost Management Prevents Budget Overruns:**
   Rigorous cost management practices are essential for keeping IT projects within budget. Organizations that excel in financial management closely track costs, implement controls, and regularly review financial performance. This discipline helps prevent budget overruns and ensures that projects are financially viable.

4. **Financial Metrics Provide Clarity and Insight:**
   Utilizing financial metrics to measure the performance of IT initiatives provides clarity and insight into their financial impact. Metrics like ROI and TCO help IT leaders demonstrate the value of IT to stakeholders, making it easier to secure support for future projects. These metrics also provide a basis for continuous improvement in financial management practices.

5. **Transparency Builds Trust with Stakeholders:**
   Transparent financial reporting is key to building and maintaining trust with stakeholders. When IT leaders provide clear, accurate, and timely financial reports, they foster confidence and ensure that stakeholders are well-informed about the financial health of IT initiatives. This transparency helps avoid misunderstandings and encourages a collaborative approach to financial management.

6. **Long-Term Planning Ensures Financial Sustainability:**
   Planning for long-term financial sustainability is essential for the continued success of IT initiatives. Successful organizations develop financial plans that account for future needs and risks, ensuring that IT investments are sustainable and aligned with the organization's strategic direction. This approach helps avoid financial shortfalls and supports the ongoing growth and development of IT capabilities.

7. **Technology Enhances Financial Management Efficiency:**
   Leveraging technology for financial management enables IT leaders to manage finances more efficiently and accurately. Tools that automate budgeting, forecasting, and reporting reduce manual errors, save time, and provide real-time insights into financial performance. This technological advantage allows IT leaders to focus on strategic financial planning and decision-making.

Mastering IT Leadership and Management, Strategies for Success in the Digital Age

By following these best practices and learning from successful IT financial management initiatives, IT leaders can ensure their organizations make the most of their IT investments, maintain financial stability, and support long-term growth and innovation.

Mastering IT Leadership and Management, Strategies for Success in the Digital Age

Conclusion

Financial management is a critical responsibility for IT leaders, directly impacting their ability to deliver value through technology while ensuring resources are utilized effectively and efficiently. In Chapter 10, we explored the key components of financial management for IT leaders, including budgeting, cost management, understanding IT financial metrics, and building a compelling case for IT investments.

Effective budgeting and cost management are foundational to financial stewardship in IT. By accurately forecasting expenses, allocating resources wisely, and monitoring spending against budgets, IT leaders can maintain financial control and ensure their departments operate within the organization's financial constraints. This financial discipline enables IT leaders to support strategic initiatives without compromising the organization's financial health.

Equally important is understanding IT financial metrics. Metrics such as Total Cost of Ownership (TCO), Return on Investment (ROI), and Cost-Benefit Analysis (CBA) provide valuable insights into the financial performance of IT initiatives. By leveraging these metrics, IT leaders can make informed decisions, prioritize projects, and demonstrate the value of IT investments to stakeholders.

Making the case for IT investments is a vital skill, especially in an environment where competition for resources is fierce. IT leaders must articulate the strategic value of technology investments, showing how they align with business goals, drive innovation, and deliver a strong return on investment. A well-prepared business case not only secures funding but also builds trust and credibility with executive leadership.

As we conclude Chapter 10, it becomes clear that financial management is not just about managing budgets and costs; it is about strategic financial stewardship that ensures IT delivers maximum value to the organization. By mastering the financial management principles discussed in this chapter, IT leaders can make sound financial decisions, justify investments, and contribute to the organization's overall financial success.

These financial management skills are essential as we progress in the book, where we will explore how IT leaders can navigate digital transformations, manage innovation, and build a resilient IT organization in the chapters that follow. With a solid foundation in financial management, IT leaders are better equipped to guide their organizations through the complexities of the digital age, ensuring both technological and financial success.

Mastering IT Leadership and Management, Strategies for Success in the Digital Age

Quizzes

I. Multiple Choice Questions:
1. What is the primary purpose of developing an IT budget?

    A. To limit spending on IT resources
    B. To ensure that IT operations and projects are financially supported and aligned with business objectives
    C. To prioritize cost-saving measures over innovation
    D. To track the salaries of IT personnel

2. Which financial metric is used to assess the total cost associated with acquiring, operating, and maintaining an IT asset over its entire lifecycle?

    A. Return on Investment (ROI)
    B. Budget Variance
    C. Payback Period
    D. Total Cost of Ownership (TCO)

3. How can IT leaders effectively demonstrate the value of IT investments to stakeholders?

    A. By focusing solely on cost reduction
    B. By emphasizing technical features over business benefits
    C. By using financial metrics like ROI and TCO, and aligning investments with business goals
    D. By minimizing stakeholder engagement

4. What is a key benefit of using technology tools in financial management?

    A. They automate decision-making, eliminating the need for human oversight
    B. They reduce the need for detailed financial reporting
    C. They enable more accurate and efficient management of IT finances through automation and real-time insights
    D. They limit the ability to track spending

II. True/False Questions:
1. Effective cost management involves both tracking expenditures and implementing cost-saving measures where possible. (True/False)
2. Financial metrics like ROI and TCO are only useful for large-scale IT projects. (True/False)

Mastering IT Leadership and Management, Strategies for Success in the Digital Age

3. A well-prepared business case should include both a detailed cost-benefit analysis and a strategic rationale for the investment. (True/False)
4. Once an IT budget is approved, there is no need to monitor it closely throughout the year. (True/False)

Exercises

I. IT Budget Development Exercise:
- **Objective:** Practice developing a comprehensive IT budget that aligns with strategic business goals.
- **Instructions:**
    1. Identify the key expenditures necessary to support both ongoing IT operations and planned projects in your organization.
    2. Develop a budget that includes these expenditures, ensuring alignment with the organization's broader strategic objectives.
    3. Present the budget to a peer or mentor for feedback, and adjust it based on their suggestions to better meet business goals.

II. Cost Management Simulation:
- **Objective:** Enhance skills in managing IT costs while maintaining service quality.
- **Instructions:**
    1. Simulate a scenario where your IT department must reduce costs by 10% without compromising critical services.
    2. Identify areas where costs can be reduced (e.g., renegotiating vendor contracts, optimizing resource allocation) and implement these measures.
    3. Analyze the impact of these cost-saving measures on service delivery and adjust your strategy as necessary to maintain quality.

III. ROI and TCO Calculation Workshop:
- **Objective:** Learn to calculate and interpret key financial metrics used in IT financial management.
- **Instructions:**
    1. Choose an IT project (real or hypothetical) and calculate its ROI by comparing the expected financial gains to the cost of the investment.
    2. Assess the TCO of the same project, considering all associated costs over its lifecycle.
    3. Use these metrics to evaluate the project's financial viability and present your findings to a peer group, explaining the significance of these metrics in decision-making.

Mastering IT Leadership and Management, Strategies for Success in the Digital Age

IV. Business Case Development Exercise:
   - **Objective:** Develop a compelling business case for a proposed IT investment.
   - **Instructions:**
     1. Select a potential IT investment and gather relevant data, including strategic alignment, cost-benefit analysis, and risk assessment.
     2. Structure the business case, starting with an executive summary and followed by detailed sections on financial analysis, strategic value, and risk mitigation.
     3. Present the business case to a group of stakeholders (real or simulated) and address their questions and concerns, refining the case based on their feedback.

V. Long-Term Financial Planning Exercise:
   - **Objective:** Create a long-term financial plan that supports the sustainability of IT initiatives.
   - **Instructions:**
     1. Identify the future technology needs and potential risks that your organization may face over the next five years.
     2. Develop a multi-year financial plan that includes budget forecasts, funding strategies, and risk mitigation measures.
     3. Ensure that the plan aligns with the organization's long-term strategic goals, and present it to senior leadership for approval.

These quizzes and exercises are designed to help readers of Chapter 10 better understand and apply the principles of financial management in IT leadership, focusing on practical application and strategic alignment.

Mastering IT Leadership and Management, Strategies for Success in the Digital Age

Conclusion of Part 3: Strategic IT Management

Strategic IT management is the backbone of successful organizations in the digital age. As IT leaders navigate the complexities of governance, project management, financial stewardship, and compliance, they must maintain a clear focus on aligning IT strategies with broader business objectives. The chapters in this section have outlined the essential frameworks, principles, and best practices that enable IT leaders to drive value and mitigate risks in an increasingly technology-driven world.

In today's rapidly evolving environment, effective IT governance is crucial for ensuring that IT resources are utilized efficiently and that technology investments deliver maximum value. By implementing robust governance frameworks and ensuring compliance with industry regulations, IT leaders can establish a foundation of trust and accountability that supports sustainable growth.

Equally important is managing IT projects and portfolios strategically. The ability to prioritize projects, manage resources effectively, and align IT initiatives with organizational goals determines the success of IT in driving business outcomes. Financial management, a critical aspect of strategic IT management, ensures that IT leaders can justify investments, manage costs, and contribute to the organization's financial health.

As we conclude Part 3, it's clear that strategic IT management requires a balance of technical expertise, leadership, and business acumen. IT leaders must be forward-thinking, adaptable, and prepared to lead their teams through both opportunities and challenges. By mastering the principles discussed in this section, IT leaders can position their organizations for long-term success, navigating the complexities of the digital landscape with confidence and strategic insight.

The journey continues as we move into the next part of the book, where we will explore the dynamic and transformative role of IT leadership in the digital age. With a solid foundation in strategic IT management, IT leaders are well-equipped to guide their organizations through the challenges and opportunities of digital transformation.

Mastering IT Leadership and Management, Strategies for Success in the Digital Age

Part 4: Navigating the Digital Transformation

"IT IS NOT THE STRONGEST COMPANIES THAT SURVIVE, NOR THE MOST INTELLIGENT, BUT THOSE MOST RESPONSIVE TO CHANGE."

— **Adapted from Charles Darwin**

Mastering IT Leadership and Management, Strategies for Success in the Digital Age

Chapter 11: Digital Leadership in the Age of Transformation

"THE GREATEST DANGER IN TIMES OF TURBULENCE IS NOT THE TURBULENCE—IT IS ACTING WITH YESTERDAY'S LOGIC."
— **Peter Drucker**

As organizations increasingly embrace digital transformation, the role of IT leaders has evolved from merely managing technology to driving business strategy. In this new landscape, IT leaders must demonstrate digital leadership, guiding their organizations through the complexities of technological change while aligning IT initiatives with broader business objectives. Digital leadership is about more than just technical expertise; it requires vision, influence, and the ability to foster innovation and collaboration. This chapter explores the key characteristics and practices of effective digital leadership in the age of transformation.

Defining Digital Leadership

Digital leadership is the ability to guide organizations through the challenges and opportunities presented by digital transformation. It requires a blend of strategic thinking, technological acumen, and the capacity to inspire and influence others.

- **Strategic Vision:** At the core of digital leadership is the ability to create and communicate a strategic vision that aligns digital initiatives with the organization's long-term goals. A digital leader understands the potential of emerging technologies to drive business growth and innovation and is skilled at translating this potential into a clear, actionable strategy.

- **Technological Expertise:** While digital leadership extends beyond technical knowledge, a deep understanding of technology is essential. Digital leaders must stay informed about the latest technological trends, tools, and platforms, and be able to assess their relevance to the organization. This expertise enables them to make informed decisions about technology investments and lead digital transformation initiatives effectively.

- **Influence and Collaboration:** Digital leaders must excel at influencing others and fostering collaboration across the organization. This involves building relationships with key stakeholders, communicating the value of digital initiatives, and creating a culture of collaboration where cross-functional teams work together to achieve common goals.

- **Adaptability and Resilience:** The digital landscape is constantly evolving, and digital leaders must be adaptable and resilient in the face of uncertainty. They need to be comfortable with ambiguity, capable of pivoting when necessary, and resilient enough to overcome setbacks and keep the organization moving forward.

Mastering IT Leadership and Management, Strategies for Success in the Digital Age

Leading Digital Transformation

Leading digital transformation requires a unique set of skills and approaches. Digital leaders must not only drive technological change but also ensure that the organization's culture, processes, and structures support the transformation.

- **Driving Innovation:** Digital leaders play a critical role in fostering innovation within the organization. This involves creating an environment where new ideas are encouraged, experimentation is valued, and failure is seen as a learning opportunity. By cultivating a culture of innovation, digital leaders can unlock their teams' creativity and drive the development of new products, services, and business models.

- **Aligning IT with Business Strategy:** A key responsibility of digital leaders is to ensure that IT initiatives align with the organization's business strategy. This requires a deep understanding of the organization's goals and challenges, as well as the ability to translate these into technology solutions that deliver value. Digital leaders must work closely with business leaders to position IT as a strategic partner, not just a service provider.

- **Managing Change:** Digital transformation often involves significant changes to the organization's processes, structures, and ways of working. Digital leaders must excel at managing change, ensuring that the transformation is implemented smoothly and that employees are supported throughout the process. This includes communicating the reasons for the change, addressing concerns, and providing the necessary training and resources to help employees adapt.

- **Building a Digital Culture:** Successful digital transformation requires a culture that supports and embraces change. Digital leaders must work to build a digital culture within the organization, where employees are encouraged to experiment, collaborate, and continuously learn. This involves promoting a mindset that values agility, innovation, and a willingness to embrace new ways of working.

Mastering IT Leadership and Management, Strategies for Success in the Digital Age

Industry Case Study: Digital Leadership in the Age of Transformation at General Electric (GE)

Situation:
In the early 2010s, General Electric (GE) recognized the need for significant transformation to remain competitive in the rapidly evolving industrial sector. The rise of digital technologies, such as the Internet of Things (IoT) and big data analytics, presented both opportunities and challenges. While GE's traditional industrial operations were highly successful, they lacked the digital capabilities necessary to thrive in this new landscape. To address this, GE embarked on a digital transformation journey, aiming to become a leader in industrial digital technology.

Task:
GE's leadership faced the task of driving this digital transformation by integrating digital technologies into its core industrial operations. This involved not only adopting new technologies but also reshaping the company's culture, business models, and value propositions. The challenge was to create a cohesive digital strategy that aligned with GE's long-term goals while fostering innovation and agility across the organization.

Action:
To achieve its transformation goals, GE's leadership took several key actions:

1. **Establishing GE Digital:**
   In 2015, GE launched GE Digital, a division focused on developing industrial software and analytics solutions. This division led the company's digital transformation efforts, including the development of Predix, a cloud-based platform for industrial IoT. GE Digital became the hub for the company's digital initiatives, driving innovation and integrating digital technologies across all business units.

2. **Visionary Leadership:**
   Jeff Immelt, then CEO of GE, played a pivotal role in articulating and driving the company's digital vision. He emphasized the importance of digital transformation for the company's future and set a clear strategic direction. Immelt's leadership was instrumental in rallying the organization around the digital transformation effort and ensuring that it became a top priority for all business units.

3. **Cultural Transformation:**
   GE recognized that digital transformation was not just about technology but also about changing the company's culture. To foster a culture of innovation and agility, GE adopted Agile methodologies and encouraged cross-functional collaboration. The company also invested in training and development programs to equip employees with the digital skills needed for the transformation.

4. **Strategic Acquisitions:**
   To accelerate its digital transformation, GE made several strategic acquisitions, including companies specializing in software development, data analytics, and

Mastering IT Leadership and Management, Strategies for Success in the Digital Age

Navigating Ethical Challenges in Digital Leadership

Digital leaders must navigate the ethical challenges that arise in the age of transformation. As organizations increasingly rely on data and technology, ethical considerations around privacy, security, and the responsible use of technology become paramount.

- **Ensuring Data Privacy and Security:** Digital leaders must prioritize data privacy and security, ensuring that the organization's data is protected from breaches and misuse. This involves implementing robust security measures, adhering to data protection regulations, and promoting a culture of privacy and security awareness across the organization.

- **Promoting Ethical AI and Automation:** As organizations adopt AI and automation technologies, digital leaders must ensure these technologies are used ethically and responsibly. This includes addressing issues such as bias in AI algorithms, the impact of automation on jobs, and the ethical implications of decisions made by AI systems. Digital leaders should promote transparency, fairness, and accountability in the use of AI and automation.

- **Balancing Innovation with Responsibility:** While innovation is critical to digital transformation, it must be balanced with responsibility. Digital leaders should consider the broader societal impacts of their decisions and ensure the organization's digital initiatives align with ethical standards and values. This might involve conducting ethical impact assessments, engaging with stakeholders, and being transparent about the organization's use of technology.

- **Leading by Example:** Digital leaders must lead by example, demonstrating ethical behavior in their decision-making and interactions. This involves being transparent, accountable, and committed to doing what is right, even when it is difficult. By modeling ethical leadership, digital leaders can build trust and set the standard for others to follow.

Mastering IT Leadership and Management, Strategies for Success in the Digital Age

Empowering Teams in the Digital Age

Empowering teams is a critical component of digital leadership. Digital leaders must create an environment where teams feel trusted, valued, and empowered to make decisions and take ownership of their work.

- **Delegating Authority:** Digital leaders should delegate authority to their teams, allowing them to make decisions and take ownership of their projects. This involves trusting teams to use their expertise and judgment to deliver results while providing the necessary support and guidance. Empowering teams in this way not only increases their engagement and motivation but also enables faster decision-making and greater agility.

- **Providing the Right Tools and Resources:** To empower teams, digital leaders must ensure they have the right tools and resources to succeed. This might involve investing in new technologies, providing access to data and analytics, or offering training and support. By equipping teams with the tools they need, digital leaders can enhance productivity and enable them to achieve their goals.

- **Encouraging Autonomy:** Empowered teams need the autonomy to experiment, innovate, and solve problems. Digital leaders should create an environment where teams are encouraged to take risks, try new approaches, and learn from their experiences. This autonomy fosters a sense of ownership and accountability, driving higher levels of performance and innovation.

- **Supporting Team Development:** Digital leaders should invest in the development of their teams, providing opportunities for learning, growth, and career advancement. This might involve offering mentorship, providing access to training and professional development, or creating opportunities for teams to take on new challenges. By supporting team development, digital leaders can build a strong, capable workforce that is equipped to navigate the complexities of digital transformation.

Mastering IT Leadership and Management, Strategies for Success in the Digital Age

Fostering a Culture of Innovation

Innovation is a key driver of digital transformation, and digital leaders must create a culture that encourages and supports innovation across the organization.

- **Encouraging Experimentation:** Digital leaders should promote experimentation by providing teams with the resources and autonomy needed to explore new ideas. This might involve setting up innovation labs, running hackathons, or creating cross-functional teams tasked with solving specific challenges. By creating a safe space for experimentation, digital leaders can foster a culture where creativity and innovation thrive.

- **Rewarding Innovation:** Recognizing and rewarding innovation is essential for building a culture of innovation. Digital leaders should celebrate successes, no matter how small, and provide incentives for teams and individuals who develop innovative solutions. This could include formal recognition programs, financial rewards, or opportunities for career advancement.

- **Promoting Collaboration:** Innovation often arises from the intersection of different ideas and perspectives. Digital leaders should encourage collaboration across departments and teams, fostering an environment where employees work together to solve problems and develop new solutions. This might involve creating cross-functional teams, using collaborative tools and platforms, or holding regular innovation workshops and brainstorming sessions.

- **Investing in Continuous Learning:** In a rapidly changing digital landscape, continuous learning is critical for innovation. Digital leaders should invest in the development of their teams by providing opportunities for training, professional development, and exposure to new ideas and technologies. This not only enhances the team's skills but also keeps the organization at the forefront of innovation.

Mastering IT Leadership and Management, Strategies for Success in the Digital Age

cybersecurity. These acquisitions helped GE build the capabilities needed to support its digital initiatives and integrate new technologies into its operations.

Result:
As a result of these efforts, GE made significant progress in its digital transformation journey. The company successfully launched Predix, which became a leading platform for industrial IoT, enabling GE and its customers to harness the power of data and analytics to improve operational efficiency and drive innovation. GE Digital became a critical part of the company's growth strategy, generating significant revenue from its software and services offerings. The cultural shift towards innovation and agility also positioned GE to respond more effectively to market changes and emerging opportunities.

However, the journey was not without challenges. GE faced difficulties scaling its digital initiatives across the organization, and eventually had to recalibrate its strategy to focus on its core industrial strengths. Despite these challenges, GE's digital transformation efforts underscored the importance of visionary leadership, cultural change, and strategic alignment in navigating the complexities of digital transformation.

This case study highlights how effective digital leadership can guide an organization through the challenges of transformation by aligning technology with business strategy, fostering a culture of innovation, and driving sustainable growth in the digital age.

Mastering IT Leadership and Management, Strategies for Success in the Digital Age

Best Practices

1. **Embrace a Visionary Approach to Digital Leadership:**
   Digital leaders must be visionaries who can anticipate future trends and drive their organizations toward innovation. IT leaders should cultivate a forward-thinking mindset, setting a clear and compelling vision for how digital transformation will reshape the business. This vision should be communicated consistently to inspire and align teams with the organization's strategic goals.

2. **Foster a Culture of Innovation:**
   A culture of innovation is essential for successful digital transformation. IT leaders should create an environment where creativity is encouraged and new ideas are welcomed. This involves empowering teams to experiment with emerging technologies, fail fast, and learn quickly. Leaders should also recognize and reward innovative thinking to sustain this culture.

3. **Lead by Example in Digital Literacy:**
   IT leaders must be champions of digital literacy within their organizations. By staying informed about the latest digital trends and demonstrating a strong understanding of emerging technologies, leaders can set the standard for their teams. Continuous learning and development should be encouraged at all levels, ensuring the organization remains competitive in the digital landscape.

4. **Drive Cross-Functional Collaboration:**
   Digital transformation often requires collaboration across multiple departments. IT leaders should facilitate cross-functional teams that bring together diverse skill sets and perspectives. By breaking down silos and encouraging collaboration, leaders can ensure that digital initiatives are holistic and aligned with broader business objectives.

5. **Navigate Ethical and Social Implications of Digital Transformation:**
   As digital transformation accelerates, ethical considerations become increasingly important. IT leaders must address issues such as data privacy, AI ethics, and the social impact of automation. Leaders should establish ethical guidelines and frameworks to guide decision-making and ensure that digital initiatives are conducted responsibly.

6. **Empower Teams with the Right Tools and Technologies:**
   Providing teams with the right tools and technologies is crucial for enabling digital transformation. IT leaders should invest in modern, scalable platforms that support innovation and collaboration. Cloud computing, AI, and data analytics are examples of technologies that can drive significant business value when leveraged effectively.

7. **Measure and Communicate the Impact of Digital Initiatives:**
   To sustain momentum in digital transformation, IT leaders must measure the impact of digital initiatives and communicate the results to stakeholders. Key performance

Mastering IT Leadership and Management, Strategies for Success in the Digital Age

indicators (KPIs) should be established to track progress, and success stories should be shared to demonstrate the tangible benefits of digital transformation.

Mastering IT Leadership and Management, Strategies for Success in the Digital Age

Lessons Learned

1. **Visionary Leadership is Critical for Digital Success:**
   Digital transformation requires a clear and compelling vision to guide the organization through change. Successful digital leaders are those who can articulate this vision and inspire their teams to work toward it. Without a strong vision, digital initiatives can become fragmented and lose direction.

2. **Innovation Must Be Cultivated and Supported:**
   Innovation doesn't happen by accident; it must be actively cultivated. Organizations that have successfully navigated digital transformation have done so by creating a culture that encourages experimentation and tolerates failure. Leaders must provide the support and resources necessary for teams to innovate effectively.

3. **Digital Literacy is a Leadership Imperative:**
   In the age of digital transformation, IT leaders must possess a deep understanding of digital technologies and trends. This literacy enables leaders to make informed decisions, guide their teams effectively, and position their organizations for success. Continuous learning is essential for maintaining this digital literacy.

4. **Collaboration Drives Comprehensive Digital Transformation:**
   Cross-functional collaboration is a key driver of successful digital transformation. When IT works closely with other departments, the organization can develop more comprehensive and integrated digital strategies. Collaboration ensures that digital initiatives align with business goals and leverage the full range of organizational expertise.

5. **Ethics Cannot Be Overlooked in Digital Initiatives:**
   Ethical considerations are paramount in digital transformation. Organizations that overlook ethics may face legal, reputational, and operational risks. Successful IT leaders establish clear ethical guidelines and ensure that digital initiatives are conducted with integrity and respect for societal values.

6. **The Right Tools Enable Digital Transformation:**
   Investing in the right tools and technologies is essential for driving digital transformation. Organizations that have successfully transformed digitally often attribute their success to the adoption of modern, flexible technologies that enable innovation and efficiency. Leaders must ensure that their teams have access to the tools they need to succeed.

7. **Communicating Success Builds Momentum:**
   Measuring and communicating the impact of digital initiatives is crucial for sustaining transformation efforts. When stakeholders see the tangible benefits of digital transformation, they are more likely to support continued investment. Sharing success stories helps build momentum and reinforces the value of digital leadership.

Mastering IT Leadership and Management, Strategies for Success in the Digital Age

By implementing these best practices and learning from successful digital leadership initiatives, IT leaders can guide their organizations through the complexities of digital transformation, ensuring that they not only survive but also thrive in the digital age.

Mastering IT Leadership and Management, Strategies for Success in the Digital Age

Conclusion

Digital transformation is redefining the business landscape, and IT leaders are at the forefront of this evolution. In Chapter 11, we explored the pivotal role digital leadership plays in guiding organizations through the complexities of transformation, integrating emerging technologies into IT strategy, and the lessons learned from successful digital transformation case studies.

As digital leaders, IT professionals are tasked with more than just implementing new technologies; they must drive a cultural shift within the organization, fostering a mindset that embraces change, innovation, and continuous improvement. This requires a deep understanding of both the technological and human aspects of transformation, balancing cutting-edge solutions with the practicalities of execution and adoption.

Integrating emerging technologies—such as AI, cloud computing, big data, and IoT—into IT strategy is a critical component of digital leadership. These technologies offer unprecedented opportunities for innovation, efficiency, and competitive advantage. However, their successful implementation requires a clear strategic vision, robust planning, and careful consideration of how they align with the organization's goals and capabilities.

The case studies examined in this chapter highlighted the importance of a holistic approach to digital transformation, where technology, people, and processes are all aligned toward a common objective. Successful digital transformation is not just about technology adoption, but about reimagining business models, enhancing customer experiences, and creating new value propositions.

As we conclude Chapter 11, it is evident that digital leadership in the age of transformation is about more than keeping pace with technological change—it is about leading that change with vision, purpose, and strategic intent. IT leaders who can successfully navigate the complexities of digital transformation will position their organizations for long-term success in a rapidly evolving digital landscape.

The insights and strategies discussed in this chapter provide a strong foundation for understanding the role of digital leadership. As we move forward in the book, these principles will continue to inform our exploration of innovation, cybersecurity leadership, and other critical aspects of IT leadership in the digital age. With a strong grasp of digital leadership, IT leaders are well-equipped to lead their organizations into the future, leveraging technology to drive transformation and achieve sustainable growth.

Mastering IT Leadership and Management, Strategies for Success in the Digital Age

Quizzes

I. Multiple Choice Questions:

1. What is a primary characteristic of effective digital leadership?

    A. Technical expertise alone
    B. A blend of strategic thinking, technological acumen, and the ability to inspire and influence others
    C. Strict adherence to traditional management practices
    D. Delegation of all leadership responsibilities to technical teams

2. Why is fostering a culture of innovation critical in digital leadership?

    A. It reduces the need for cross-functional collaboration
    B. It allows the organization to remain stagnant in its practices
    C. It unlocks the creativity of teams, driving new products, services, and business models
    D. It eliminates the need for continuous learning

3. Which approach is essential for aligning IT initiatives with business strategy?

    A. Prioritizing technical advancements without considering business impact
    B. Ensuring IT operates independently of other business functions
    C. Collaborating with business leaders to ensure IT is seen as a strategic partner
    D. Limiting IT's role to support functions only

4. What role does adaptability play in digital leadership?

    A. It allows leaders to ignore market changes
    B. It enables leaders to pivot and remain resilient in the face of uncertainty
    C. It minimizes the need for innovation
    D. It focuses solely on maintaining existing systems

II. True/False Questions:

1. Digital leadership requires more than just technical expertise; it involves vision, influence, and fostering collaboration. (True/False)
2. A key role of digital leaders is to resist any changes in the technological landscape. (True/False)
3. Building a digital culture within the organization is essential for successful digital transformation. (True/False)

Mastering IT Leadership and Management, Strategies for Success in the Digital Age

4. Digital leaders should discourage experimentation to avoid the risk of failure. (True/False)

Exercises

I. Strategic Vision Development:
   - **Objective:** Create a strategic vision for digital transformation in your organization.
   - **Instructions:**
     1. Define a clear and compelling strategic vision that aligns digital initiatives with your organization's long-term goals.
     2. Outline how this vision will be communicated to different stakeholders to gain their buy-in.
     3. Develop a roadmap that includes key initiatives, timelines, and milestones to achieve this vision.

II. Innovation Culture Workshop:
   - **Objective:** Foster a culture of innovation within your team or organization.
   - **Instructions:**
     1. Identify current barriers to innovation within your organization.
     2. Propose initiatives to overcome these barriers, such as setting up innovation labs or running hackathons.
     3. Implement a pilot program to encourage experimentation and assess its impact on team creativity and productivity.

III. Cross-Functional Collaboration Exercise:
   - **Objective:** Improve collaboration across different departments to support digital transformation.
   - **Instructions:**
     1. Identify key departments that should be involved in your organization's digital transformation efforts.
     2. Design a cross-functional team structure that facilitates collaboration, ensuring that IT initiatives align with broader business objectives.
     3. Plan and conduct a workshop with these teams to develop integrated strategies for digital transformation.

IV. Adaptability and Resilience Simulation:
   - **Objective:** Practice adaptability and resilience in the face of digital disruption.
   - **Instructions:**

Mastering IT Leadership and Management, Strategies for Success in the Digital Age

1. Create a scenario where a significant technological change disrupts your organization's operations.
2. Role-play how digital leaders should respond, including how to communicate the change, pivot strategies, and maintain team morale.
3. Reflect on the exercise and identify key takeaways for improving adaptability and resilience in your leadership approach.

V. Ethical Digital Leadership Case Study:
- **Objective:** Navigate the ethical challenges associated with digital transformation.
- **Instructions:**
    1. Review a case study where ethical considerations played a critical role in digital transformation (e.g., data privacy, AI ethics).
    2. Analyze the decisions made by leaders in the case study, identifying both successful and problematic approaches.
    3. Develop a set of ethical guidelines for your organization to follow during digital transformation initiatives, ensuring alignment with societal values and legal requirements.

These quizzes and exercises are designed to help readers of Chapter 11 better understand and apply the principles of digital leadership in the age of transformation, focusing on practical application, strategic alignment, and ethical considerations.

Mastering IT Leadership and Management, Strategies for Success in the Digital Age

Chapter 12: Navigating Digital Transformation

"IT IS NOT THE STRONGEST OF THE SPECIES THAT SURVIVE, NOR THE MOST INTELLIGENT, BUT THE ONE MOST RESPONSIVE TO CHANGE."

— **Charles Darwin**

Digital transformation is no longer just a buzzword—it's a strategic imperative for organizations looking to stay competitive in a rapidly evolving marketplace. For IT leaders, guiding their organizations through the complexities of digital transformation requires not only technical expertise but also a deep understanding of business processes, cultural dynamics, and change management. This chapter explores the key aspects of digital transformation, from setting the vision and strategy to executing initiatives that drive innovation, efficiency, and value.

Setting the Vision for Digital Transformation

The foundation of any successful digital transformation is a clear and compelling vision that aligns with the organization's long-term goals. As an IT leader, your role is to define this vision and articulate how digital transformation will enhance the organization's ability to achieve its objectives.

- **Aligning with Business Goals:**
  The digital transformation vision must be directly aligned with the organization's business goals. Whether the objective is to improve customer experience, increase operational efficiency, drive innovation, or enter new markets, the vision should clearly demonstrate how digital initiatives will support these goals. IT leaders should work closely with senior management to ensure that the digital transformation vision is integrated into the broader business strategy.

- **Communicating the Vision:**
  Once the vision is established, it's crucial to communicate it effectively across the organization. This involves not just sharing the high-level goals but also explaining the specific ways in which digital transformation will impact different departments, teams, and roles. Clear communication helps to build buy-in and ensures that everyone understands the purpose and benefits of the transformation.

- **Creating a Roadmap:**
  A digital transformation vision without a roadmap is just an aspiration. IT leaders must develop a detailed roadmap that outlines the key initiatives, timelines, and milestones required to achieve the vision. The roadmap should include short-term wins that build momentum, as well as long-term goals that require sustained effort and investment.

Mastering IT Leadership and Management, Strategies for Success in the Digital Age

Driving Innovation Through Technology

Innovation is at the heart of digital transformation. As IT leaders, fostering a culture of innovation and leveraging emerging technologies to drive business value are key responsibilities. This section explores how to use technology as a catalyst for innovation.

- **Identifying Emerging Technologies:**
  Staying ahead of the curve requires a keen eye on emerging technologies that have the potential to disrupt industries and create new opportunities. These might include artificial intelligence, machine learning, blockchain, the Internet of Things (IoT), and cloud computing. IT leaders should regularly assess how these technologies can be integrated into the organization's digital transformation efforts to drive innovation and create competitive advantages.

- **Encouraging Experimentation:**
  Innovation often stems from experimentation and taking calculated risks. IT leaders should create an environment where teams are encouraged to experiment with new ideas, technologies, and processes. This might involve setting up innovation labs, running pilot projects, or creating cross-functional teams to explore new concepts. By fostering a culture of experimentation, IT leaders can unlock creativity and discover new ways to deliver value.

- **Scaling Innovation:**
  Once innovative ideas have been tested and proven, the next challenge is scaling them across the organization. IT leaders must develop strategies for scaling successful initiatives, whether through the deployment of new technologies, the adoption of new processes, or the introduction of new products or services. Scaling innovation requires careful planning, resource allocation, and change management to ensure the benefits are realized organization-wide.

Mastering IT Leadership and Management, Strategies for Success in the Digital Age

Managing Cultural Change in Digital Transformation

Digital transformation is as much about people and culture as it is about technology. Successfully navigating cultural change is essential to ensuring that digital initiatives are embraced and sustained over the long term.

- **Understanding Organizational Culture:**
  Every organization has its own unique culture, shaped by its history, values, and people. IT leaders must take the time to understand the existing culture and how it might support or hinder digital transformation efforts. This involves assessing the organization's readiness for change, identifying potential cultural barriers, and developing strategies to address them.

- **Engaging Employees in the Transformation Process:**
  Employees are the backbone of any digital transformation effort. IT leaders should actively engage employees in the process, involving them in decision-making, soliciting their feedback, and addressing their concerns. When employees feel they are part of the journey, they are more likely to embrace the changes and contribute to the transformation's success.

- **Promoting a Digital Mindset:**
  A successful digital transformation requires a shift in mindset across the organization. IT leaders must promote a digital mindset that values agility, innovation, collaboration, and continuous learning. This can be achieved through targeted training programs, leadership development, and the establishment of digital champions who model and reinforce the desired behaviors.

- **Overcoming Resistance to Change:**
  Resistance to change is a common challenge in digital transformation. IT leaders must be prepared to address this resistance by clearly communicating the benefits of the transformation, providing support and resources to help employees adapt, and addressing any fears or concerns head-on. By building trust and demonstrating the positive impact of digital initiatives, IT leaders can reduce resistance and increase buy-in.

Mastering IT Leadership and Management, Strategies for Success in the Digital Age

Executing Digital Transformation Initiatives

The execution of digital transformation initiatives is where vision and strategy come to life. This section explores best practices for executing these initiatives effectively, ensuring they deliver the desired outcomes.

- **Prioritizing Initiatives:**
  Not all digital initiatives can be executed simultaneously. IT leaders must prioritize initiatives based on their strategic importance, potential impact, and feasibility. This involves assessing the resources required, the risks involved, and the expected benefits. By prioritizing initiatives, IT leaders can focus on those that will deliver the greatest value and set the stage for further transformation.

- **Agile Project Management:**
  Digital transformation requires a flexible and adaptive approach to project management. Agile methodologies, such as Scrum or Kanban, are well-suited to digital initiatives because they emphasize iterative development, continuous feedback, and rapid adaptation to change. IT leaders should adopt Agile practices to manage digital transformation projects, ensuring they can respond quickly to new challenges and opportunities.

- **Leveraging Data and Analytics:**
  Data is a powerful tool for driving digital transformation. IT leaders should leverage data and analytics to inform decision-making, measure progress, and optimize initiatives. This might involve using advanced analytics to gain insights into customer behavior, optimizing operations through data-driven process improvements, or using predictive analytics to anticipate market trends and opportunities.

- **Ensuring Integration and Interoperability:**
  As digital initiatives are executed, it's important to ensure that new technologies, systems, and processes are integrated seamlessly with existing ones. Interoperability is key to ensuring that digital transformation efforts work together harmoniously and deliver a cohesive experience for customers and employees alike. IT leaders must focus on integration strategies, such as using APIs, adopting cloud-based platforms, or implementing middleware solutions to connect disparate systems.

- **Measuring Success and ROI:**
  To ensure that digital transformation initiatives are delivering value, IT leaders must establish clear metrics for success and regularly measure their performance. This might include key performance indicators (KPIs) related to customer satisfaction, operational efficiency, revenue growth, or employee engagement. By measuring ROI and other success metrics, IT leaders can demonstrate the impact of digital transformation and make data-driven decisions about future initiatives.

Mastering IT Leadership and Management, Strategies for Success in the Digital Age

Sustaining Digital Transformation

Digital transformation is not a one-time effort but an ongoing journey. Sustaining the momentum of digital transformation requires continuous improvement, adaptability, and a commitment to innovation.

- **Continuous Improvement:**
  Digital transformation initiatives should be continuously evaluated and refined to ensure they continue to deliver value. IT leaders should implement processes for regularly reviewing and improving digital initiatives, whether through iterative development cycles, customer feedback loops, or internal audits. Continuous improvement helps organizations stay agile and responsive in a rapidly changing environment.

- **Adapting to Changing Market Conditions:**
  The digital landscape is constantly evolving, and organizations must be prepared to adapt to new market conditions, technologies, and customer expectations. IT leaders should maintain a forward-looking perspective, staying informed about emerging trends and being ready to pivot when necessary. This adaptability is key to sustaining digital transformation and maintaining a competitive edge.

- **Building a Culture of Innovation:**
  Sustaining digital transformation requires an organizational culture that values and supports innovation. IT leaders should continue to promote a culture of experimentation, where new ideas are encouraged and tested. This might involve fostering cross-functional collaboration, investing in research and development, or establishing innovation hubs within the organization. By embedding innovation into the organization's DNA, IT leaders can ensure that digital transformation remains a dynamic and ongoing process.

- **Maintaining Leadership Commitment:**
  The success of digital transformation depends on the continued commitment of senior leadership. IT leaders must keep digital transformation on the leadership agenda by regularly reporting on progress, demonstrating value, and advocating for ongoing investment in digital initiatives. Leadership commitment is essential for sustaining the momentum of digital transformation and ensuring that it continues to drive business success.

Mastering IT Leadership and Management, Strategies for Success in the Digital Age

Industry Case Study: Navigating Digital Transformation at Honeywell

Situation:
Honeywell, a global conglomerate with interests in aerospace, building technologies, performance materials, and safety solutions, recognized the need to embark on a digital transformation journey in the mid-2010s. The company aimed to leverage digital technologies to enhance operational efficiency, improve customer experience, and drive innovation. However, Honeywell faced significant challenges, including integrating digital technologies into its legacy systems, managing cultural change across its diverse global operations, and ensuring that its digital initiatives aligned with its strategic business goals.

Task:
Honeywell's IT leadership was tasked with successfully navigating the digital transformation journey by developing and executing a comprehensive strategy that would integrate digital technologies into all aspects of the business. This involved setting a clear vision for digital transformation, driving innovation through technology, managing cultural change, and ensuring that digital initiatives delivered measurable business value.

Action:
To achieve these objectives, Honeywell's IT leadership implemented several key strategies:

1. **Setting a Vision for Digital Transformation:**
   Honeywell's leadership articulated a clear and compelling vision for digital transformation, emphasizing the importance of digital technologies in driving the company's future growth. This vision was closely aligned with Honeywell's overall business strategy, ensuring that digital initiatives supported the company's long-term goals.

2. **Driving Innovation Through Technology:**
   Honeywell invested heavily in emerging technologies such as the Internet of Things (IoT), artificial intelligence (AI), and advanced data analytics. The company developed and launched several digital platforms, including Honeywell Forge, an enterprise performance management solution that leverages IoT and AI to optimize building operations, energy efficiency, and safety. These platforms were designed to deliver significant value to customers by improving operational efficiency and reducing costs.

3. **Managing Cultural Change:**
   Recognizing that digital transformation was as much about people as it was about technology, Honeywell's IT leaders focused on managing cultural change across the organization. This involved engaging employees at all levels, promoting a digital mindset, and providing training and support to help employees adapt to new technologies. Honeywell also established a network of "digital champions" within the organization to drive change and foster a culture of innovation.

4. **Executing and Sustaining Digital Transformation:**
   Honeywell implemented Agile project management methodologies to ensure that

Mastering IT Leadership and Management, Strategies for Success in the Digital Age

digital initiatives were executed effectively and delivered the desired outcomes. The company continuously monitored the progress of its digital transformation efforts, using data and analytics to measure success and make data-driven adjustments as needed. Honeywell's leadership remained committed to the digital transformation journey, regularly reviewing and refining the strategy to ensure it remained aligned with the company's goals.

Result:
As a result of these actions, Honeywell successfully navigated its digital transformation journey, achieving significant improvements in operational efficiency, customer satisfaction, and innovation. The company's investment in digital technologies enabled it to launch new products and services that provided substantial value to customers, enhancing Honeywell's competitive position in the market. By effectively managing cultural change and sustaining its digital transformation efforts, Honeywell created a more agile, innovative, and resilient organization, well-positioned to thrive in the digital age.

This case study illustrates the importance of a comprehensive and well-executed digital transformation strategy. Honeywell's success demonstrates how IT leaders can drive innovation, manage change, and achieve strategic business goals by navigating the complexities of digital transformation.

Mastering IT Leadership and Management, Strategies for Success in the Digital Age

Best Practices

1. **Start with a Clear Digital Transformation Strategy:**
   A successful digital transformation begins with a well-defined strategy that outlines the organization's vision, goals, and roadmap for change. IT leaders should collaborate with executive leadership to ensure that the digital transformation strategy aligns with the overall business strategy. This strategy should identify key areas for digital innovation, the technologies to be adopted, and the expected outcomes.

2. **Prioritize Customer-Centricity:**
   Customer needs should be at the center of digital transformation efforts. IT leaders should focus on how digital initiatives can enhance the customer experience, improve service delivery, and meet changing customer expectations. By prioritizing customer-centric solutions, organizations can drive greater engagement, loyalty, and satisfaction.

3. **Adopt an Agile Approach to Transformation:**
   Digital transformation is a dynamic and ongoing process that requires flexibility and adaptability. IT leaders should adopt an Agile approach, allowing for iterative development, continuous feedback, and rapid adjustments. This approach enables organizations to respond quickly to changes in technology, market conditions, and customer preferences.

4. **Invest in Employee Skills and Digital Literacy:**
   The success of digital transformation depends on the skills and capabilities of the workforce. IT leaders should invest in training and development programs that enhance digital literacy across the organization. Empowering employees with the knowledge and skills to leverage new technologies ensures they can contribute effectively to digital initiatives.

5. **Leverage Data Analytics for Informed Decision-Making:**
   Data is a critical asset in digital transformation. IT leaders should establish robust data analytics capabilities to inform decision-making, identify opportunities, and track the success of digital initiatives. By leveraging data, organizations can gain valuable insights, optimize processes, and drive innovation.

6. **Foster a Culture of Change and Innovation:**
   Digital transformation requires a cultural shift that embraces change, innovation, and continuous improvement. IT leaders should work to create an organizational culture that supports experimentation, values learning from failure, and encourages creative problem-solving. This culture of innovation is essential for sustaining momentum and achieving long-term success.

7. **Ensure Strong Leadership and Governance:**
   Effective leadership and governance are crucial for navigating digital transformation. IT leaders should establish clear governance structures, define roles and

responsibilities, and ensure strong executive sponsorship for digital initiatives. This leadership provides direction, ensures accountability, and helps manage risks throughout the transformation process.

8. **Collaborate Across the Organization:**
    Digital transformation is not just an IT initiative; it requires collaboration across all functions of the organization. IT leaders should work closely with other departments to ensure that digital initiatives are integrated, aligned with business goals, and supported by the entire organization. Cross-functional teams can bring diverse perspectives and expertise to drive successful transformation.

Mastering IT Leadership and Management, Strategies for Success in the Digital Age

Lessons Learned

1. **Strategic Alignment is Critical for Success:**
   Digital transformation efforts that are closely aligned with the organization's strategic objectives are more likely to succeed. When digital initiatives support business goals, they gain stronger backing from leadership and are more likely to deliver meaningful results. Strategic alignment ensures that digital transformation is not just about technology but also about achieving business outcomes.

2. **Customer-Centric Solutions Drive Engagement:**
   Organizations that prioritize customer-centric digital solutions see greater engagement and satisfaction from their customers. Successful digital transformations enhance the customer experience, making it easier and more enjoyable for customers to interact with the business. This focus on the customer helps differentiate the organization in a competitive market.

3. **Agility is Key to Navigating Change:**
   The fast pace of technological change requires an Agile approach to digital transformation. Organizations that are flexible and responsive are better able to navigate the complexities of transformation. Agile methodologies allow teams to iterate quickly, incorporate feedback, and adapt to evolving circumstances, ensuring that digital initiatives remain relevant and effective.

4. **Investing in People is Essential:**
   Digital transformation is as much about people as it is about technology. Organizations that invest in upskilling their workforce and enhancing digital literacy are better positioned to succeed. Employees who are confident and capable in using new technologies can drive innovation, improve processes, and contribute to the organization's digital transformation goals.

5. **Data-Driven Decisions Lead to Better Outcomes:**
   Leveraging data analytics to inform decision-making is a powerful tool in digital transformation. Organizations that base their strategies and actions on data-driven insights are more likely to achieve their desired outcomes. Data analytics provides a clear picture of what is working and what needs adjustment, enabling continuous improvement.

6. **Cultural Change is Necessary for Transformation:**
   Successful digital transformation requires a shift in organizational culture. A culture that embraces change, encourages innovation, and values learning is essential for sustaining transformation efforts. Leaders who foster this culture create an environment where digital initiatives can thrive, and employees are motivated to contribute to the organization's success.

7. **Strong Governance Ensures Accountability:**
   Clear governance structures and strong leadership are essential for managing the complexities of digital transformation. Organizations that establish well-defined

Mastering IT Leadership and Management, Strategies for Success in the Digital Age

roles, responsibilities, and decision-making processes are better equipped to navigate challenges, manage risks, and ensure that digital initiatives are executed effectively.

8. **Collaboration Across Functions Enhances Success:**
   Cross-functional collaboration is a key driver of successful digital transformation. When IT works closely with other departments, digital initiatives are more likely to be comprehensive, aligned with business objectives, and supported across the organization. Collaboration ensures that digital transformation is a collective effort, leading to more holistic and sustainable outcomes.

By adopting these best practices and learning from successful digital transformation initiatives, IT leaders can guide their organizations through the complexities of transformation, ensuring they emerge stronger, more competitive, and better positioned for the future.

Mastering IT Leadership and Management, Strategies for Success in the Digital Age

Conclusion

Navigating digital transformation is one of the most significant challenges—and opportunities—facing IT leaders today. In Chapter 12, we explored the strategies and skills required to effectively guide organizations through this complex and often disruptive process. From fostering a culture of innovation to leveraging cutting-edge technologies like AI, cloud computing, and big data, digital transformation is about reshaping business models, enhancing customer experiences, and driving competitive advantage.

At the heart of successful digital transformation is the ability to foster a culture of innovation within the organization. IT leaders must create an environment where creativity and experimentation are encouraged, and where teams feel empowered to explore new ideas and challenge the status quo. This cultural shift is crucial for driving the continuous improvement and agility needed to thrive in the digital age.

Leveraging emerging technologies is another critical component of digital transformation. By strategically integrating technologies such as AI, cloud computing, and big data into the organization's IT infrastructure, leaders can unlock new opportunities for efficiency, scalability, and innovation. However, successful adoption of these technologies requires careful planning, clear alignment with business objectives, and a focus on building the necessary skills and capabilities within the IT team.

Managing innovation teams and projects is also essential for navigating digital transformation. IT leaders must be adept at leading cross-functional teams, managing the risks associated with innovation, and ensuring that new initiatives are delivered on time and within budget. This requires a blend of strong leadership, strategic vision, and the ability to adapt to changing circumstances.

As we conclude Chapter 12, it is clear that navigating digital transformation is not just about implementing new technologies—it is about reimagining the entire business in the context of the digital age. IT leaders who can successfully navigate this transformation will position their organizations to capitalize on new opportunities, respond effectively to market changes, and achieve sustainable growth.

The insights and strategies discussed in this chapter provide a comprehensive framework for understanding and leading digital transformation. As we continue to explore the evolving role of IT leadership, these principles will be crucial for addressing the challenges and opportunities that lie ahead. With a solid foundation in navigating digital transformation, IT leaders are well-prepared to drive their organizations toward a future defined by innovation, agility, and success.

Mastering IT Leadership and Management, Strategies for Success in the Digital Age

Quizzes

I. Multiple Choice Questions:

1. What is the first step in setting a vision for digital transformation?

    A. Implementing new technology without considering business goals
    B. Aligning the digital transformation vision with the organization's long-term business goals
    C. Outsourcing all IT functions
    D. Reducing IT staff to cut costs

2. Which of the following is essential for driving innovation through technology?

    A. Avoiding new technologies to minimize risks
    B. Identifying emerging technologies that can disrupt industries and create new opportunities
    C. Implementing technology only after competitors do
    D. Maintaining the status quo to ensure stability

3. What is a key strategy for managing cultural change in digital transformation?

    A. Ignoring resistance to change
    B. Promoting a digital mindset that values agility, innovation, and continuous learning
    C. Mandating changes without employee input
    D. Focusing solely on technological advancements without considering people

4. Why is it important to measure success and ROI in digital transformation?

    A. To justify the cancellation of ongoing initiatives
    B. To ensure digital transformation initiatives are delivering value and to inform future decisions
    C. To maintain a static budget for IT
    D. To reduce the frequency of digital initiatives

II. True/False Questions:

1. A digital transformation vision that is not aligned with business goals can still be successful. (True/False)
2. Innovation in digital transformation should be limited to proven technologies to minimize risks. (True/False)
3. Continuous improvement is essential for sustaining digital transformation. (True/False)

Mastering IT Leadership and Management, Strategies for Success in the Digital Age

4. Measuring the success of digital transformation initiatives is unnecessary once they are implemented. (True/False)

Exercises

I. Digital Transformation Vision Exercise:
   - **Objective:** Develop a clear and aligned vision for digital transformation in your organization.
   - **Instructions:**
     1. Identify the long-term business goals of your organization.
     2. Create a vision statement for digital transformation that aligns with these goals.
     3. Outline the key initiatives and technologies that will support this vision.
     4. Present the vision to stakeholders for feedback and refine it as necessary.

II. Innovation Workshop:
   - **Objective:** Foster a culture of innovation through the exploration of emerging technologies.
   - **Instructions:**
     1. Research emerging technologies relevant to your industry, such as AI, blockchain, or IoT.
     2. Organize a workshop where team members can brainstorm potential applications of these technologies within your organization.
     3. Develop a pilot project based on one of the ideas generated, focusing on its potential impact and feasibility.
     4. Present the pilot project plan to leadership for approval and support.

III. Cultural Change Management Simulation:
   - **Objective:** Practice managing cultural change during digital transformation.
   - **Instructions:**
     1. Create a scenario where a significant digital transformation initiative is introduced in your organization.
     2. Role-play the scenario with colleagues, focusing on addressing resistance and promoting a digital mindset.
     3. Develop a plan to engage employees in the transformation process, including communication strategies, training programs, and leadership involvement.
     4. Reflect on the simulation and identify key takeaways for managing cultural change in real-world situations.

Mastering IT Leadership and Management, Strategies for Success in the Digital Age

IV. Data-Driven Decision-Making Exercise:
- **Objective:** Leverage data and analytics to inform decision-making during digital transformation.
- **Instructions:**
    1. Identify a digital transformation initiative within your organization that would benefit from data-driven insights.
    2. Collect relevant data, such as customer behavior, operational metrics, or market trends.
    3. Use data analytics tools to analyze the data and generate actionable insights.
    4. Present your findings to the project team and propose data-driven adjustments to the initiative based on the analysis.

V. Continuous Improvement Plan:
- **Objective:** Create a plan to sustain digital transformation through continuous improvement.
- **Instructions:**
    1. Review ongoing digital transformation initiatives in your organization.
    2. Develop a continuous improvement plan that includes regular reviews, feedback loops, and iterative development cycles.
    3. Establish key performance indicators (KPIs) to measure the success of the initiatives.
    4. Implement the plan and monitor progress, making adjustments as necessary to ensure sustained transformation.

These quizzes and exercises are designed to help readers of Chapter 12 better understand and apply the principles of navigating digital transformation, with a focus on strategic alignment, innovation, cultural change, and continuous improvement.

Mastering IT Leadership and Management, Strategies for Success in the Digital Age

Chapter 13: Building a Cybersecurity Strategy

"SECURITY IS NOT A PRODUCT; IT IS A PROCESS."
— **Bruce Schneier**

As the digital landscape evolves, cybersecurity has emerged as a top priority for organizations across all industries. IT leaders are responsible for developing and implementing robust strategies to protect sensitive data, ensure regulatory compliance, and safeguard the organization's reputation. This chapter explores the key components of an effective cybersecurity strategy, including risk assessment, threat management, incident response, and fostering a culture of security within the organization.

Understanding the Cybersecurity Landscape

The first step in building a cybersecurity strategy is to understand the current cybersecurity landscape. Cyber threats are constantly evolving, and IT leaders must stay informed about the latest trends, risks, and best practices to protect their organizations effectively.

- **Evolving Threats:**
  Cyber threats are becoming increasingly sophisticated, with attackers employing advanced techniques such as phishing, ransomware, and zero-day exploits to breach systems. IT leaders must stay vigilant to these evolving threats and understand how they could impact the organization's operations, data, and reputation.

- **Regulatory Requirements:**
  Compliance with cybersecurity regulations and standards is essential for avoiding legal penalties and maintaining customer trust. IT leaders must stay up to date with relevant regulations, such as GDPR, HIPAA, and PCI DSS, ensuring their cybersecurity strategies align with these requirements.

- **Industry Best Practices:**
  Industry frameworks and best practices, such as the NIST Cybersecurity Framework, ISO 27001, and CIS Controls, offer valuable guidance for building a comprehensive cybersecurity strategy. IT leaders should leverage these resources to ensure their cybersecurity programs align with industry standards and best practices.

Mastering IT Leadership and Management, Strategies for Success in the Digital Age

Conducting a Cybersecurity Risk Assessment

A comprehensive cybersecurity risk assessment forms the foundation of an effective cybersecurity strategy. It involves identifying, assessing, and prioritizing risks to the organization's information assets and IT infrastructure.

- **Identifying Assets and Vulnerabilities:**
  Begin by identifying the organization's critical information assets, such as customer data, intellectual property, and financial records. Then, evaluate the vulnerabilities in the IT infrastructure that could be exploited by attackers, such as unpatched software, weak passwords, or misconfigured systems.

- **Assessing Threats and Risks:**
  Once vulnerabilities are identified, assess the potential threats that could exploit them. This includes both external threats, such as cybercriminals and nation-state actors, and internal threats, such as disgruntled employees or accidental data breaches. Evaluate the likelihood and impact of these threats to determine the level of risk they pose to the organization.

- **Prioritizing Risks:**
  Not all risks are equal, so it's crucial to prioritize them based on their potential impact on the organization. High-priority risks should be addressed immediately, while lower-priority risks can be managed over time. This prioritization ensures that resources are allocated efficiently to mitigate the most significant risks.

Mastering IT Leadership and Management, Strategies for Success in the Digital Age

Developing a Comprehensive Cybersecurity Strategy

With a clear understanding of the organization's risks, IT leaders can develop a comprehensive cybersecurity strategy that addresses these risks and protects the organization's information assets.

- **Establishing Security Policies and Procedures:**
Security policies and procedures are the backbone of any cybersecurity strategy. These documents outline the rules and guidelines for protecting the organization's information assets. Key policies may include data protection, access control, and incident response procedures. IT leaders must ensure these policies are clearly communicated to all employees and enforced consistently.

- **Implementing Security Controls:**
Security controls are the technical and administrative measures that protect the organization's information assets from cyber threats. These controls may include firewalls, encryption, multi-factor authentication, intrusion detection systems, and security awareness training. IT leaders should adopt a layered approach to security, combining multiple controls to provide comprehensive protection against a wide range of threats.

- **Aligning Security with Business Objectives:**
A successful cybersecurity strategy must align with the organization's broader business objectives. IT leaders should collaborate with business leaders to ensure that security measures support the organization's goals, such as protecting customer data, maintaining regulatory compliance, and enabling digital transformation. Security should be viewed as an enabler of business success, not an obstacle.

Mastering IT Leadership and Management, Strategies for Success in the Digital Age

Building an Incident Response Plan

Despite the best efforts to prevent cyber incidents, breaches can and do happen. Having a well-defined incident response plan is crucial for minimizing the impact of a cyber incident and ensuring a swift recovery.

- **Defining Roles and Responsibilities:**
  An effective incident response plan clearly defines the roles and responsibilities of the incident response team. This team should include representatives from IT, legal, communications, and senior management. Each team member must understand their role during an incident and be trained on how to respond effectively.

- **Establishing Incident Response Procedures:**
  The incident response plan should include detailed procedures for detecting, reporting, and responding to cyber incidents. These may include steps for isolating affected systems, conducting forensic investigations, communicating with stakeholders, and restoring normal operations. IT leaders should ensure that these procedures are regularly tested and updated to reflect the latest threats and best practices.

- **Communicating with Stakeholders:**
  Communication is a critical component of incident response. IT leaders must ensure that all stakeholders, including employees, customers, regulators, and the media, are informed of the incident in a timely and transparent manner. Clear and accurate communication helps maintain trust and minimize reputational damage.

- **Learning from Incidents:**
  After an incident has been resolved, conducting a post-incident review is essential to identify lessons learned and improve the organization's security posture. This may involve updating security policies, enhancing security controls, or providing additional training to employees. By learning from incidents, IT leaders can continuously improve their cybersecurity strategy and reduce the likelihood of future breaches.

Mastering IT Leadership and Management, Strategies for Success in the Digital Age

Fostering a Culture of Security

Building a strong cybersecurity culture is essential for the success of any cybersecurity strategy. Employees at all levels of the organization play a critical role in protecting information assets, and IT leaders must ensure that everyone understands the importance of cybersecurity.

- **Providing Security Awareness Training:**
  Security awareness training is crucial for educating employees about the risks they face and the actions they can take to protect the organization. Training should cover topics such as phishing, password management, and safe internet practices. IT leaders must ensure that training is ongoing and tailored to the specific needs and risks of the organization.

- **Encouraging Secure Behavior:**
  IT leaders should promote secure behavior by encouraging best practices and recognizing employees who follow security policies. This may involve rewarding employees for reporting phishing attempts, using strong passwords, or adhering to data protection guidelines. By making security an integral part of the organization's culture, IT leaders can reduce the risk of human error and create a more resilient organization.

- **Engaging Leadership:**
  Senior leadership plays a crucial role in fostering a culture of security. IT leaders should engage executives in cybersecurity initiatives, ensuring they understand the importance of security and fully support the organization's efforts to protect its information assets. Leadership commitment is vital for creating a security-conscious organization.

- **Promoting Accountability:**
  Accountability is a key component of a strong security culture. IT leaders must ensure that employees understand their responsibilities in protecting information assets and that there are consequences for failing to follow security policies. This could involve implementing security metrics to track performance or conducting regular security audits to ensure compliance.

Mastering IT Leadership and Management, Strategies for Success in the Digital Age

Industry Case Study: Building a Cybersecurity Strategy at Equifax

Situation:
In 2017, Equifax, one of the largest credit reporting agencies in the United States, experienced a massive data breach that exposed the personal information of approximately 147 million people. The breach resulted from vulnerabilities in Equifax's cybersecurity defenses, including outdated software and inadequate security protocols. This incident underscored the critical importance of having a robust and proactive cybersecurity strategy in place to protect sensitive data and maintain trust with customers and stakeholders.

Task:
In the aftermath of the breach, Equifax's IT leadership faced the urgent task of rebuilding the company's cybersecurity strategy from the ground up. This involved identifying and addressing existing vulnerabilities, implementing new security measures, and restoring trust with the public and regulatory bodies. The company needed to ensure that such a breach would not occur again, which required a comprehensive overhaul of its cybersecurity practices.

Action:
To address these challenges, Equifax implemented several key initiatives:

1. **Conducting a Comprehensive Risk Assessment:**
   Equifax's IT team began by conducting a thorough risk assessment to identify the root causes of the breach and understand the full scope of their cybersecurity vulnerabilities. This assessment included evaluating the company's existing security infrastructure, identifying outdated or unpatched software, and mapping out the data flows that were most at risk.

2. **Implementing Advanced Security Controls:**
   In response to the identified risks, Equifax invested heavily in upgrading its security infrastructure. This included deploying advanced security controls such as multi-factor authentication, encryption of sensitive data, and intrusion detection systems. The company also introduced regular security audits and vulnerability assessments to ensure its defenses remained robust over time.

3. **Developing a Strong Incident Response Plan:**
   Equifax recognized the importance of having a well-defined incident response plan to quickly and effectively manage future security incidents. The new plan included clear roles and responsibilities for all team members, as well as detailed procedures for isolating affected systems, conducting forensic investigations, and communicating with stakeholders.

4. **Fostering a Culture of Security:**
   To ensure long-term success, Equifax placed a strong emphasis on building a culture of security across the organization. This included regular training for employees on cybersecurity best practices and increasing awareness of the importance of data

protection. The company also engaged senior leadership in cybersecurity initiatives, ensuring that security became a top priority at all levels of the organization.

Result:
As a result of these efforts, Equifax significantly strengthened its cybersecurity posture. The company's new security measures helped prevent further breaches and restored some level of public trust. While the breach had a lasting impact on the company's reputation, the steps taken by Equifax's IT leadership demonstrated a commitment to protecting customer data and complying with regulatory requirements. The case of Equifax highlights the importance of a proactive and comprehensive approach to cybersecurity, particularly in industries that handle sensitive personal information.

This example illustrates how critical it is for organizations to build and maintain a robust cybersecurity strategy. Through effective risk assessment, the implementation of advanced security controls, and fostering a culture of security, IT leaders can protect their organizations from evolving cyber threats and ensure long-term resilience.

Mastering IT Leadership and Management, Strategies for Success in the Digital Age

Best Practices

1. **Adopt a Risk-Based Approach to Cybersecurity:**
   A successful cybersecurity strategy begins with a risk-based approach. IT leaders should assess the organization's risk landscape, identifying its most critical assets and potential threats. By prioritizing risks based on their potential impact and likelihood, organizations can allocate resources more effectively to protect their most valuable assets.

2. **Develop a Comprehensive Security Framework:**
   A well-defined security framework is essential for guiding the organization's cybersecurity efforts. IT leaders should adopt industry-recognized frameworks such as NIST, ISO 27001, or CIS Controls to structure their security practices. These frameworks provide a systematic approach to managing cybersecurity risks, ensuring that all aspects of security are addressed.

3. **Implement a Multi-Layered Defense Strategy:**
   Cybersecurity should not rely on a single line of defense. IT leaders should implement a multi-layered defense strategy that includes firewalls, intrusion detection systems, encryption, multi-factor authentication, and regular security audits. This approach provides multiple barriers to potential attackers, reducing the likelihood of a successful breach.

4. **Focus on Continuous Monitoring and Incident Response:**
   Cybersecurity is an ongoing process, not a one-time effort. IT leaders should establish continuous monitoring systems to detect and respond to threats in real time. An effective incident response plan is crucial for minimizing the impact of security breaches. Regular testing and updates of the incident response plan ensure the organization is prepared to respond swiftly and effectively to any security incidents.

5. **Promote a Security-Aware Culture:**
   Human error is often the weakest link in cybersecurity. IT leaders should work to build a security-aware culture where employees understand the importance of cybersecurity and their role in protecting the organization. Regular training, phishing simulations, and clear communication of security policies help embed security consciousness into the organization's culture.

6. **Collaborate with External Partners and Experts:**
   Cybersecurity is a complex and rapidly evolving field. It's essential for organizations to collaborate with external partners and experts. IT leaders should engage with cybersecurity vendors, industry groups, and government agencies to stay informed about the latest threats, best practices, and technological advancements. This collaboration helps organizations stay ahead of emerging threats.

7. **Ensure Compliance with Regulations and Standards:**
   Compliance with relevant cybersecurity regulations and standards is a critical

component of any cybersecurity strategy. IT leaders must ensure the organization meets all legal and regulatory requirements, such as GDPR, HIPAA, or SOX, depending on the industry. Regular audits and reviews help maintain compliance and avoid legal penalties.

8. **Invest in Cybersecurity Innovation:**
   Cyber threats are constantly evolving, and IT leaders must be proactive in adopting new technologies and approaches to stay ahead. Investing in cybersecurity innovation, such as AI-driven threat detection, advanced encryption methods, and zero-trust architectures, provides a significant advantage in protecting the organization from sophisticated attacks.

Mastering IT Leadership and Management, Strategies for Success in the Digital Age

Lessons Learned

1. **Risk-Based Prioritization Enhances Resource Allocation:**
   Organizations that adopt a risk-based approach to cybersecurity are better positioned to allocate resources where they are needed most. By focusing on the most critical risks, these organizations can effectively protect key assets while optimizing their cybersecurity budgets. This prioritization helps balance security needs with business objectives.

2. **A Structured Framework Ensures Comprehensive Security:**
   Implementing a comprehensive security framework ensures that all aspects of cybersecurity are systematically addressed. Organizations that follow established frameworks, such as NIST or ISO 27001, are better equipped to manage cybersecurity risks effectively, as these frameworks provide a proven structure for security governance, risk management, and compliance.

3. **Layered Defense is Essential for Resilience:**
   A multi-layered defense strategy is crucial for building resilience against cyber threats. Organizations that implement multiple security measures create a more robust defense, reducing the risk of a single point of failure. This approach ensures that even if one security layer is breached, others remain in place to protect the organization.

4. **Proactive Monitoring and Response Mitigate Impact:**
   Continuous monitoring and a well-prepared incident response plan are key to minimizing the impact of cybersecurity incidents. Organizations that invest in real-time threat detection and regularly update their incident response plans can respond quickly to breaches, minimizing damage and recovery time. This proactive approach is essential for maintaining business continuity.

5. **Security Awareness Reduces Human Error:**
   Building a security-aware culture significantly reduces the risk of human error, a common cause of cybersecurity incidents. Organizations that prioritize employee training and awareness are more likely to prevent breaches caused by phishing, weak passwords, or other avoidable mistakes. This cultural shift is a critical component of a strong cybersecurity strategy.

6. **External Collaboration Strengthens Cyber Defenses:**
   Collaborating with external partners and experts enhances an organization's ability to defend against cyber threats. Organizations that engage with cybersecurity vendors, industry peers, and government agencies gain access to valuable intelligence, tools, and best practices. This collaboration helps ensure that security measures remain up-to-date and aligned with the latest developments in the field.

7. **Regulatory Compliance Protects Against Legal Risks:**
   Compliance with cybersecurity regulations and standards is essential for protecting the organization from legal risks and penalties. Organizations that maintain

Mastering IT Leadership and Management, Strategies for Success in the Digital Age

compliance with relevant laws, such as GDPR or HIPAA, are better positioned to avoid costly fines and reputational damage. Regular audits and compliance reviews help ensure that security practices meet regulatory requirements.

8. **Innovation is Key to Staying Ahead of Threats:**
   Investing in cybersecurity innovation is crucial for staying ahead of evolving threats. Organizations that embrace new technologies, such as AI-driven threat detection and zero-trust architectures, are better equipped to defend against sophisticated attacks. This commitment to innovation helps future-proof the organization's cybersecurity strategy and ensures long-term resilience.

By adopting these best practices and learning from successful cybersecurity initiatives, IT leaders can build a robust and adaptive cybersecurity strategy that protects their organizations from current and emerging threats, ensuring the safety and integrity of critical assets in the digital age.

Mastering IT Leadership and Management, Strategies for Success in the Digital Age

Conclusion

In today's digital landscape, cybersecurity is not just a technical necessity—it is a strategic imperative. Chapter 13 has explored the critical components of building a robust cybersecurity strategy, highlighting the pivotal role IT leaders play in safeguarding their organizations against an ever-evolving array of cyber threats. As digital transformation accelerates, the importance of a comprehensive, proactive approach to cybersecurity cannot be overstated.

A well-crafted cybersecurity strategy begins with a thorough understanding of the current threat landscape. IT leaders must stay informed about emerging risks, from sophisticated malware and ransomware to insider threats and supply chain vulnerabilities. By maintaining vigilant awareness of these threats, organizations can better anticipate potential attacks and respond with agility and precision.

Risk assessment and management are foundational to any effective cybersecurity strategy. Identifying and prioritizing risks based on their potential impact enables IT leaders to allocate resources efficiently and implement the most appropriate security measures. This risk-based approach ensures the protection of an organization's most critical assets while optimizing its overall security posture.

Implementing a layered defense strategy is another key aspect of cybersecurity. By deploying multiple layers of security controls—such as firewalls, encryption, intrusion detection systems, and regular security audits—IT leaders can create a robust defense-in-depth approach that minimizes the likelihood of a successful breach. This multi-faceted strategy also includes educating employees on best practices, as human error often remains the weakest link in the cybersecurity chain.

Incident response planning is equally critical. IT leaders must ensure their organizations are prepared to respond quickly and effectively to security breaches. This includes developing and regularly testing incident response plans, establishing clear communication channels, and ensuring that all relevant stakeholders understand their roles and responsibilities during a cybersecurity incident.

As we conclude Chapter 13, it is clear that building a cybersecurity strategy is not a one-time task but an ongoing commitment. The rapidly evolving nature of cyber threats requires continuous monitoring, adaptation, and improvement of security measures. IT leaders who prioritize cybersecurity as a strategic concern will not only protect their organizations from potential harm but also build trust with customers, partners, and stakeholders.

The principles and strategies discussed in this chapter are essential for any IT leader aiming to secure their organization in the digital age. Moving forward, these cybersecurity insights will continue to guide our exploration of IT leadership, ensuring that security remains at the forefront of technological innovation and business strategy. With a strong cybersecurity strategy in place, IT leaders can confidently navigate the challenges of the digital world, knowing that their organizations are well-protected against the ever-present threat of cyberattacks.

Mastering IT Leadership and Management, Strategies for Success in the Digital Age

Quizzes

I. Multiple Choice Questions:

1. What is the first step in building an effective cybersecurity strategy?

    A. Implementing advanced security technologies
    B. Conducting a thorough risk assessment
    C. Training employees on cybersecurity awareness
    D. Outsourcing security functions to third parties

2. Which of the following best describes the concept of "layered defense" in cybersecurity?

    A. Using a single, highly secure system to protect all data
    B. Implementing multiple, overlapping security measures to protect information assets
    C. Relying solely on encryption to secure data
    D. Segregating data into different security levels based on sensitivity

3. What is the primary goal of an incident response plan in cybersecurity?

    A. To prevent all cyber incidents from occurring
    B. To ensure a quick and effective response to security breaches
    C. To outsource all incident management to external vendors
    D. To minimize the financial impact of security investments

4. Why is fostering a culture of security important in an organization?

    A. It shifts all responsibility for cybersecurity to the IT department
    B. It reduces the risk of human error and strengthens overall security
    C. It allows for flexible and inconsistent application of security policies
    D. It eliminates the need for advanced security technologies

II. True/False Questions:

1. A comprehensive risk assessment should identify both internal and external threats to the organization. (True/False)
2. Regular training and security awareness programs are optional for maintaining a strong cybersecurity posture. (True/False)
3. An effective cybersecurity strategy should be aligned with the organization's business objectives. (True/False)
4. Incident response plans should be static documents that do not require regular updates or testing. (True/False)

Mastering IT Leadership and Management, Strategies for Success in the Digital Age

Exercises

I. Cybersecurity Risk Assessment Exercise:
   - **Objective:** Conduct a risk assessment to identify and prioritize cybersecurity threats.
   - **Instructions:**
     1. Identify the critical information assets in your organization, such as customer data, intellectual property, and financial records.
     2. Assess potential vulnerabilities in your IT infrastructure that could be exploited by attackers.
     3. Evaluate both internal and external threats, considering factors such as cybercriminal activity, employee errors, and system vulnerabilities.
     4. Prioritize the identified risks based on their potential impact on the organization, and develop a plan to mitigate the highest-priority risks.

II. Incident Response Planning Workshop:
   - **Objective:** Develop a comprehensive incident response plan for a simulated cyber incident.
   - **Instructions:**
     1. Create a scenario involving a significant cyber incident, such as a data breach or ransomware attack.
     2. Assemble a cross-functional incident response team, including representatives from IT, legal, communications, and senior management.
     3. Define the roles and responsibilities of each team member, and outline the steps for detecting, reporting, and responding to the incident.
     4. Conduct a tabletop exercise to simulate the response to the incident, and refine the incident response plan based on lessons learned.

III. Building a Security-Aware Culture Exercise:
   - **Objective:** Foster a culture of security awareness across the organization.
   - **Instructions:**
     1. Develop a security awareness training program tailored to your organization's specific needs and risks.
     2. Implement regular training sessions covering topics such as phishing, password management, and safe internet practices.
     3. Introduce initiatives to encourage secure behavior, such as recognizing employees who follow security best practices or report phishing attempts.
     4. Engage senior leadership in promoting the importance of cybersecurity and ensuring accountability at all levels of the organization.

Mastering IT Leadership and Management, Strategies for Success in the Digital Age

IV. Layered Defense Strategy Development:
- **Objective:** Design a multi-layered defense strategy to protect the organization's information assets.
- **Instructions:**
    1. Identify the key security controls that should be implemented across the organization, including firewalls, encryption, intrusion detection systems, and multi-factor authentication.
    2. Develop a plan to integrate these controls into a cohesive, multi-layered defense strategy that addresses various types of cyber threats.
    3. Ensure the strategy includes regular security audits and vulnerability assessments to maintain the effectiveness of defense measures.
    4. Present the strategy to stakeholders and gather feedback to further refine the approach.

V. Cybersecurity Innovation Investment Proposal:
- **Objective:** Explore and propose investments in innovative cybersecurity technologies.
- **Instructions:**
    1. Research emerging cybersecurity technologies, such as AI-driven threat detection, advanced encryption methods, or zero-trust architectures.
    2. Evaluate the potential benefits and challenges of implementing these technologies within your organization.
    3. Develop a proposal for investing in one or more of these innovations, including a cost-benefit analysis and alignment with the organization's security goals.
    4. Present the proposal to senior leadership and advocate for the adoption of the recommended technologies.

These exercises are designed to help readers of Chapter 13 better understand and apply the principles of building a robust cybersecurity strategy, focusing on practical application, strategic alignment, and continuous improvement.

Mastering IT Leadership and Management, Strategies for Success in the Digital Age

Conclusion of Part 4: Navigating the Digital Transformation

Digital transformation is reshaping the way businesses operate, compete, and deliver value, making it a critical focus for IT leaders. Throughout Part 4 of this book, we have explored the multifaceted role of IT leadership in guiding organizations through the complexities of digital transformation. This section has emphasized the importance of strategic vision, innovative thinking, and the effective integration of emerging technologies to drive successful digital change.

In Chapter 11, we examined the role of digital leadership, highlighting the need for IT leaders to not only understand the technological landscape but also inspire and lead their organizations through change. Digital leadership is about setting a clear vision for transformation, aligning it with business objectives, and fostering a culture that embraces innovation and continuous improvement.

Chapter 12 explored strategies for navigating digital transformation, stressing the need to balance technological advancements with organizational readiness. Successful digital transformation requires a holistic approach, where technology, people, and processes are aligned toward achieving strategic goals. IT leaders must be skilled in managing this balance, ensuring that new technologies are implemented in ways that enhance business performance and drive growth.

In Chapter 13, the focus shifted to building a robust cybersecurity strategy—an essential component of any digital transformation effort. As organizations become more reliant on digital technologies, the risks associated with cyber threats increase. IT leaders must ensure that cybersecurity is embedded into the digital transformation strategy from the outset, protecting the organization's assets, reputation, and customer trust.

As we conclude Part 4, it is clear that navigating digital transformation presents both a challenge and an opportunity for IT leaders. Those who can effectively guide their organizations through this journey will unlock new avenues for innovation, efficiency, and competitive advantage. The insights and strategies discussed in this section provide a comprehensive framework for understanding and leading digital transformation in the modern business landscape.

With a strong grasp of digital leadership, strategic planning, and cybersecurity, IT leaders are well-positioned to drive successful digital transformation efforts. As we move into the next part of the book, these principles will remain essential as we explore how IT leadership adapts to new working environments, manages talent, and prepares for the future of technology and business. The journey of digital transformation is ongoing, and the skills and strategies discussed here will continue to be crucial as organizations evolve in the digital age.

Mastering IT Leadership and Management, Strategies for Success in the Digital Age

Part 5: Leading in a Hybrid and Remote Work Environment

"THE MEASURE OF INTELLIGENCE IS THE ABILITY TO CHANGE."

—Albert Einstein

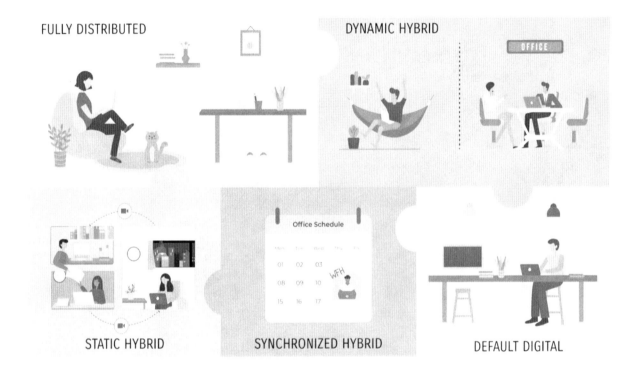

Mastering IT Leadership and Management, Strategies for Success in the Digital Age

Chapter 14: IT Leadership in a Hybrid Work World

"THE KEY TO SUCCESS IS NOT JUST MANAGING WORK, BUT MANAGING HOW AND WHERE WORK HAPPENS."
—**Unknown**

The COVID-19 pandemic accelerated the adoption of hybrid work models, transforming how businesses operate and how employees engage with their work. As organizations increasingly embrace hybrid work, IT leaders face the unique challenge of supporting a distributed workforce while ensuring security, productivity, and collaboration. This chapter explores the key aspects of IT leadership in a hybrid work environment, from enabling remote work technologies to fostering a strong organizational culture and addressing security concerns.

Enabling Remote Work Technologies

One of the primary responsibilities of IT leaders in a hybrid work environment is to provide the technology infrastructure necessary to support both remote and on-site employees effectively. This involves selecting, implementing, and managing the tools and platforms that enable seamless communication, collaboration, and productivity.

- **Cloud-Based Solutions:** Cloud technology is the backbone of hybrid work, enabling employees to access applications, data, and services from anywhere. IT leaders should prioritize implementing cloud-based solutions that support remote access to critical business systems, such as document management, CRM, and project management tools. These solutions must be scalable, secure, and user-friendly, ensuring that employees can work efficiently regardless of their location.

- **Unified Communication and Collaboration Tools:** Effective communication and collaboration are essential for hybrid teams. IT leaders should implement unified communication platforms that integrate messaging, video conferencing, and collaboration tools into a single, cohesive solution. Tools like Microsoft Teams, Slack, and Zoom can help bridge the gap between remote and in-office workers, fostering real-time communication and collaboration.

- **Remote Access and Virtual Desktops:** For employees who require access to on-premises applications and systems, IT leaders should consider implementing remote access solutions such as Virtual Private Networks (VPNs) or Virtual Desktop Infrastructure (VDI). These technologies enable employees to securely access corporate resources from any location while maintaining the performance and reliability of on-premises systems.

- **Device Management and Support:** Managing a diverse range of devices, from corporate-issued laptops to employee-owned smartphones, is a critical aspect of supporting hybrid work. IT leaders should implement mobile device management

Mastering IT Leadership and Management, Strategies for Success in the Digital Age

(MDM) and endpoint management solutions that allow them to monitor, manage, and secure devices remotely. Additionally, providing robust IT support for remote employees is essential to minimize downtime and ensure that technical issues are resolved quickly.

Fostering a Strong Organizational Culture

Maintaining a strong organizational culture is challenging in a hybrid work environment, where employees may feel disconnected from their colleagues and the company's mission. IT leaders play a crucial role in fostering a sense of community, engagement, and alignment among distributed teams.

- **Promoting Communication and Engagement:** Regular communication is key to keeping employees engaged and connected in a hybrid work environment. IT leaders should encourage the use of communication platforms that facilitate both formal and informal interactions, such as virtual town halls, team meetings, and social channels. These platforms should be used to share company news, celebrate achievements, and provide opportunities for employees to connect on a personal level.

- **Supporting Team Collaboration:** Collaborative work is essential for innovation and problem-solving, but it can be more challenging in a hybrid environment. IT leaders should implement collaboration tools that allow teams to work together seamlessly, regardless of location. Features like shared workspaces, real-time document editing, and integrated task management can help teams stay aligned and productive.

- **Reinforcing Company Values and Mission:** In a hybrid work world, it's important to ensure that employees feel connected to the company's values and mission. IT leaders can support this by creating digital platforms and content that reinforce the company's culture and purpose. This might include intranet sites with company news, virtual onboarding programs that introduce new hires to the company's values, and online training programs that emphasize the organization's commitment to its mission.

- **Creating Opportunities for Social Interaction:** Social interaction is a vital component of a strong organizational culture. IT leaders should support virtual social events, such as online coffee breaks, happy hours, or team-building activities, to help employees build relationships and foster a sense of belonging. Additionally, hybrid work policies should include provisions for in-person meetings and events when safe and feasible, allowing employees to connect face-to-face.

Mastering IT Leadership and Management, Strategies for Success in the Digital Age

Ensuring Security in a Hybrid Work Environment

Security is a top concern for IT leaders in a hybrid work world. The distributed nature of hybrid work presents new challenges in securing data, networks, and devices, requiring IT leaders to implement robust security measures that protect the organization's assets while enabling remote work.

- **Zero Trust Security Model:** The Zero Trust security model is particularly well-suited to hybrid work environments. This model assumes that no user or device is trusted by default, regardless of whether they are inside or outside the corporate network. IT leaders should implement Zero Trust principles by verifying the identity of users and devices, enforcing least-privilege access, and continuously monitoring for suspicious activity. This approach minimizes the risk of unauthorized access and data breaches.

- **Multi-Factor Authentication (MFA):** Multi-factor authentication is a critical security measure for hybrid work. IT leaders should ensure that MFA is implemented for all remote access to corporate systems, requiring employees to verify their identity using multiple factors, such as passwords, biometrics, or security tokens. MFA significantly reduces the risk of compromised credentials and unauthorized access.

- **Data Encryption and Protection:** Protecting sensitive data is essential in a hybrid work environment, where data is often transmitted and stored across various devices and networks. IT leaders should implement end-to-end encryption for data in transit and at rest, ensuring that sensitive information remains secure. Additionally, data loss prevention (DLP) solutions can help monitor and control the transfer of sensitive data, preventing unauthorized sharing or leakage.

- **Endpoint Security:** With employees accessing corporate resources from various devices, endpoint security becomes a critical concern. IT leaders should implement endpoint protection solutions that provide real-time threat detection, antivirus protection, and automated patch management. These solutions help secure employee devices against malware, ransomware, and other cyber threats.

- **Employee Security Awareness Training:** Human error is one of the leading causes of security breaches. IT leaders should implement regular security awareness training programs that educate employees about the risks associated with hybrid work, such as phishing attacks, weak passwords, and unsafe Wi-Fi networks. Training should be interactive and tailored to the specific challenges of remote work, ensuring that employees are equipped to recognize and respond to potential threats.

Mastering IT Leadership and Management, Strategies for Success in the Digital Age

Supporting Employee Well-Being and Work-Life Balance

The shift to hybrid work has blurred the boundaries between work and personal life, making it essential for IT leaders to support employee well-being and promote a healthy work-life balance.

- **Implementing Flexible Work Policies:** Flexibility is one of the primary benefits of hybrid work, and IT leaders should support policies that allow employees to choose where and when they work. This may include flexible hours, the ability to work from home on certain days, or the option to work from different locations. By providing this flexibility, IT leaders can help employees balance their work and personal responsibilities, reducing stress and increasing job satisfaction.

- **Promoting the Use of Wellness Tools:** Technology can play a crucial role in supporting employee well-being. IT leaders should encourage the use of wellness tools and apps that help employees manage stress, stay active, and maintain a healthy work-life balance. These might include meditation apps, fitness trackers, or platforms that promote regular breaks and time away from screens.

- **Monitoring Workload and Burnout:** The always-on nature of hybrid work can lead to burnout if not properly managed. IT leaders should monitor employee workloads and watch for signs of burnout, such as decreased productivity, disengagement, or increased absenteeism. Implementing tools that track work hours and provide insights into employee well-being can help managers intervene early and offer support when needed.

- **Encouraging Time Off and Disconnecting:** IT leaders should actively encourage employees to take time off and disconnect from work. This could involve promoting the use of vacation days, setting clear expectations about after-hours work, or implementing policies that limit work-related communications outside regular hours. Encouraging time off helps employees recharge and return to work with renewed energy and focus.

Mastering IT Leadership and Management, Strategies for Success in the Digital Age

Leading with Empathy and Inclusion

Empathy and inclusion are critical components of effective leadership in a hybrid work world. IT leaders must create an environment where all employees feel valued, supported, and included, regardless of their location.

- **Practicing Empathetic Leadership:** Empathetic leadership involves understanding and addressing the unique challenges employees face in a hybrid work environment. IT leaders should actively listen to employees' concerns, provide support, and show understanding of their individual circumstances. By leading with empathy, IT leaders can build trust and foster a more positive work environment.

- **Promoting Inclusivity in Hybrid Meetings:** Hybrid meetings can inadvertently exclude remote participants if not managed properly. IT leaders should promote inclusivity by ensuring that remote employees have equal opportunities to participate and contribute. This might involve using technology to facilitate collaboration, providing clear agendas and meeting materials in advance, and encouraging active participation from all attendees.

- **Supporting Diversity and Inclusion Initiatives:** Diversity and inclusion are vital in any work environment, and IT leaders should continue to support these initiatives in a hybrid work setting. This could include implementing policies that promote equal access to opportunities, providing diversity training, and ensuring all voices are heard and valued in decision-making processes.

- **Creating a Sense of Belonging:** In a hybrid work environment, it's essential to create a sense of belonging for all employees, regardless of their location. IT leaders can achieve this by fostering a strong organizational culture, promoting open communication, and creating opportunities for employees to connect and build relationships. A sense of belonging enhances employee engagement and contributes to a positive work environment.

Mastering IT Leadership and Management, Strategies for Success in the Digital Age

Industry Case Study: IT Leadership in a Hybrid Work World at Microsoft

Situation:
The COVID-19 pandemic in 2020 forced companies worldwide to rapidly adopt remote and hybrid work models. Microsoft, a global technology giant, was not only a leader in the technology space but also needed to navigate this significant shift in work dynamics within its organization. As a company that provides tools and platforms for remote work, Microsoft's leadership needed to set an example by effectively managing its distributed workforce while continuing to innovate and support its global customer base.

Task:
Microsoft's leadership was tasked with implementing a hybrid work model that ensured employee productivity, maintained team cohesion, and supported employee well-being. This involved rethinking traditional management practices, adopting new technologies, and fostering a culture that embraced flexibility and inclusivity. The challenge was to manage a global workforce effectively, ensuring that all employees, regardless of location, had the tools and support they needed to succeed.

Action:
To address these challenges, Microsoft implemented several strategic actions:

1. **Adopting a Hybrid Work Strategy:**
   Microsoft introduced a flexible work policy allowing employees to work remotely part-time on a permanent basis. The company provided guidelines and resources to help managers support their teams in this new hybrid environment. This policy emphasized trust and accountability, granting employees the autonomy to choose how and where they worked most effectively.

2. **Deploying Technology to Support Hybrid Work:**
   As a leading provider of collaboration tools, Microsoft leveraged its own technology, such as Microsoft Teams, to facilitate communication and collaboration across dispersed teams. The company invested in enhancing these tools to support hybrid work, adding features like Together Mode in Teams, which helped recreate the feeling of working together in a shared space. Microsoft also implemented security measures to protect its data and systems from the increased risks associated with remote access.

3. **Fostering a Culture of Inclusion and Well-Being:**
   Microsoft's leadership recognized the importance of employee well-being and inclusivity in a hybrid work model. The company introduced initiatives to support mental health, such as virtual meditation sessions and resources for managing stress. Additionally, Microsoft promoted an inclusive culture by ensuring that remote employees were equally involved in meetings and decision-making processes. Training was provided for managers on how to lead with empathy and support diverse teams.

Mastering IT Leadership and Management, Strategies for Success in the Digital Age

4. **Supporting Continuous Learning and Development:**
   To ensure employees could adapt to the new hybrid work environment, Microsoft invested in continuous learning and development. The company offered training on using new collaboration tools, as well as courses on effective remote working strategies. Microsoft also encouraged a growth mindset, fostering an environment where employees were empowered to learn, innovate, and grow in their roles.

Result:
As a result of these actions, Microsoft successfully transitioned to a hybrid work model that supported productivity, innovation, and employee well-being. The company's flexible work policies and robust technology infrastructure enabled it to maintain business continuity and customer support during the pandemic. Microsoft's emphasis on inclusion and well-being helped maintain high levels of employee engagement and morale, despite the challenges of remote work. The company's ability to navigate the shift to hybrid work not only strengthened its internal operations but also set a positive example for its customers and partners around the world.

This case study illustrates how IT leadership at Microsoft successfully managed the transition to a hybrid work model by leveraging technology, fostering an inclusive culture, and supporting continuous learning. These strategies helped Microsoft maintain its competitive edge while ensuring that its workforce remained engaged, productive, and resilient in a rapidly changing environment.

Mastering IT Leadership and Management, Strategies for Success in the Digital Age

Best Practices

1. **Prioritize Flexibility and Adaptability:** In a hybrid work environment, flexibility is key. IT leaders should focus on creating an adaptable infrastructure that supports both in-office and remote work seamlessly. This includes investing in cloud-based solutions, remote collaboration tools, and secure access technologies that allow employees to work effectively from any location.

2. **Ensure Robust Cybersecurity for Remote Work:** The shift to hybrid work has expanded the cybersecurity perimeter, making it essential to implement robust security measures. IT leaders should prioritize securing remote connections through VPNs, multi-factor authentication, endpoint protection, and regular security training for employees. This approach helps mitigate the increased risk of cyber threats in a dispersed workforce.

3. **Promote Clear Communication and Collaboration:** Effective communication is crucial in a hybrid work environment. IT leaders should ensure their teams have access to reliable communication and collaboration tools, such as video conferencing, chat platforms, and project management software. Establishing clear communication protocols and encouraging regular check-ins helps maintain team cohesion and alignment, regardless of physical location.

4. **Foster an Inclusive Work Culture:** A successful hybrid work strategy requires an inclusive culture where all employees, whether remote or in-office, feel equally valued and connected. IT leaders should implement practices that promote inclusivity, such as virtual team-building activities, recognition programs, and ensuring remote employees have equal access to growth and development opportunities.

5. **Support Employee Well-Being and Work-Life Balance:** The hybrid work model can blur the lines between work and personal life. IT leaders should promote policies and tools that support employee well-being and help maintain a healthy work-life balance. This includes encouraging regular breaks, setting clear boundaries for work hours, and providing access to wellness resources and programs.

6. **Enable Continuous Learning and Development:** In a hybrid work world, continuous learning and development are more important than ever. IT leaders should ensure employees have access to online training resources, virtual workshops, and opportunities for professional growth. This commitment to learning helps employees stay up to date with the latest technologies and industry trends, enhancing their performance and engagement.

7. **Leverage Data to Monitor and Optimize Performance:** IT leaders should use data analytics to monitor productivity, engagement, and overall performance in a hybrid work environment. By analyzing data on tool usage, communication patterns, and project outcomes, leaders can identify areas for improvement and optimize

processes to support hybrid work. This data-driven approach ensures that the hybrid model remains effective and efficient.

8. **Communicate and Reinforce Company Culture:** Maintaining a strong company culture in a hybrid work environment can be challenging. IT leaders should actively communicate and reinforce the organization's values, mission, and culture through regular virtual meetings, newsletters, and other digital platforms. Consistently emphasizing the company culture helps keep all employees aligned and engaged, no matter where they work.

Mastering IT Leadership and Management, Strategies for Success in the Digital Age

Lessons Learned

1. **Flexibility is a Competitive Advantage:** Organizations that prioritize flexibility in their IT infrastructure and work policies are better positioned to thrive in a hybrid work world. Flexibility allows employees to choose the work environment that best suits their needs, leading to higher productivity, job satisfaction, and retention. Successful IT leaders recognize the value of flexibility as a key driver of organizational success.

2. **Security Must Evolve with the Work Environment:** The transition to hybrid work has highlighted the need for stronger cybersecurity measures. Organizations that have successfully navigated this transition have invested in comprehensive security solutions that address the unique risks of remote work. Continuous monitoring and regular updates to security protocols are essential for safeguarding the organization in a hybrid model.

3. **Communication is Key to Team Cohesion:** Clear and consistent communication is vital for maintaining team cohesion and productivity in a hybrid work environment. IT leaders who prioritize communication and provide the necessary tools for collaboration help ensure that all team members stay connected and informed. This focus on communication prevents misunderstandings and keeps projects on track.

4. **Inclusivity Drives Engagement and Retention:** An inclusive culture is essential for the success of a hybrid work model. Organizations that actively promote inclusivity and ensure that remote employees feel connected and valued see higher levels of engagement and retention. IT leaders must be intentional in creating an environment where all employees can thrive, regardless of their location.

5. **Well-Being is Critical to Sustained Performance:** Supporting employee well-being is crucial in a hybrid work environment. Organizations that prioritize work-life balance and provide resources for mental and physical health observe higher levels of employee satisfaction and sustained performance. IT leaders who champion well-being initiatives help create a resilient and motivated workforce.

6. **Continuous Learning Fuels Innovation:** The need for ongoing learning and development has become more pronounced in a hybrid work world. Organizations that invest in continuous learning opportunities for their employees are better equipped to adapt to changes and innovate. IT leaders play a critical role in facilitating access to training and development resources, ensuring that their teams remain competitive and future-ready.

7. **Data-Driven Decision-Making Enhances Effectiveness:** Leveraging data to monitor and optimize hybrid work practices has proven effective in maintaining productivity and engagement. Organizations that use data to inform their decisions can quickly identify challenges and implement solutions that enhance the hybrid

Mastering IT Leadership and Management, Strategies for Success in the Digital Age

work experience. IT leaders who embrace data-driven approaches are better positioned to navigate the complexities of hybrid work.

8. **Culture Requires Intentional Effort:** Maintaining a strong company culture in a hybrid environment requires intentional and consistent effort. Successful organizations make culture a priority, using digital tools and regular communication to reinforce their values and mission. IT leaders who actively work to sustain and evolve the company culture ensure that all employees, whether remote or on-site, feel connected to the organization's goals and values.

By implementing these best practices and learning from successful IT initiatives in a hybrid work world, IT leaders can effectively manage the challenges of hybrid work, create a supportive and inclusive environment, and drive sustained success for their organizations.

Mastering IT Leadership and Management, Strategies for Success in the Digital Age

Conclusion

The shift to a hybrid work environment has fundamentally changed the way organizations operate, presenting new challenges and opportunities for IT leaders. In Chapter 14, we explored how IT leadership must adapt to effectively manage and support teams in this new work paradigm. As hybrid work becomes a permanent fixture in the modern workplace, IT leaders are tasked with ensuring that technology not only supports productivity but also fosters collaboration, engagement, and a strong organizational culture.

Adapting leadership styles for remote and hybrid teams is crucial in this environment. IT leaders must develop the flexibility to lead teams dispersed across various locations, understanding the unique challenges and needs of remote workers. This includes fostering trust, maintaining open lines of communication, and providing the support necessary to ensure that all team members feel connected and valued, regardless of where they work.

The tools and technologies that enable effective remote IT management are another critical aspect of leading in a hybrid work world. IT leaders must stay ahead of the curve by implementing and optimizing tools that facilitate collaboration, secure communication, and seamless access to resources. This includes not only selecting the right technologies but also ensuring that teams are well-trained and comfortable using them, while implementing robust security measures to protect the organization's digital assets.

Maintaining team cohesion and culture in a hybrid work environment is perhaps one of the most significant challenges IT leaders face. As teams become more geographically dispersed, it is essential to cultivate a sense of belonging and shared purpose. This requires intentional efforts to create opportunities for virtual collaboration, team-building, and regular check-ins that reinforce the organization's values and goals.

As we conclude Chapter 14, it's clear that IT leadership in a hybrid work world demands a rethinking of traditional management approaches. The ability to lead effectively in this environment will be a key determinant of organizational success in the years to come. By embracing the challenges of hybrid work and leveraging the right tools, strategies, and leadership practices, IT leaders can create a resilient, adaptive, and high-performing workforce that thrives in the new normal.

The insights and strategies discussed in this chapter provide a solid foundation for navigating the complexities of hybrid work. As we move forward in the book, these principles will continue to be essential as we explore talent management, diversity, and the future trends that will shape the next generation of IT leadership. With the right approach, IT leaders can ensure that their organizations are not only prepared for the hybrid work world but are also poised to excel within it.

Mastering IT Leadership and Management, Strategies for Success in the Digital Age

Quizzes

1. Multiple Choice Questions:
    1. Which technology is considered the backbone of hybrid work, enabling employees to access applications and data from anywhere?

        A. On-premises servers
        B. Cloud-based solutions
        C. Local area networks (LANs)
        D. USB flash drives

    2. Why is it crucial for IT leaders to implement multi-factor authentication (MFA) in a hybrid work environment?

        A. To simplify the login process for remote workers
        B. To reduce the risk of compromised credentials and unauthorized access
        C. To eliminate the need for passwords
        D. To increase employee productivity by reducing security protocols

    3. Which approach is essential for fostering a strong organizational culture in a hybrid work environment?

        A. Focusing solely on remote employees
        B. Ignoring informal social interactions
        C. Promoting regular communication and engagement across all team members
        D. Limiting collaboration tools to in-office use

    4. What is the main purpose of implementing endpoint security in a hybrid work environment?

        A. To reduce the cost of IT infrastructure
        B. To secure employee devices against malware, ransomware, and other cyber threats
        C. To simplify the IT management process
        D. To enable remote desktop access for all employees

2. True/False Questions:
    1. IT leaders should prioritize employee well-being and work-life balance in a hybrid work environment. (True/False)
    2. Fostering an inclusive culture in hybrid meetings involves ensuring that remote employees have equal opportunities to participate. (True/False)

Mastering IT Leadership and Management, Strategies for Success in the Digital Age

3. Security measures in a hybrid work environment can remain static and do not need regular updates. (True/False)
4. Flexibility is a disadvantage in a hybrid work environment. (True/False)

Exercises

I. Remote Work Technology Evaluation:
   - **Objective:** Assess the effectiveness of your organization's current remote work technologies.
   - **Instructions:**
     1. Identify the key technologies your organization uses to support remote work, such as cloud-based solutions, communication tools, and security measures.
     2. Evaluate the effectiveness of each technology in terms of usability, security, and scalability.
     3. Identify any gaps or areas for improvement and propose solutions to enhance the remote work experience for your team.

II. Hybrid Meeting Inclusivity Workshop:
   - **Objective:** Improve the inclusivity of hybrid meetings in your organization.
   - **Instructions:**
     1. Analyze recent hybrid meetings to identify any instances where remote participants were excluded or disadvantaged.
     2. Develop a set of best practices to ensure inclusivity in hybrid meetings, such as clear agendas, advance sharing of materials, and active facilitation.
     3. Conduct a workshop with your team to discuss these best practices and implement them in future meetings.

III. Security Awareness Training Simulation:
   - **Objective:** Increase awareness of cybersecurity risks in a hybrid work environment.
   - **Instructions:**
     1. Develop a cybersecurity training module that focuses on the unique risks associated with hybrid work, such as phishing, unsecured networks, and device security.
     2. Simulate a cybersecurity incident, such as a phishing attempt, and guide your team through the appropriate response.
     3. Evaluate the team's performance and provide feedback to strengthen their security awareness.

Mastering IT Leadership and Management, Strategies for Success in the Digital Age

IV. Employee Well-Being Plan Development:
- **Objective:** Create a plan to support employee well-being in a hybrid work environment.
- **Instructions:**
    1. Conduct a survey to assess the well-being and work-life balance of your remote and in-office employees.
    2. Based on the survey results, develop a well-being plan that includes initiatives such as flexible work hours, wellness tools, and regular check-ins.
    3. Implement the plan and monitor its impact on employee satisfaction and productivity.

V. Building a Sense of Belonging Exercise:
- **Objective:** Foster a sense of belonging among remote and in-office employees.
- **Instructions:**
    1. Organize virtual social events, such as online coffee breaks or team-building activities, to help employees build relationships.
    2. Encourage team members to share their experiences and stories, promoting open communication and mutual understanding.
    3. Regularly assess the sense of belonging among employees and make adjustments to the activities to ensure everyone feels included.

These quizzes and exercises are designed to help readers of Chapter 14 better understand and apply the principles of IT leadership in a hybrid work environment, focusing on technology implementation, inclusivity, security, and employee well-being.

Mastering IT Leadership and Management, Strategies for Success in the Digital Age

Chapter 15: Talent Management and Development

"THE GROWTH AND DEVELOPMENT OF PEOPLE IS THE HIGHEST CALLING OF LEADERSHIP."

—**Harvey S. Firestone**

In the rapidly evolving landscape of IT and digital transformation, talent management and development have become critical priorities for organizations. The success of any technology-driven initiative depends on the skills, knowledge, and motivation of the workforce. As IT leaders, it is essential to focus on attracting, developing, and retaining top talent while fostering a culture of continuous learning and growth. This chapter explores the key aspects of talent management and development, including strategies for recruiting IT talent, developing skills and competencies, and creating a culture of engagement and retention.

Recruiting Top IT Talent

Attracting top talent is the first step in building a high-performing IT team. As the demand for skilled IT professionals continues to grow, IT leaders must adopt innovative recruitment strategies to attract the best candidates.

- **Understanding the Talent Landscape:** The IT talent market is highly competitive, with certain skills in particularly high demand, such as cybersecurity, data science, cloud computing, and AI. IT leaders must stay informed about industry trends and understand the specific skills and competencies required for their organization's digital transformation efforts. This knowledge allows for targeted recruitment efforts focused on the most critical areas.

- **Building a Strong Employer Brand:** A strong employer brand is crucial for attracting top IT talent. IT leaders should work closely with HR and marketing teams to create a compelling narrative about the organization's mission, values, and culture. Highlighting opportunities for growth, innovation, and impact within the organization can make it an attractive destination for skilled IT professionals.

- **Leveraging Multiple Recruitment Channels:** To reach a diverse pool of candidates, IT leaders should leverage multiple recruitment channels, including job boards, social media, professional networks like LinkedIn, and industry-specific platforms. Additionally, attending industry conferences, hackathons, and networking events can help build relationships with potential candidates and showcase the organization's commitment to technology and innovation.

- **Creating an Inclusive Hiring Process:** Inclusivity is a key factor in successful talent acquisition. IT leaders should ensure that the hiring process is free from bias and actively encourages applications from diverse candidates. This includes using inclusive language in job descriptions, ensuring diverse interview panels, and

Mastering IT Leadership and Management, Strategies for Success in the Digital Age

providing equal opportunities for all candidates to demonstrate their skills and potential.

Developing IT Skills and Competencies

Once top talent has been recruited, the focus shifts to developing their skills and competencies. In the fast-paced world of IT, continuous learning and development are essential for keeping up with technological advancements and ensuring that the organization remains competitive.

- **Implementing a Continuous Learning Culture:** A culture of continuous learning is vital for the ongoing development of IT professionals. IT leaders should encourage employees to take ownership of their learning and provide access to a variety of resources, including online courses, certifications, workshops, and conferences. By promoting a mindset of lifelong learning, IT leaders can ensure their teams are always equipped with the latest skills and knowledge.

- **Creating Personalized Development Plans:** Every IT professional has unique strengths, interests, and career goals. IT leaders should work with employees to create personalized development plans that align with both individual aspirations and organizational needs. These plans should outline specific learning objectives, opportunities for skill development, and pathways for career advancement.

- **Providing Access to Cutting-Edge Tools and Technologies:** Hands-on experience with the latest tools and technologies is one of the most effective ways for IT professionals to develop new skills. IT leaders should provide opportunities for employees to work on innovative projects, experiment with new technologies, and collaborate with cross-functional teams. Access to advanced tools and platforms not only enhances technical skills but also fosters creativity and innovation.

- **Encouraging Cross-Training and Knowledge Sharing:** Cross-training and knowledge sharing are valuable strategies for building a versatile and resilient IT team. IT leaders should encourage employees to learn from one another by rotating roles, participating in mentorship programs, and holding regular knowledge-sharing sessions. This approach helps break down silos, builds a broader skill set across the team, and prepares employees for new challenges and opportunities.

Mastering IT Leadership and Management, Strategies for Success in the Digital Age

Retaining Top IT Talent

Retaining top IT talent is as important as attracting and developing it. High turnover can disrupt projects, diminish morale, and lead to a loss of institutional knowledge. IT leaders must focus on creating an environment where employees feel valued, supported, and motivated to stay with the organization.

- **Fostering a Positive Work Environment:** A positive work environment is key to employee satisfaction and retention. IT leaders should work to create a culture that values collaboration, transparency, and respect. This includes promoting work-life balance, providing flexible work arrangements, and recognizing and rewarding employees for their contributions.

- **Offering Competitive Compensation and Benefits:** Compensation and benefits are critical factors in retaining top IT talent. IT leaders should ensure that their organization offers competitive salaries, bonuses, and benefits packages that reflect the value of their employees' skills and contributions. Additionally, offering non-monetary benefits, such as professional development opportunities, wellness programs, and employee recognition initiatives, can enhance job satisfaction and loyalty.

- **Providing Clear Career Paths:** Career development is a top priority for many IT professionals. IT leaders should provide clear career paths that outline opportunities for advancement within the organization. This includes offering leadership development programs, succession planning, and opportunities for employees to take on new challenges and responsibilities. By showing employees that there is room for growth within the organization, IT leaders can increase engagement and reduce turnover.

- **Building Strong Relationships:** Strong relationships between employees and their managers are a key driver of retention. IT leaders should prioritize regular one-on-one meetings, open communication, and active listening to understand employees' needs, concerns, and aspirations. By building trust and rapport, IT leaders can create a supportive environment where employees feel valued and connected to the organization.

Mastering IT Leadership and Management, Strategies for Success in the Digital Age

Managing and Developing IT Leadership

Developing the next generation of IT leaders is essential for sustaining an organization's long-term success. IT leaders must focus on identifying, mentoring, and developing high-potential employees who can step into leadership roles in the future.

- **Identifying Leadership Potential:** Identifying employees with leadership potential is the first step in developing future IT leaders. IT leaders should look for individuals who demonstrate strong problem-solving skills, the ability to influence others, and a commitment to continuous learning. These employees should be given opportunities to lead projects, mentor others, and take on increasing levels of responsibility.

- **Providing Leadership Development Programs:** Leadership development programs are critical for preparing employees for future leadership roles. IT leaders should offer a range of development opportunities, including formal training programs, executive coaching, and mentorship. These programs should focus on building both technical expertise and soft skills, such as communication, emotional intelligence, and strategic thinking.

- **Encouraging Leadership Experience:** Hands-on leadership experience is invaluable for developing future IT leaders. IT leaders should provide opportunities for high-potential employees to lead teams, manage projects, and make strategic decisions. This might involve assigning them to cross-functional teams, rotating them through different departments, or giving them responsibility for key initiatives. Real-world experience helps build confidence and prepares employees for leadership roles.

- **Mentoring and Coaching:** Mentorship and coaching are powerful tools for developing IT leaders. IT leaders should act as mentors to high-potential employees, providing guidance, support, and feedback as they navigate their career paths. Additionally, executive coaching can help employees develop the specific skills and behaviors needed for leadership roles, such as decision-making, conflict resolution, and strategic planning.

Mastering IT Leadership and Management, Strategies for Success in the Digital Age

Creating a Culture of Engagement and Retention

Engagement and retention go hand in hand, and both are essential for building a high-performing IT team. IT leaders must create a culture that fosters employee engagement, where employees are motivated, committed, and invested in the organization's success.

- **Promoting Employee Engagement:** Employee engagement is driven by a sense of purpose, meaningful work, and opportunities for growth. IT leaders should ensure that employees understand how their work contributes to the organization's goals and provide opportunities for them to take on challenging and rewarding projects. Regular feedback, recognition, and career development opportunities also contribute to higher levels of engagement.

- **Building a Sense of Purpose:** A sense of purpose is a powerful motivator for employees. IT leaders should communicate the organization's mission, vision, and values clearly and regularly, ensuring that employees understand how their work aligns with the organization's broader goals. When employees feel that their work is meaningful and contributes to a greater purpose, they are more likely to be engaged and committed to the organization.

- **Fostering Team Collaboration:** Collaboration is essential for fostering a sense of belonging and connection among employees. IT leaders should create opportunities for team collaboration through cross-functional projects, team-building activities, and collaborative tools and platforms. By encouraging teamwork and cooperation, IT leaders can build strong relationships within the team and create a positive work environment.

- **Measuring and Improving Retention:** Retention should be regularly measured and analyzed to identify areas for improvement. IT leaders should track turnover rates, conduct exit interviews, and gather feedback from employees to understand the factors that influence retention. By addressing the root causes of turnover and implementing strategies to improve retention, IT leaders can build a more stable and committed IT team.

Mastering IT Leadership and Management, Strategies for Success in the Digital Age

Industry Case Study: Talent Management and Development at Google

Situation:
Google, one of the world's leading technology companies, has consistently been recognized as a top employer due to its innovative approach to talent management and development. As Google expanded rapidly, it faced the challenge of attracting, retaining, and developing top talent in an extremely competitive market. The company needed to ensure that its workforce remained motivated, engaged, and equipped with the skills necessary to drive continuous innovation.

Task:
Google's leadership needed to create a comprehensive talent management and development strategy that would not only attract top talent but also foster continuous learning and development within the organization. This strategy needed to align with Google's mission to organize the world's information and make it universally accessible and useful, while also supporting the company's rapid growth and innovation objectives.

Action:
Google implemented several key initiatives as part of its talent management and development strategy:

1. **Attracting Top Talent with a Strong Employer Brand:**
   Google invested heavily in building a strong employer brand that emphasizes its culture of innovation, creativity, and employee empowerment. The company offers competitive compensation packages, unique perks (such as on-site wellness programs and gourmet meals), and a work environment that encourages collaboration and experimentation. Google's recruitment efforts are also bolstered by its reputation for challenging projects and opportunities for growth.

2. **Fostering a Culture of Continuous Learning:**
   Google promotes a culture of continuous learning through various programs and initiatives. One of the most notable is its "20% time" policy, which allows employees to spend 20% of their work time on projects they are passionate about, even if they are not directly related to their job responsibilities. This policy encourages innovation and personal growth. Additionally, Google offers a wide range of learning and development resources, including access to online courses, workshops, and mentorship programs.

3. **Promoting Diversity and Inclusion:**
   Google has made significant efforts to promote diversity and inclusion within its workforce. The company has implemented initiatives to recruit from a diverse talent pool, such as partnering with organizations that focus on underrepresented groups in tech. Google also fosters an inclusive work environment through employee resource groups, unconscious bias training, and programs aimed at supporting diverse perspectives and experiences.

Mastering IT Leadership and Management, Strategies for Success in the Digital Age

4. **Implementing Leadership Development Programs:**
   Google invests in developing its future leaders through structured leadership development programs. These programs include training on key leadership skills such as communication, decision-making, and team management, as well as opportunities for emerging leaders to take on challenging projects and roles within the company. By preparing high-potential employees for leadership positions, Google ensures it has a strong pipeline of leaders ready to guide the company through future challenges.

Result:
As a result of these initiatives, Google has been able to attract and retain top talent in the tech industry, maintaining its position as a leader in innovation and employee satisfaction. The company's focus on continuous learning and development has led to a highly skilled and motivated workforce capable of driving Google's mission forward. Moreover, Google's commitment to diversity and inclusion has contributed to a dynamic and creative work environment that values different perspectives and ideas.

This case study illustrates how Google's comprehensive talent management and development strategy has been instrumental in its success. By prioritizing employee growth, fostering an inclusive culture, and developing strong leaders, Google has created an environment where top talent thrives, driving continuous innovation and long-term business success.

Mastering IT Leadership and Management, Strategies for Success in the Digital Age

Best Practices

1. **Develop a Strategic Talent Management Plan:** A strategic approach to talent management is essential for aligning the organization's human capital with its business goals. IT leaders should create a comprehensive talent management plan that includes recruitment, development, retention, and succession planning. This plan should be closely aligned with the organization's strategic objectives and anticipate future skills needs.

2. **Focus on Continuous Learning and Development:** In the fast-paced IT industry, continuous learning is critical. IT leaders should foster a culture of continuous learning by providing employees with access to ongoing training, certifications, and professional development opportunities. Encouraging employees to upskill and reskill ensures the organization remains competitive and its workforce is equipped to handle emerging technologies and challenges.

3. **Implement a Robust Recruitment and Onboarding Process:** Attracting and retaining top talent starts with an effective recruitment and onboarding process. IT leaders should develop recruitment strategies that target diverse talent pools and highlight the organization's culture, values, and opportunities for growth. A comprehensive onboarding program that integrates new hires quickly and effectively helps ensure long-term retention and engagement.

4. **Promote a Culture of Inclusion and Diversity:** A diverse and inclusive workforce is more innovative and better equipped to solve complex problems. IT leaders should prioritize diversity and inclusion (D&I) in their talent management strategies, ensuring that recruitment, development, and retention practices reflect the organization's commitment to D&I. Promoting a culture where all employees feel valued and included drives higher levels of engagement and performance.

5. **Leverage Technology for Talent Management:** Technology can play a crucial role in managing talent effectively. IT leaders should utilize talent management systems (TMS), learning management systems (LMS), and other digital tools to streamline recruitment, track employee development, and manage performance. These tools provide valuable data and insights that help leaders make informed decisions about talent management.

6. **Provide Clear Career Development Pathways:** Employees are more likely to stay with an organization when they see clear opportunities for career growth. IT leaders should create and communicate transparent career development pathways that outline the skills, experiences, and milestones needed for advancement. Regular career planning discussions and mentorship programs can help employees navigate these pathways and achieve their professional goals.

7. **Recognize and Reward Performance:** Recognition and rewards are powerful motivators that can drive employee engagement and retention. IT leaders should implement recognition programs that celebrate both individual and team

achievements. Providing meaningful rewards, such as bonuses, promotions, or professional development opportunities, reinforces a culture of excellence and motivates employees to perform at their best.

8. **Support Work-Life Balance and Employee Well-Being:** Talent management in the modern workplace must consider the well-being of employees. IT leaders should promote policies and practices that support work-life balance, such as flexible working hours, remote work options, and wellness programs. A focus on employee well-being not only enhances job satisfaction but also reduces burnout and turnover.

Mastering IT Leadership and Management, Strategies for Success in the Digital Age

Lessons Learned

1. **Strategic Alignment is Key to Talent Management:** Successful organizations align their talent management strategies with their business goals. By anticipating future skills needs and aligning recruitment and development efforts accordingly, IT leaders can ensure the organization has the talent required to achieve its strategic objectives. This alignment also helps create a workforce that is agile and responsive to changes in the market.

2. **Continuous Learning Fuels Innovation:** Continuous learning is essential for maintaining a competitive edge in the IT industry. Organizations that invest in ongoing training and development for their employees are better positioned to innovate and adapt to new technologies. IT leaders who prioritize learning and development foster a culture of growth that drives both individual and organizational success.

3. **Effective Recruitment and Onboarding Drive Retention:** A strong recruitment and onboarding process is crucial for attracting and retaining top talent. Organizations that effectively integrate new hires into the company culture and provide them with the tools and support they need from day one are more likely to retain those employees. IT leaders who invest in these processes lay the foundation for long-term employee engagement and success.

4. **Diversity and Inclusion Enhance Performance:** A commitment to diversity and inclusion leads to a more innovative and high-performing workforce. Organizations that prioritize D&I in their talent management strategies are better able to attract diverse talent, foster creativity, and address complex challenges. IT leaders who champion D&I create a more dynamic and resilient organization.

5. **Technology is a Game-Changer for Talent Management:** Leveraging technology for talent management provides significant advantages in recruitment, development, and performance management. Organizations that utilize digital tools and systems for talent management gain insights that inform better decision-making and improve efficiency. IT leaders who embrace these technologies can enhance their talent management practices and outcomes.

6. **Career Development Opportunities Retain Top Talent:** Employees are more likely to stay with an organization when they see clear opportunities for career advancement. Organizations that provide transparent career development pathways and support employees' professional growth through mentorship and training programs experience higher retention rates. IT leaders who prioritize career development help build a loyal and motivated workforce.

7. **Recognition and Rewards Drive Engagement:** Recognizing and rewarding employee achievements is essential for maintaining high levels of engagement and performance. Organizations that implement meaningful recognition and reward

programs see increased employee satisfaction and productivity. IT leaders who celebrate successes and provide tangible rewards foster a culture of excellence.

8. **Well-Being is Essential for Talent Retention:** Supporting employee well-being is critical for reducing turnover and maintaining a healthy, productive workforce. Organizations that prioritize work-life balance and employee wellness create an environment where employees feel valued and supported. IT leaders who focus on well-being initiatives help retain top talent and enhance overall organizational performance.

By adopting these best practices and learning from successful talent management and development initiatives, IT leaders can build a strong, motivated, and capable workforce that drives the organization's success in the digital age.

Mastering IT Leadership and Management, Strategies for Success in the Digital Age

Conclusion

Talent management and development are critical components of IT leadership, directly impacting the success and sustainability of an organization in the rapidly evolving digital landscape. In Chapter 15, we explored the strategies and best practices IT leaders can employ to attract, retain, and develop top IT talent while fostering a diverse and inclusive work environment.

Attracting and retaining top IT talent is more important than ever in a competitive job market where skilled professionals are in high demand. IT leaders must create an appealing workplace that offers not only competitive compensation but also opportunities for growth, innovation, and meaningful work. By building a strong employer brand and actively engaging with potential candidates, organizations can position themselves as desirable places to work.

Professional development and succession planning are equally essential in ensuring the organization is prepared for future challenges. Investing in the continuous learning and development of IT professionals not only enhances their skills but also increases job satisfaction and loyalty. Succession planning, on the other hand, ensures the organization has a pipeline of capable leaders ready to step into critical roles as the company grows and evolves.

Diversity and inclusion are foundational to building a strong, innovative, and resilient IT team. A diverse workforce brings a wide range of perspectives, experiences, and ideas, which are crucial for driving creativity and problem-solving in the IT domain. IT leaders must proactively create an inclusive culture where all employees feel valued, respected, and empowered to contribute to the organization's success.

As we conclude Chapter 15, it is clear that effective talent management and development are not just HR responsibilities—they are strategic imperatives for IT leaders. By prioritizing the attraction, retention, and development of top talent, while fostering diversity and inclusion, IT leaders can build a high-performing team capable of driving the organization's success in the digital age.

The strategies and practices discussed in this chapter provide a comprehensive framework for managing IT talent effectively. As we continue to explore the future of IT leadership in the following chapters, these principles will remain central to building teams that are not only skilled and capable but also aligned with the organization's long-term goals and values. With the right approach to talent management and development, IT leaders can ensure their organizations are well-equipped to navigate the challenges and seize the opportunities of the future.

Mastering IT Leadership and Management, Strategies for Success in the Digital Age

Quizzes

I. Multiple Choice Questions:

1. What is the most critical factor in attracting top IT talent in a competitive job market?

    A. Offering the highest salaries in the industry
    B. Providing flexible work hours
    C. Building a strong employer brand that highlights opportunities for growth and innovation
    D. Relying on traditional recruitment channels

2. Which strategy is essential for fostering a culture of continuous learning within an IT team?

    A. Limiting training opportunities to senior staff only
    B. Encouraging employees to take ownership of their learning and providing access to diverse learning resources
    C. Focusing solely on mandatory certifications
    D. Offering training sessions only during onboarding

3. How can IT leaders ensure high retention rates among their top talent?

    A. Offering competitive compensation and benefits
    B. Requiring employees to work long hours
    C. Limiting career development opportunities to avoid internal competition
    D. Focusing on short-term incentives

4. Why is diversity and inclusion important in building a strong IT team?

    A. It reduces the need for training programs
    B. It helps attract talent from the same backgrounds
    C. It fosters creativity and problem-solving by bringing in diverse perspectives and experiences
    D. It simplifies decision-making by limiting differing opinions

II. True/False Questions:

1. Career development opportunities have little impact on employee retention. (True/False)
2. A strong employer brand can help attract top IT talent by showcasing the organization's culture and growth opportunities. (True/False)

Mastering IT Leadership and Management, Strategies for Success in the Digital Age

3. Continuous learning and upskilling are only necessary during the early stages of an IT professional's career. (True/False)
4. Inclusive hiring practices are crucial for attracting a diverse pool of candidates. (True/False)

Exercises

I. Talent Acquisition Strategy Development:
   - **Objective:** Develop a strategic plan for attracting top IT talent to your organization.
   - **Instructions:**
     1. Identify the key skills and competencies required for your organization's digital transformation initiatives.
     2. Create a recruitment plan that includes building a strong employer brand, leveraging multiple recruitment channels, and implementing inclusive hiring practices.
     3. Outline steps to ensure a smooth onboarding process that integrates new hires effectively and fosters long-term engagement.

II. Continuous Learning Program Design:
   - **Objective:** Design a continuous learning program that keeps your IT team up to date with the latest industry trends and technologies.
   - **Instructions:**
     1. Assess the current learning needs of your IT team by identifying skill gaps and future technology trends.
     2. Develop a continuous learning program that includes access to online courses, certifications, workshops, and mentorship opportunities.
     3. Implement the program and establish a feedback mechanism to continuously improve the learning experience.

III. Employee Retention Analysis:
   - **Objective:** Analyze factors that influence employee retention and develop strategies to improve it.
   - **Instructions:**
     1. Conduct a survey or hold focus group discussions with employees to understand their satisfaction levels and retention factors.
     2. Analyze the survey results to identify common themes, such as career development opportunities, work-life balance, and recognition.
     3. Based on your analysis, develop a retention strategy that addresses key concerns and enhances the overall employee experience.

Mastering IT Leadership and Management, Strategies for Success in the Digital Age

IV. Diversity and Inclusion Initiative:
  - **Objective:** Promote diversity and inclusion within your IT team.
  - **Instructions:**
    1. Evaluate your current recruitment, development, and retention practices for inclusivity.
    2. Develop initiatives to improve diversity within the team, such as partnering with organizations focused on underrepresented groups, providing unconscious bias training, and creating employee resource groups.
    3. Implement these initiatives and measure their impact on team diversity and performance.

V. Leadership Development Plan:
  - **Objective:** Prepare a leadership development plan to cultivate the next generation of IT leaders within your organization.
  - **Instructions:**
    1. Identify high-potential employees within your IT team who demonstrate leadership qualities.
    2. Develop a leadership development program that includes mentorship, leadership training, and opportunities for hands-on leadership experience.
    3. Monitor the progress of participants and adjust the program as needed to ensure their growth into leadership roles.

These quizzes and exercises are designed to help readers of Chapter 15 better understand and apply the principles of talent management and development, focusing on practical application and strategic alignment.

Mastering IT Leadership and Management, Strategies for Success in the Digital Age

Conclusion of Part 5: Leading in a Hybrid and Remote Work Environment

The shift to hybrid and remote work environments has transformed the way organizations operate, challenging IT leaders to rethink traditional leadership and management practices. Throughout Part 5 of this book, we have explored the critical aspects of leading IT teams in this new work paradigm, focusing on adapting leadership styles, leveraging technology, maintaining team cohesion, and managing talent in a dispersed workforce.

In Chapter 14, we examined how IT leaders must adapt their leadership approaches to effectively manage teams that are no longer centralized in a single location. The flexibility to lead both in-person and remote teams, understanding the unique challenges of each, and fostering a culture of trust and accountability are key to ensuring that all team members remain engaged and productive, regardless of where they work.

Chapter 15 delved into the vital role of talent management and development in a hybrid and remote work environment. Attracting and retaining top IT talent, investing in continuous professional development, and fostering a diverse and inclusive work culture are all essential for building resilient and high-performing teams. IT leaders must be proactive in creating opportunities for growth, collaboration, and innovation, ensuring their teams are well-equipped to navigate the complexities of the digital age.

Maintaining team cohesion and a strong organizational culture in a dispersed workforce is perhaps one of the most significant challenges IT leaders face. As teams become more geographically spread out, IT leaders must find new ways to build connections, foster collaboration, and reinforce shared goals and values. The strategies discussed in this part of the book emphasize the importance of communication, regular check-ins, and the use of technology to bridge the gap between remote and in-person team members.

As we conclude Part 5, it is evident that leading in a hybrid and remote work environment requires a new set of skills and strategies. IT leaders who can successfully adapt to these changes will be well-positioned to guide their organizations through the ongoing evolution of the workplace. The insights and approaches discussed in this section provide a solid foundation for navigating the challenges of hybrid and remote work, ensuring that teams remain cohesive, engaged, and aligned with the organization's goals.

As we move into the final part of the book, focusing on future trends in IT leadership, the lessons learned from leading in a hybrid and remote environment will continue to be relevant. The ability to lead effectively in this new work paradigm will be a key determinant of success as organizations continue to evolve in response to changing technological, economic, and social dynamics. With the right leadership approach, IT leaders can ensure that their teams and organizations are not only resilient but also poised to thrive in the future of work.

Mastering IT Leadership and Management, Strategies for Success in the Digital Age

Part 6: Future Trends in IT Leadership

"THE FUTURE OF IT LEADERSHIP BELONGS TO THOSE WHO NOT ONLY EMBRACE EMERGING TECHNOLOGIES BUT ALSO FORESEE THE ETHICAL, STRATEGIC, AND HUMAN IMPACTS OF INNOVATION. TRUE LEADERS WILL NAVIGATE THE DIGITAL FRONTIER WITH VISION, AGILITY, AND A DEEP COMMITMENT TO GUIDING THEIR ORGANIZATIONS THROUGH UNCHARTED TERRITORIES."

—The Author

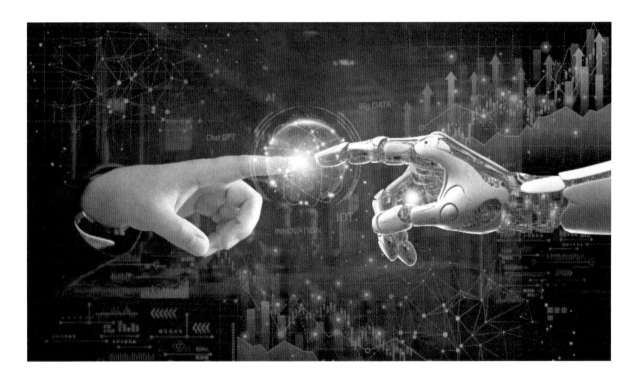

Mastering IT Leadership and Management, Strategies for Success in the Digital Age

Chapter 16: The Future of IT Leadership

"THE FUTURE BELONGS TO THOSE WHO PREPARE FOR IT TODAY."

—**Malcolm X**

The role of IT leadership is undergoing a profound transformation as organizations continue to navigate the complexities of the digital age. As technology becomes increasingly integral to every aspect of business, IT leaders are no longer just custodians of technology; they are strategic partners, innovators, and drivers of change. This chapter explores the future of IT leadership, examining the trends, challenges, and opportunities that will shape the role in the coming years. It also provides insights into how IT leaders can prepare themselves and their organizations for the future.

Evolving Role of IT Leaders

The future of IT leadership will be defined by a broader, more strategic role within the organization. IT leaders will need to move beyond managing technology and focus on driving business outcomes, fostering innovation, and leading digital transformation.

- **From Technology Management to Business Leadership:** IT leaders are increasingly expected to contribute to business strategy and drive organizational success. This shift requires IT leaders to develop a deep understanding of the business, its goals, and its challenges. They must translate technological capabilities into business value and align IT initiatives with the organization's strategic objectives. In the future, IT leaders will be seen as business leaders who leverage technology to create competitive advantages and drive growth.

- **Focus on Innovation and Digital Transformation:** As organizations continue to embrace digital transformation, IT leaders will play a central role in fostering innovation. This involves identifying emerging technologies, experimenting with new ideas, and scaling successful innovations across the organization. IT leaders will need to create a culture that encourages experimentation, rewards creativity, and embraces change. Their ability to drive innovation will be a key factor in the organization's success in the digital age.

- **Leading Cross-Functional Teams:** The future of IT leadership will involve greater collaboration across departments and functions. IT leaders will need to work closely with other business leaders, such as marketing, finance, and operations, to deliver integrated solutions that meet the organization's needs. This cross-functional approach requires IT leaders to build strong relationships, communicate effectively, and align diverse teams around common goals.

Mastering IT Leadership and Management, Strategies for Success in the Digital Age

Navigating Emerging Technologies

The rapid pace of technological change presents both opportunities and challenges for IT leaders. Staying ahead of emerging technologies and understanding their implications for the organization will be critical for future success.

- **Adopting Artificial Intelligence and Machine Learning:** Artificial intelligence (AI) and machine learning (ML) are transforming industries and creating new opportunities for innovation. IT leaders will need to understand the potential of these technologies, identify use cases, and integrate AI and ML into their organization's processes and systems. This requires a focus on data management, algorithm development, and ethical considerations to ensure AI and ML are used responsibly and effectively.

- **Leveraging Blockchain and Decentralized Technologies:** Blockchain and other decentralized technologies are poised to disrupt traditional business models, particularly in areas such as finance, supply chain, and data management. IT leaders must explore the potential of these technologies, assess their impact on the organization, and develop strategies for their adoption. This may involve partnering with external experts, investing in research and development, and experimenting with pilot projects.

- **Embracing the Internet of Things (IoT):** The Internet of Things (IoT) is expanding the reach of digital technologies into the physical world, creating new opportunities for data collection, automation, and customer engagement. IT leaders will need to develop strategies for managing IoT devices, securing data, and integrating IoT with existing systems. As IoT continues to grow, IT leaders will play a key role in ensuring the organization can harness its potential while mitigating risks.

- **Preparing for Quantum Computing:** Quantum computing is still in its early stages, but it has the potential to revolutionize computing power and solve complex problems that are currently beyond the reach of classical computers. IT leaders should monitor developments in quantum computing, explore potential applications, and prepare for its eventual adoption. This may involve building partnerships with academic institutions, investing in quantum research, and developing the skills needed to leverage quantum technology in the future.

Mastering IT Leadership and Management, Strategies for Success in the Digital Age

Addressing Ethical and Social Implications

As technology continues to evolve, IT leaders will face increasing responsibility for addressing the ethical and social implications of their decisions. The future of IT leadership will require a strong focus on ethics, privacy, and the impact of technology on society.

- **Ensuring Ethical AI and Automation:** As AI and automation become more prevalent, IT leaders must ensure these technologies are used ethically and responsibly. This includes addressing issues such as bias in AI algorithms, the impact of automation on employment, and the transparency of decision-making processes. IT leaders should develop ethical guidelines for the use of AI and automation, promote fairness and accountability, and engage with stakeholders to address concerns.

- **Protecting Data Privacy and Security:** Data privacy and security will continue to be top priorities for IT leaders in the future. As data collection and processing become more pervasive, IT leaders must ensure their organizations comply with data protection regulations and implement robust security measures. This involves developing privacy-first strategies, investing in cybersecurity, and educating employees about the importance of data protection.

- **Navigating the Digital Divide:** The digital divide—disparities in access to technology and digital skills—remains a significant challenge. IT leaders must consider the impact of their decisions on different groups within the organization and society at large. This includes promoting digital inclusion, providing access to training and resources, and advocating for policies that bridge the digital divide. By addressing these issues, IT leaders can help create a more equitable and inclusive digital future.

- **Fostering Digital Responsibility:** IT leaders will need to champion digital responsibility, ensuring technology is used in ways that benefit society and the environment. This includes promoting sustainable IT practices, reducing the organization's carbon footprint, and supporting initiatives that use technology for social good. By leading with purpose, IT leaders can build trust and create long-term value for their organizations and communities.

Mastering IT Leadership and Management, Strategies for Success in the Digital Age

Developing Future IT Leaders

The future of IT leadership also involves preparing the next generation of leaders. IT leaders must focus on identifying and developing talent, creating opportunities for growth, and fostering a culture of leadership development.

- **Identifying and Nurturing Talent:** IT leaders should actively identify high-potential employees who possess the skills and mindset needed for leadership roles. This involves recognizing individuals who demonstrate strategic thinking, adaptability, and a commitment to continuous learning. Once identified, these employees should be given opportunities to lead projects, take on new responsibilities, and develop their leadership skills.

- **Providing Leadership Development Programs:** Leadership development programs are essential for preparing future IT leaders. These programs should focus on both technical and soft skills, including communication, emotional intelligence, and decision-making. IT leaders should also provide access to mentorship, coaching, and networking opportunities that allow emerging leaders to learn from experienced professionals.

- **Promoting a Culture of Learning:** A culture of learning is critical for developing future leaders. IT leaders should encourage continuous learning and provide resources for employees to expand their knowledge and skills. This might include offering access to online courses, certifications, and workshops, as well as creating opportunities for cross-functional collaboration and knowledge sharing.

- **Succession Planning:** Succession planning is essential for ensuring continuity in IT leadership. IT leaders should develop succession plans that identify potential successors for key leadership roles and outline the steps needed to prepare them for these positions. By proactively planning for leadership transitions, IT leaders can ensure their organizations are well-prepared for the future.

Mastering IT Leadership and Management, Strategies for Success in the Digital Age

Building Resilience and Agility

The future of IT leadership will be defined by the ability to build resilience and agility within the organization. As technology and business environments continue to change rapidly, IT leaders must ensure their organizations can adapt and thrive in the face of uncertainty.

- **Developing a Resilient IT Infrastructure:** A resilient IT infrastructure is essential for maintaining business continuity and protecting against disruptions. IT leaders should focus on building redundancy into systems, implementing robust disaster recovery plans, and continuously monitoring for vulnerabilities. By creating a resilient infrastructure, IT leaders can minimize the impact of outages, cyberattacks, and other disruptions.

- **Fostering Organizational Agility:** Agility is the ability to respond quickly and effectively to changing circumstances. IT leaders should promote agile practices within their teams, such as iterative development, rapid prototyping, and cross-functional collaboration. This approach allows organizations to pivot quickly in response to new opportunities or challenges, ensuring they remain competitive and innovative.

- **Preparing for Future Disruptions:** IT leaders must be proactive in anticipating and preparing for future disruptions. This involves staying informed about emerging trends, conducting scenario planning, and developing contingency plans. By thinking ahead and planning for the unexpected, IT leaders can ensure their organizations are ready to respond to whatever the future may hold.

- **Leading Through Change:** The ability to lead through change is a critical skill for future IT leaders. This involves communicating a clear vision, managing resistance, and supporting employees through transitions. IT leaders must be skilled at guiding their organizations through periods of uncertainty, ensuring they remain focused, motivated, and aligned with the organization's goals.

Mastering IT Leadership and Management, Strategies for Success in the Digital Age

Industry Case Study: The Future of IT Leadership at IBM

Situation:
In recent years, IBM has undergone a significant transformation, shifting its focus from traditional hardware and software solutions to becoming a leader in cloud computing, artificial intelligence (AI), and quantum computing. This transformation was driven by the recognition that the future of technology lies in these emerging fields and that IBM needed to position itself as a leader in these areas to remain competitive. The challenge for IBM's IT leadership was to navigate this transition while maintaining the company's core strengths and continuing to deliver value to its customers.

Task:
IBM's IT leadership was tasked with leading the company through this transformation by developing a strategic vision for the future, investing in emerging technologies, and fostering a culture of innovation. This involved not only adopting new technologies but also rethinking IBM's business model, organizational structure, and approach to talent management. The goal was to ensure that IBM could continue to thrive in a rapidly changing technological landscape.

Action:
To achieve these goals, IBM's leadership took several key actions:

1. **Strategic Focus on Emerging Technologies:**
   IBM made a strategic decision to focus on AI, cloud computing, and quantum computing as the pillars of its future growth. The company invested heavily in research and development in these areas, acquiring leading companies and talent to bolster its capabilities. For example, IBM's acquisition of Red Hat in 2019 was a significant move to strengthen its position in the cloud computing market.

2. **Cultural Transformation:**
   Recognizing that technology alone would not drive success, IBM's leadership embarked on a cultural transformation to foster innovation and agility within the organization. This included encouraging cross-functional collaboration, embracing Agile methodologies, and promoting a mindset of continuous learning and experimentation.

3. **Leadership Development and Succession Planning:**
   IBM prioritized the development of future IT leaders by implementing robust leadership development programs. These programs focused on equipping leaders with the skills needed to navigate the complexities of emerging technologies and lead in a fast-paced, innovative environment. IBM also focused on succession planning to ensure a smooth transition of leadership as the company evolved.

4. **Ethical Leadership and Social Responsibility:**
   As a leader in AI and other advanced technologies, IBM has been at the forefront of addressing the ethical implications of technology. The company developed clear

Mastering IT Leadership and Management, Strategies for Success in the Digital Age

guidelines for the ethical use of AI and has been an advocate for transparency, fairness, and accountability in AI development. This focus on ethical leadership has helped IBM build trust with stakeholders and position itself as a responsible leader in the tech industry.

Result:
As a result of these actions, IBM successfully repositioned itself as a leader in AI, cloud computing, and quantum computing. The company's focus on innovation and ethical leadership has allowed it to maintain a competitive edge in the technology industry while also addressing the evolving needs of its customers. IBM's cultural transformation has fostered a more agile and innovative workforce, enabling the company to adapt quickly to new challenges and opportunities.

The strategic investments in leadership development have ensured that IBM is well-prepared for the future, with a strong pipeline of leaders ready to guide the company through the next phase of its evolution.

This case study illustrates how IBM's IT leadership successfully navigated the challenges of a rapidly changing technological landscape by focusing on emerging technologies, fostering a culture of innovation, and prioritizing ethical leadership. These strategies have positioned IBM to continue leading in the digital age.

Mastering IT Leadership and Management, Strategies for Success in the Digital Age

Best Practices

1. **Embrace Emerging Technologies and Innovation:** The future of IT leadership is closely tied to the ability to understand and leverage emerging technologies such as artificial intelligence, blockchain, quantum computing, and advanced data analytics. IT leaders should stay informed about technological advancements and proactively explore how these innovations can create value for their organizations. This requires a commitment to continuous learning and a willingness to experiment with new tools and methodologies.

2. **Develop Strategic Vision and Forward-Thinking Leadership:** IT leaders of the future must possess a strategic vision that goes beyond immediate technical challenges. They should be able to anticipate trends, forecast technological impacts, and align IT initiatives with the organization's long-term goals. Being a forward-thinking leader involves not just responding to changes but driving them, ensuring that the organization remains competitive and innovative.

3. **Cultivate Agile and Adaptive Leadership:** The rapidly changing technological landscape demands leaders who are agile and adaptive. IT leaders should cultivate flexibility in their leadership style, enabling them to respond quickly to new opportunities and challenges. This involves fostering an organizational culture that embraces change, encourages innovation, and values quick iterations and learning from failure.

4. **Focus on Ethical Leadership and Responsible Innovation:** As technology becomes increasingly integrated into all aspects of business and society, ethical considerations are paramount. Future IT leaders must prioritize ethical leadership, ensuring that decisions regarding technology usage and innovation are guided by a strong moral compass. This includes addressing issues such as data privacy, AI ethics, and the social impact of technology on communities.

5. **Build Cross-Functional Collaboration and Partnerships:** IT leadership will increasingly involve collaboration across various functions within the organization, as well as with external partners. IT leaders should work closely with business units, HR, marketing, finance, and other departments to ensure that technology initiatives are integrated and aligned with organizational objectives. Building strong partnerships with external vendors, industry peers, and academic institutions will also be crucial for staying ahead of technological trends.

6. **Prioritize Talent Development and Leadership Succession:** Preparing the next generation of IT leaders is critical for long-term success. IT leaders should focus on identifying and nurturing talent within their teams, providing opportunities for professional growth, and creating a clear path for leadership succession. This includes mentoring emerging leaders, offering leadership development programs, and fostering a culture of continuous learning.

Mastering IT Leadership and Management, Strategies for Success in the Digital Age

7. **Leverage Data-Driven Decision Making:** Data will continue to play a central role in IT leadership. Future IT leaders should excel in using data analytics to inform decision-making processes, optimize operations, and drive innovation. Developing strong data literacy within the IT function and across the organization is essential for leveraging data effectively and making informed, strategic decisions.

8. **Champion Sustainability and Social Responsibility:** Sustainability and social responsibility will become increasingly important in IT leadership. IT leaders should prioritize environmentally sustainable practices, such as reducing the carbon footprint of data centers and promoting energy-efficient technologies. Additionally, they should advocate for the use of technology to address social challenges, such as bridging the digital divide and enhancing access to education and healthcare.

Mastering IT Leadership and Management, Strategies for Success in the Digital Age

Lessons Learned

1. **Proactive Adoption of Emerging Technologies Yields Competitive Advantage:** Organizations that proactively adopt and experiment with emerging technologies are better positioned to gain a competitive edge. IT leaders who are early adopters of innovative solutions can drive significant business value and differentiate their organizations in the market. Staying ahead of the technology curve is essential for long-term success.

2. **Strategic Vision Aligns IT with Business Success:** IT leaders who possess a strong strategic vision are better able to align technology initiatives with business objectives, ensuring that IT contributes to the overall success of the organization. This forward-thinking approach enables leaders to anticipate changes and position the organization to capitalize on future opportunities.

3. **Agility Enables Resilience in a Changing Landscape:** The ability to adapt quickly to changing circumstances is a key trait of successful IT leaders. Organizations that foster an agile mindset within their IT teams can navigate disruptions more effectively and maintain resilience in the face of uncertainty. This adaptability is critical for thriving in a dynamic technological environment.

4. **Ethical Leadership Builds Trust and Long-Term Success:** As technology increasingly influences every aspect of life, ethical leadership becomes more important than ever. IT leaders who prioritize ethics in their decision-making processes build trust with stakeholders and ensure their organizations use technology responsibly. Ethical leadership is essential for maintaining a positive reputation and achieving long-term success.

5. **Cross-Functional Collaboration Enhances Innovation:** Collaboration across functions within the organization drives more comprehensive and innovative solutions. IT leaders who actively engage with other departments and external partners create synergies that lead to better outcomes. This collaborative approach ensures that technology initiatives are well-integrated and aligned with broader business goals.

6. **Talent Development is Key to Future Leadership:** Nurturing the next generation of IT leaders is essential for sustaining organizational success. Organizations that invest in leadership development and succession planning are better equipped to maintain continuity and drive future growth. IT leaders who mentor and develop their teams contribute to a culture of leadership excellence.

7. **Data-Driven Decisions Lead to Better Outcomes:** Leveraging data to inform decision-making processes results in more accurate and effective outcomes. IT leaders who excel in data analytics can optimize operations, identify new opportunities, and drive innovation. A data-driven approach is critical for making informed decisions that align with the organization's strategic goals.

Mastering IT Leadership and Management, Strategies for Success in the Digital Age

8. **Sustainability and Social Responsibility Enhance Brand Value:** Organizations that prioritize sustainability and social responsibility not only contribute to a better world but also enhance their brand value. IT leaders who advocate for environmentally sustainable practices and use technology to address social challenges position their organizations as responsible and forward-thinking. This focus on sustainability and responsibility is increasingly important for attracting customers, employees, and investors.

By embracing these best practices and learning from successful IT initiatives, future IT leaders can effectively navigate the complexities of the digital age, drive innovation, and ensure their organizations thrive in an ever-evolving technological landscape.

Mastering IT Leadership and Management, Strategies for Success in the Digital Age

Conclusion

As technology continues to evolve at an unprecedented pace, the role of IT leadership is undergoing a profound transformation. In Chapter 16, we explored the emerging trends reshaping the landscape of IT leadership, the impact of AI and automation, and the preparations necessary to develop the next generation of IT leaders. Understanding these trends is crucial for IT leaders who aim to remain relevant and effective in the face of continuous change.

The emergence of new technologies, such as artificial intelligence, machine learning, and blockchain, is not only transforming how businesses operate but also redefining the skills and competencies required of IT leaders. The future of IT leadership will increasingly demand a blend of technical expertise, strategic vision, and the ability to navigate complex ethical and regulatory landscapes. IT leaders must be agile, forward-thinking, and ready to embrace innovation while managing the risks and challenges that come with it.

AI and automation are particularly influential forces shaping the future of IT leadership. These technologies promise to revolutionize industries by automating routine tasks, enhancing decision-making, and enabling new business models. However, they also raise important questions about job displacement, data privacy, and the ethical use of technology. IT leaders must balance the potential benefits of AI and automation with the responsibility to manage these technologies in a way that is transparent, fair, and aligned with organizational values.

Preparing for the next generation of IT leaders is another critical focus. As current IT leaders transition out of their roles, it is essential to cultivate a pipeline of future leaders equipped to handle the challenges of a rapidly changing technological environment. This involves not only providing the necessary training and development opportunities but also fostering a culture of continuous learning and adaptability. Mentorship, leadership development programs, and succession planning will be key strategies for ensuring a smooth transition to the next era of IT leadership.

As we conclude Chapter 16, it is clear that the future of IT leadership will be shaped by both opportunities and challenges. The ability to anticipate and adapt to emerging trends, leverage new technologies responsibly, and prepare the next generation of leaders will be crucial for navigating the future successfully. IT leaders who embrace these changes with a proactive and strategic mindset will position their organizations for sustained success in the digital age.

The insights and strategies discussed in this chapter provide a roadmap for understanding the future of IT leadership. As we continue to explore the importance of continuous learning and adaptation in the final chapter of this book, the principles outlined here will serve as a foundation for building resilient, forward-looking IT leadership ready to meet the challenges of tomorrow.

Mastering IT Leadership and Management, Strategies for Success in the Digital Age

Quizzes

I. Multiple-Choice Questions

1. What is a key responsibility of future IT leaders?
- A. Managing day-to-day technology operations
- B. Focusing solely on cost-cutting measures
- C. Driving business outcomes and fostering innovation
- D. Avoiding collaboration with other business departments

2. How should IT leaders approach the integration of Artificial Intelligence (AI) and Machine Learning (ML) into their organizations?
- A. By only using AI in non-critical business functions
- B. By ensuring strong data management, algorithm development, and ethical considerations
- C. By outsourcing all AI and ML efforts
- D. By focusing only on algorithm development without considering data quality

3. Which of the following is a recommended strategy for fostering innovation in IT leadership?
- A. Encouraging only proven solutions and avoiding risks
- B. Experimenting with new ideas and scaling successful innovations
- C. Avoiding collaboration with other business units
- D. Restricting the team to traditional methods and processes

4. Why is ethical leadership important in the context of AI and automation?
- A. It helps to increase profitability by cutting down on human oversight
- B. It ensures fairness, transparency, and accountability in the use of technology
- C. It focuses on maximizing automation without considering human job displacement
- D. It is only important for large enterprises

5. What is one of the challenges IT leaders must address when adopting blockchain technology?
- A. Focusing solely on external consultants
- B. Partnering with experts and experimenting with pilot projects
- C. Replacing all traditional systems immediately with blockchain
- D. Reducing innovation efforts in other technological fields

6. What should be the focus of leadership development programs for future IT leaders?
- A. Only technical skills
- B. Soft skills, such as communication and emotional intelligence
- C. Technical and soft skills, along with mentorship opportunities
- D. Restricting leadership roles to external hires

Mastering IT Leadership and Management, Strategies for Success in the Digital Age

7. How can IT leaders contribute to organizational resilience in the face of technological changes?
   A. By sticking to traditional methods and resisting new technologies
   B. By developing a resilient IT infrastructure and promoting organizational agility
   C. By focusing only on current technologies
   D. By avoiding collaboration with non-IT departments

II. True/False Questions

1. Future IT leaders should focus solely on managing technology infrastructure and not on aligning IT with business strategies. (True/False)
2. **Artificial Intelligence (AI) and Machine Learning (ML) offer organizations opportunities for innovation, but they also require ethical considerations regarding bias and transparency. (True/False)**
3. IT leaders should focus exclusively on their own department and avoid collaboration with other business units to drive technological innovation. (True/False)
4. **To ensure long-term success, IT leaders must foster a culture of continuous learning and development within their teams. (True/False)**
5. The rise of emerging technologies like blockchain and quantum computing means that IT leaders must continuously explore their potential business applications. (True/False)
6. **Ethical leadership in IT is only necessary when handling confidential customer data. (True/False)**
7. IT leaders need to be adaptable and agile in their approach to lead teams through periods of rapid technological change. (True/False)
8. **IT leaders should focus only on technical skills when developing the next generation of IT leaders. (True/False)**
9. Developing a resilient IT infrastructure that can handle disruptions is a key responsibility of future IT leaders. (True/False)
10. **A strong focus on sustainability and responsibility is expected to become a growing priority for IT leaders in the future. (True/False)**

These questions cover a variety of topics from Chapter 16 and can be used to test understanding of the key concepts discussed.

Mastering IT Leadership and Management, Strategies for Success in the Digital Age

Exercises

I. Reflective Essay:
   - Write an essay (500-700 words) on how the evolving role of IT leadership will influence your approach to leading your current team. Consider how you would adapt to the increased demand for business strategy involvement and the integration of emerging technologies.

II. Case Study Analysis:
   - Review the industry case study of IBM's approach to future IT leadership as discussed in the chapter. Identify the key strategies IBM implemented to stay ahead in the rapidly changing technology landscape. Then, describe how you could apply similar strategies within your organization.

III. Group Discussion:
   - Organize a group discussion where participants explore the ethical implications of AI and automation in IT leadership. Discuss potential challenges, such as job displacement and data privacy, and how IT leaders can address these concerns.

IV. Scenario-Based Role Play:
   - Role-play a scenario where you are the IT leader of a company facing rapid technological changes. Present a plan to your executive team outlining how you will navigate emerging technologies, manage ethical concerns, and prepare the next generation of IT leaders.

V. Strategic Planning Exercise:
   - Develop a strategic plan that outlines how your organization can leverage emerging technologies such as AI, blockchain, and machine learning. Include potential challenges, opportunities, and ethical considerations that need to be addressed in the plan.

These quizzes and exercises are designed to help readers apply the concepts of future IT leadership in practical scenarios, preparing them to lead effectively in an evolving digital landscape.

Mastering IT Leadership and Management, Strategies for Success in the Digital Age

Chapter 17: Continuous Learning and Adaptation

"IN A WORLD THAT IS CONSTANTLY CHANGING, THE GREATEST SKILL IS THE ABILITY TO LEARN."
—Unknown

In an era of rapid technological advancements and constant change, continuous learning and adaptation have become essential for both individuals and organizations. For IT leaders, fostering a culture of continuous learning and ensuring that teams remain adaptable are critical components of long-term success. This chapter explores the importance of continuous learning and adaptation, strategies for cultivating these qualities within teams, and how IT leaders can position their organizations to thrive in an ever-evolving landscape.

The Importance of Continuous Learning

Continuous learning is the process of constantly acquiring new knowledge and skills to stay relevant and competitive in a dynamic environment. In the context of IT and digital transformation, continuous learning is vital for keeping pace with technological innovations and ensuring that teams have the expertise needed to drive business success.

- **Keeping Up with Technological Advancements:**
  The IT industry is characterized by rapid innovation, with new technologies, tools, and methodologies emerging regularly. Continuous learning allows IT professionals to stay current with these advancements, ensuring they can leverage the latest technologies to improve efficiency, enhance security, and deliver innovative solutions. IT leaders must prioritize continuous learning to ensure their teams are equipped with the skills needed to capitalize on new opportunities.

- **Adapting to Changing Business Needs:**
  As business environments evolve, so do the demands placed on IT teams. Continuous learning enables IT professionals to adapt to changing business needs by acquiring the skills required to support new initiatives, address emerging challenges, and contribute to the organization's strategic goals. IT leaders must encourage continuous learning to ensure their teams remain agile and responsive to business changes.

- **Driving Innovation and Growth:**
  Innovation is often driven by the ability to see new possibilities and apply fresh knowledge to solve problems. Continuous learning fosters a mindset of curiosity and creativity, empowering IT professionals to explore new ideas, experiment with new approaches, and drive innovation within the organization. By promoting continuous learning, IT leaders can create an environment where innovation thrives.

Mastering IT Leadership and Management, Strategies for Success in the Digital Age

Fostering a Culture of Continuous Learning

Building a culture of continuous learning requires deliberate effort from IT leaders. This culture must be embedded in the organization's values, practices, and behaviors, encouraging employees to take ownership of their learning and development.

- **Promoting a Growth Mindset:**
  A growth mindset is the belief that abilities and intelligence can be developed through dedication and hard work. IT leaders should promote this mindset within their teams by encouraging employees to embrace challenges, learn from failures, and view learning as a lifelong journey. This shift can help employees overcome the fear of failure and become more open to learning new skills and taking on new challenges.

- **Providing Access to Learning Resources:**
  To support continuous learning, IT leaders must provide employees with access to a wide range of learning resources, including online courses, webinars, workshops, certifications, and conferences. Additionally, IT leaders should encourage the use of internal knowledge-sharing platforms, such as wikis or forums, where employees can share insights, best practices, and lessons learned.

- **Encouraging Self-Directed Learning:**
  While formal training programs are valuable, self-directed learning is equally important in fostering continuous growth. IT leaders should empower employees to take charge of their own learning by setting personal development goals, exploring topics of interest, and seeking learning opportunities that align with their career aspirations. This approach encourages autonomy and accountability in the learning process.

- **Recognizing and Rewarding Learning Achievements:**
  Recognizing and rewarding employees for their learning achievements is a powerful way to reinforce the value of continuous learning. IT leaders should celebrate milestones such as completing certifications, acquiring new skills, or applying new knowledge to solve business problems. Recognition can take many forms, from formal awards and promotions to informal praise and acknowledgment.

Mastering IT Leadership and Management, Strategies for Success in the Digital Age

Strategies for Organizational Adaptation

Adaptation is the ability of an organization to adjust to changes in its environment, whether driven by technological advancements, market shifts, or internal challenges. For IT leaders, fostering adaptability within their teams is crucial for navigating uncertainty and driving long-term success.

- **Embracing Agile Methodologies:**
  Agile methodologies, such as Scrum or Kanban, are designed to promote flexibility, collaboration, and rapid iteration. IT leaders should adopt agile practices within their teams to enhance their ability to respond to changes quickly and efficiently. This involves breaking down projects into smaller, manageable tasks, encouraging cross-functional collaboration, and continuously seeking feedback to improve processes.

- **Encouraging Experimentation and Innovation:**
  Adaptability is closely linked to the willingness to experiment and innovate. IT leaders should create an environment where teams are encouraged to test new ideas, take calculated risks, and learn from both successes and failures. By fostering a culture of experimentation, IT leaders can drive continuous improvement and ensure their teams are always seeking better ways to achieve their goals.

- **Building Resilience in Teams:**
  Resilience is the ability to bounce back from setbacks and continue moving forward. IT leaders should focus on building resilience within their teams by promoting a positive work environment, providing support during challenging times, and encouraging a focus on solutions rather than problems. Resilient teams are better equipped to adapt to change and maintain high performance, even in the face of adversity.

- **Leveraging Data-Driven Decision-Making:**
  In a rapidly changing environment, making informed decisions is critical for successful adaptation. IT leaders should leverage data and analytics to guide decision-making, identify trends, and anticipate future challenges. By using data to inform strategies and actions, IT leaders can enhance their organization's ability to adapt to changes and seize new opportunities.

Mastering IT Leadership and Management, Strategies for Success in the Digital Age

Preparing for Future Challenges

The future is unpredictable, but IT leaders can position their organizations for success by preparing for potential challenges and uncertainties. This involves proactive planning, continuous monitoring, and a commitment to ongoing learning and adaptation.

- **Anticipating Technological Disruptions:**
  Technological disruptions can significantly impact business operations and competitive positioning. IT leaders must stay informed about emerging technologies and assess their potential impact on the organization. This includes conducting regular technology assessments, engaging with industry experts, and exploring pilot projects to test new technologies. By anticipating disruptions, IT leaders can develop strategies to mitigate risks and capitalize on new opportunities.

- **Developing Scenario Planning:**
  Scenario planning is a strategic tool that helps organizations prepare for different future scenarios. IT leaders should use scenario planning to explore various possibilities, such as economic downturns, regulatory changes, or shifts in customer behavior. This process allows IT leaders to identify potential risks and opportunities, develop contingency plans, and ensure that the organization is ready to adapt to different circumstances.

- **Investing in Workforce Development:**
  The skills required in the IT industry are constantly evolving. IT leaders must invest in workforce development to ensure their teams have the capabilities needed to meet future challenges. This includes providing ongoing training, encouraging cross-skilling, and fostering a culture of continuous learning. By developing a skilled and adaptable workforce, IT leaders can ensure their organization remains competitive in a rapidly changing landscape.

- **Cultivating Leadership Agility:**
  Leadership agility is the ability to lead effectively in a rapidly changing environment. IT leaders must cultivate their own agility by staying open to new ideas, seeking feedback, and continuously improving their leadership skills. This involves embracing change, making quick and informed decisions, and empowering teams to take initiative. Agile leaders are better equipped to navigate uncertainty and guide their organizations through periods of transformation.

Mastering IT Leadership and Management, Strategies for Success in the Digital Age

Embracing Lifelong Learning

Lifelong learning is the ongoing, voluntary, and self-motivated pursuit of knowledge for personal and professional development. For IT leaders and their teams, embracing lifelong learning is essential for staying relevant and achieving long-term success.

- **Setting an Example as a Lifelong Learner:**
  IT leaders must lead by example by actively engaging in lifelong learning themselves. This involves staying current with industry trends, attending conferences, pursuing certifications, and continuously expanding their knowledge base. By demonstrating a commitment to lifelong learning, IT leaders can inspire their teams to do the same.

- **Creating Learning Pathways:**
  IT leaders should create clear learning pathways that guide employees in their professional development. These pathways should outline the skills and knowledge required for different roles, provide access to relevant learning resources, and offer opportunities for career advancement. By providing a structured approach to learning, IT leaders can help employees achieve their goals and contribute to the organization's success.

- **Encouraging Knowledge Sharing:**
  Knowledge sharing is a key component of lifelong learning. IT leaders should encourage employees to share their expertise and insights with others through mentoring, workshops, and collaborative projects. This not only enhances the collective knowledge of the team but also fosters a culture of continuous learning and collaboration.

- **Supporting Learning Beyond the Workplace:**
  Lifelong learning extends beyond the workplace. IT leaders should support employees in pursuing learning opportunities outside of work, such as enrolling in online courses, attending industry events, or participating in professional associations. By encouraging learning in all areas of life, IT leaders can help employees develop a well-rounded skill set that benefits both their personal and professional growth.

Mastering IT Leadership and Management, Strategies for Success in the Digital Age

Industry Case Study: Continuous Learning and Adaptation at IBM

Situation:
In the rapidly evolving tech industry, IBM, a global leader in technology and consulting, recognized the need for continuous learning and adaptation to maintain its competitive edge. The company faced the challenge of keeping its workforce up-to-date with emerging technologies such as cloud computing, artificial intelligence, and blockchain. As these technologies began to reshape the industry, IBM needed to ensure that its employees had the skills necessary to lead in these new areas.

Task:
IBM's leadership was tasked with creating a robust strategy for continuous learning and adaptation that would enable its workforce to stay ahead of technological trends. This strategy needed to support skill development across the organization, encourage innovation, and ensure that IBM remained a leader in the rapidly changing tech landscape.

Action:
To address these challenges, IBM implemented several key initiatives:

1. **Creating a Culture of Continuous Learning:**
   IBM established a culture of continuous learning by encouraging employees to take ownership of their professional development. The company provided access to a wide range of learning resources, including online courses, certifications, and workshops. IBM's "Think Academy" was a key initiative, offering employees a platform to access educational content on emerging technologies and business strategies. Additionally, IBM promoted a growth mindset across the organization, encouraging employees to embrace challenges and view learning as an ongoing journey.

2. **Leveraging Technology for Learning:**
   IBM utilized advanced technologies to enhance its learning and development programs. The company introduced AI-driven learning platforms that personalized learning experiences for employees based on their roles, skills, and career goals. These platforms recommended relevant courses, learning paths, and opportunities for skill development, making it easier for employees to stay current with industry trends.

3. **Fostering Innovation through Experimentation:**
   IBM encouraged a culture of experimentation by allowing employees to apply their new skills in real-world projects. The company implemented initiatives such as hackathons, innovation labs, and cross-functional collaboration projects, which provided employees with opportunities to experiment with new ideas and technologies. This approach not only facilitated learning but also drove innovation within the organization.

4. **Supporting Leadership Development:**
   Recognizing the importance of leadership in driving continuous learning, IBM

Mastering IT Leadership and Management, Strategies for Success in the Digital Age

invested in leadership development programs. These programs focused on developing future leaders who could guide their teams through the complexities of technological change. IBM provided mentoring, coaching, and leadership training to prepare high-potential employees for leadership roles, ensuring a strong pipeline of leaders ready to navigate future challenges.

Result:
As a result of these initiatives, IBM successfully built a culture of continuous learning and adaptation. The company's workforce became more agile and equipped to handle the demands of the rapidly changing tech landscape. IBM's focus on innovation and experimentation led to the development of new products and services that kept the company at the forefront of technological advancements.

By investing in leadership development, IBM ensured that its leaders were prepared to guide the organization through ongoing change, maintaining IBM's position as a global leader in technology.

This case study highlights the importance of continuous learning and adaptation in the tech industry. IBM's approach demonstrates how a commitment to learning, supported by advanced technologies and a culture of innovation, can drive long-term success in a rapidly evolving environment.

Mastering IT Leadership and Management, Strategies for Success in the Digital Age

Best Practices

1. **Foster a Culture of Continuous Learning:**
   Successful IT organizations prioritize continuous learning as a core value. IT leaders should create an environment where learning is encouraged and supported at all levels. This includes providing access to training programs, online courses, certifications, and learning resources. By fostering a learning culture, organizations can stay ahead of technological advancements and maintain a competitive edge.

2. **Encourage Cross-Training and Skill Diversification:**
   In a rapidly changing IT landscape, a diverse skill set is invaluable. IT leaders should encourage cross-training among team members, allowing them to gain expertise in different areas of IT. This approach builds a more versatile workforce and enhances collaboration and innovation, as employees bring varied perspectives to problem-solving.

3. **Leverage Real-World Projects for Learning:**
   Practical, hands-on experience is one of the most effective ways to learn. IT leaders should leverage real-world projects as opportunities for employees to apply new skills and technologies. Assigning team members to stretch projects or roles slightly outside their comfort zones can accelerate learning and help them adapt to new challenges.

4. **Implement Mentorship and Knowledge Sharing Programs:**
   Mentorship and knowledge sharing are critical components of continuous learning. IT leaders should establish mentorship programs where experienced professionals guide less experienced team members. Additionally, fostering a culture of knowledge sharing through regular team meetings, brown-bag sessions, and internal workshops helps disseminate expertise throughout the organization.

5. **Stay Updated on Industry Trends and Emerging Technologies:**
   Keeping pace with industry trends and emerging technologies is essential for continuous adaptation. IT leaders should encourage team members to attend conferences, webinars, and industry events, and to read relevant publications. Staying informed helps the organization anticipate changes and be proactive in adopting new technologies and practices.

6. **Promote a Growth Mindset:**
   A growth mindset—the belief that skills and abilities can be developed through dedication and hard work—is crucial for continuous learning and adaptation. IT leaders should promote this mindset by recognizing and rewarding efforts to learn and grow. Encouraging a growth mindset helps employees embrace challenges, persist through setbacks, and view learning as a lifelong journey.

7. **Utilize Data to Inform Learning Strategies:**
   Data-driven decision-making can also be applied to learning and development. IT leaders should use data to assess the effectiveness of training programs, identify skill

gaps, and tailor learning strategies to the needs of the team. By leveraging data, organizations can optimize their learning initiatives and ensure they are meeting workforce needs.

8. **Adapt Learning to Changing Business Needs:**
   Continuous learning should be closely aligned with the organization's evolving business needs. IT leaders should regularly reassess the skills required to meet current and future business challenges and adapt learning programs accordingly. This ensures that the workforce remains relevant and capable of driving the organization's success.

Mastering IT Leadership and Management, Strategies for Success in the Digital Age

Lessons Learned

1. **A Learning Culture Drives Innovation and Agility:**
   Organizations that prioritize continuous learning are more innovative and agile. By fostering a culture that values learning, IT leaders enable their teams to quickly adapt to new technologies and methodologies, driving continuous improvement and innovation. This culture of learning also enhances the organization's ability to respond to market changes and seize new opportunities.

2. **Skill Diversification Enhances Resilience:**
   Cross-training and skill diversification build a more resilient workforce. Employees with a broad range of skills are better equipped to handle diverse challenges and can step into different roles as needed. This versatility is especially valuable in a rapidly changing IT environment, where the ability to adapt quickly is crucial for success.

3. **Hands-On Experience Accelerates Learning:**
   Real-world projects provide invaluable learning opportunities that theoretical training alone cannot match. IT leaders who incorporate hands-on experience into their learning programs see faster skill development and greater retention of knowledge. This practical approach to learning helps employees build confidence and apply new skills effectively.

4. **Mentorship Strengthens Organizational Knowledge:**
   Mentorship programs enhance the transfer of knowledge within an organization. Experienced mentors can provide guidance, share insights, and help mentees navigate challenges. Organizations that invest in mentorship see stronger employee development, greater knowledge retention, and a more collaborative work environment.

5. **Staying Informed Keeps the Organization Competitive:**
   Keeping up with industry trends and emerging technologies is critical for maintaining a competitive edge. IT leaders who encourage their teams to stay informed and engaged with the broader industry ensure that their organization is not caught off guard by technological advancements. This proactive approach helps the organization stay ahead of competitors and remain relevant in a fast-paced market.

6. **A Growth Mindset Fuels Continuous Improvement:**
   A growth mindset is a powerful driver of continuous learning and adaptation. Employees who believe in their ability to learn and grow are more likely to embrace new challenges, seek out learning opportunities, and persist in the face of setbacks. IT leaders who cultivate a growth mindset within their teams foster a culture of continuous improvement and resilience.

7. **Data-Driven Learning Optimizes Development Efforts:**
   Using data to inform learning strategies ensures that development efforts are targeted and effective. Organizations that leverage data to identify skill gaps,

Mastering IT Leadership and Management, Strategies for Success in the Digital Age

measure the impact of training programs, and tailor learning initiatives to individual needs see better outcomes. This data-driven approach helps maximize the return on investment in learning and development.

8. **Aligning Learning with Business Needs Ensures Relevance:**
   Continuous learning must be aligned with the organization's evolving business needs to remain relevant and impactful. IT leaders who regularly reassess the skills required to meet business challenges can adapt their learning programs to ensure the workforce is prepared for future demands. This alignment between learning and business needs is key to sustaining organizational success in a dynamic environment.

By embracing these best practices and learning from successful continuous learning and adaptation initiatives, IT leaders can ensure their teams are well-prepared to meet future challenges, driving sustained growth and innovation in the digital age.

Mastering IT Leadership and Management, Strategies for Success in the Digital Age

Conclusion

Continuous learning and adaptation are the cornerstones of successful IT leadership in an era defined by rapid technological change and constant innovation. In Chapter 17, we explored the importance of lifelong learning for IT leaders, the need to adapt to rapid technological changes, and the strategies for building resilience and agility within leadership roles.

In the fast-paced world of IT, the ability to continuously learn and adapt is not just a competitive advantage—it's a necessity. As technology evolves, so too must the skills and knowledge of IT leaders. This chapter emphasized the critical need for IT leaders to commit to lifelong learning, staying current with emerging technologies, industry trends, and best practices. By fostering a culture of continuous learning within their teams, IT leaders can ensure that their organizations remain at the forefront of innovation and are prepared to capitalize on new opportunities.

Adapting to rapid technological changes requires more than just technical knowledge; it demands a mindset that is open to change, experimentation, and growth. IT leaders must be flexible and forward-thinking, able to pivot quickly in response to new challenges and opportunities. This chapter highlighted the importance of developing an adaptive leadership style that balances strategic planning with the agility to respond to unforeseen developments. This adaptability will be crucial in navigating the uncertainties of the digital age.

Building resilience and agility within IT leadership roles is essential for sustaining long-term success. Resilient leaders are those who can withstand and recover from setbacks, while agile leaders are those who can anticipate and respond to change with speed and efficiency. This chapter provided strategies for cultivating these qualities, such as embracing a growth mindset, encouraging innovation, and fostering a supportive and collaborative work environment.

As we conclude Chapter 17, it is clear that continuous learning and adaptation are not just final steps in the journey of IT leadership—they are ongoing commitments that will define the effectiveness and relevance of IT leaders in the years to come. The ability to learn, adapt, and evolve in response to technological advancements and shifting business landscapes will determine the success of IT leaders and their organizations in the digital future.

The principles and strategies discussed in this chapter serve as a capstone to the leadership journey explored throughout this book. By embracing continuous learning and adaptation, IT leaders can not only navigate the challenges of today but also prepare for the opportunities of tomorrow. As we conclude this book, these enduring qualities will remain central to the practice of IT leadership, ensuring that leaders are equipped to drive innovation, resilience, and success in the ever-changing world of technology.

Mastering IT Leadership and Management, Strategies for Success in the Digital Age

Quizzes

I. Multiple Choice Questions:

1. **What is one of the primary benefits of continuous learning in IT leadership?**
   A. Reducing employee turnover
   B. Keeping up with technological advancements
   C. Increasing the budget for IT departments
   D. Decreasing collaboration within teams

2. **Which of the following is a key strategy for fostering continuous learning within an IT team?**
   A. Limiting access to learning resources
   B. Encouraging employees to take ownership of their learning
   C. Focusing only on formal training sessions
   D. Promoting a fixed mindset

3. **What is one of the main purposes of implementing agile methodologies in IT leadership?**
   A. To avoid experimenting with new ideas
   B. To improve employee satisfaction only
   C. To enhance flexibility and collaboration
   D. To reduce the need for training

4. **Why is scenario planning important for IT leaders?**
   A. It helps avoid new technological innovations
   B. It allows leaders to plan for different future possibilities
   C. It focuses only on regulatory compliance
   D. It reduces the need for employee feedback

5. **What is the benefit of leveraging real-world projects for learning?**
   A. It eliminates the need for formal training
   B. It accelerates skill development and knowledge retention
   C. It reduces the time spent on collaboration
   D. It simplifies decision-making processes

6. **Which mindset should IT leaders promote to foster continuous learning and adaptability?**
   A. Fixed mindset
   B. Short-term mindset
   C. Growth mindset
   D. Risk-averse mindset

7. **Why is it essential for IT leaders to embrace lifelong learning?**

Mastering IT Leadership and Management, Strategies for Success in the Digital Age

   A. To focus solely on internal company training
   B. To maintain their competitive advantage in a rapidly changing world
   C. To avoid experimenting with new technologies
   D. To ensure that IT projects are completed on time

8. What role does resilience play in IT leadership?
   A. It helps leaders avoid taking risks
   B. It ensures that teams maintain high levels of performance during challenges
   C. It decreases the need for cross-functional collaboration
   D. It focuses solely on team satisfaction

9. Why is knowledge sharing important for IT teams?
   A. It decreases the need for external training
   B. It enhances collaboration and promotes continuous learning
   C. It reduces the number of required formal meetings
   D. It focuses only on top-level management

10. How can IT leaders prepare for technological disruptions?
    A. By avoiding new technologies until fully developed
    B. By investing only in current technology
    C. By conducting regular technology assessments and exploring pilot projects
    D. By limiting experimentation and innovation within teams

---

II. True/False Questions:

1. Continuous learning and adaptation are essential for IT leaders to navigate rapid technological change and innovation effectively. (True/False)
2. **Adopting agile methodologies helps IT leaders enhance their team's ability to respond quickly and efficiently to changes. (True/False)**
3. IT leaders do not need to anticipate technological disruptions to ensure organizational success. (True/False)
4. **Mentorship programs are not a necessary part of continuous learning for IT leaders and their teams. (True/False)**
5. Fostering a growth mindset within teams is key to promoting continuous learning and innovation. (True/False)
6. **Resilience in IT teams means the ability to adapt to change while maintaining high performance. (True/False)**
7. Leveraging data to inform decision-making is not crucial for the successful adaptation of IT teams to changes. (True/False)
8. **Encouraging experimentation and calculated risk-taking is essential for driving continuous improvement in IT teams. (True/False)**

These questions cover various aspects of leadership strategies discussed in the chapter related to continuous learning, adaptability, and the evolving role of IT leaders.

Mastering IT Leadership and Management, Strategies for Success in the Digital Age

Exercises

I. Reflective Essay:
- Write a short essay (300-500 words) discussing how continuous learning has impacted your career in IT. What steps have you taken to ensure you stay updated with industry trends, and how has this influenced your leadership style?

II. Case Study Analysis:
- Review the Industry Case Study on continuous learning and adaptation at IBM as discussed in the chapter. Identify the key strategies IBM implemented to foster continuous learning. Then, describe how you would apply similar strategies in your organization.

III. Group Discussion:
- Organize a discussion group where participants share the continuous learning practices in their respective organizations. Discuss the challenges they face in implementing these practices and brainstorm solutions to overcome these challenges.

IV. Action Plan Development:
- Develop a personal continuous learning plan that outlines your learning objectives for the next 12 months. Include specific goals, the resources you will use, and a timeline for achieving these objectives.

V. Scenario-Based Role Play:
- Imagine you are the IT leader of a company undergoing a major technological transformation. Role-play a meeting where you introduce a new learning initiative aimed at upskilling the team. Prepare a presentation that highlights the importance of this initiative and addresses potential concerns from team members.

These quizzes and exercises are designed to reinforce the concepts of continuous learning and adaptation, helping readers apply the knowledge in practical, real-world scenarios.

Mastering IT Leadership and Management, Strategies for Success in the Digital Age

Conclusion of Part 6: Future Trends in IT Leadership

As we conclude Part 6 of this book, it is evident that the future of IT leadership will be shaped by unprecedented technological advancements, evolving business needs, and the continuous demand for adaptability and innovation. The chapters in this section have explored the emerging trends that will define the next generation of IT leaders, the transformative impact of AI and automation, and the critical importance of continuous learning and adaptation.

The future of IT leadership will be marked by a profound shift in the skills and competencies required to lead effectively. IT leaders will need to navigate a landscape where technology is not just a support function but a core driver of business strategy and competitive advantage. This shift will require leaders to balance deep technical expertise with strategic vision, business acumen, and the ability to manage complex ethical and regulatory challenges.

The rise of AI and automation will continue to reshape industries, offering both opportunities and challenges for IT leaders. While these technologies promise significant efficiencies and new capabilities, they also raise important considerations around job displacement, data privacy, and ethical use. IT leaders must guide their organizations through this transformation with a focus on responsible innovation, ensuring that technology is leveraged in ways that align with organizational values and societal expectations.

Continuous learning and adaptation will be the foundation of future IT leadership. As technology evolves at an ever-increasing pace, IT leaders must commit to lifelong learning, staying ahead of industry trends and emerging technologies. The ability to adapt to rapid change, embrace new challenges, and foster a culture of innovation and agility within their teams will be essential for sustaining success in the digital age.

As we close this final part of the book, it is clear that the future of IT leadership is both challenging and full of potential. Those who can anticipate and respond to emerging trends, harness the power of new technologies, and lead with resilience and adaptability will be well-positioned to drive their organizations toward continued success. The insights and strategies discussed in this section provide a roadmap for navigating the future, empowering IT leaders to lead with confidence in a world defined by constant change and innovation.

The journey of IT leadership does not end here; it is an ongoing process of growth, learning, and adaptation. As you move forward, the principles outlined in this book will serve as a guide to help you navigate the complexities of the digital future, ensuring that you and your organization are prepared to thrive in the years to come.

Mastering IT Leadership and Management, Strategies for Success in the Digital Age

Conclusion
Recap of Key Concepts

As we reach the conclusion of this book, it's important to revisit the key concepts discussed throughout the chapters. These concepts form the foundation of effective IT leadership and are essential for guiding organizations through the complexities of digital transformation, fostering innovation, and driving business success. Below is a recap of the critical ideas and strategies explored in each chapter.

Chapter 1: The Evolving Role of IT Leadership

- **Strategic Partnership:** IT leaders are no longer just technology managers; they are strategic partners who drive business outcomes and contribute to the organization's overall strategy.
- **Digital Transformation:** IT leaders play a pivotal role in leading digital transformation efforts, aligning technology initiatives with business goals to create competitive advantages.
- **Innovation and Change Management:** Embracing innovation and effectively managing change are key responsibilities for IT leaders in today's dynamic business environment.

Chapter 2: Building a Visionary IT Strategy

- **Vision Alignment:** A clear IT vision aligned with business objectives is critical for guiding technology investments and initiatives.
- **Strategic Planning:** IT leaders must develop comprehensive strategic plans that outline the roadmap for achieving the organization's IT goals.
- **Continuous Review:** Regularly reviewing and adjusting the IT strategy ensures that it remains relevant and responsive to changing business needs.

Chapter 3: IT Governance and Compliance

- **Governance Frameworks:** Implementing robust IT governance frameworks ensures that technology decisions align with business goals and comply with regulatory requirements.
- **Risk Management:** Effective risk management practices are essential for identifying, assessing, and mitigating IT-related risks.
- **Compliance:** IT leaders must ensure that the organization's IT practices comply with relevant laws, regulations, and industry standards.

Mastering IT Leadership and Management, Strategies for Success in the Digital Age

Chapter 4: Managing IT Operations and Infrastructure

- **Operational Efficiency:** Optimizing IT operations and infrastructure is crucial for ensuring reliability, performance, and cost-effectiveness.
- **Automation and Process Improvement:** Leveraging automation and continuous process improvement enhances operational efficiency and reduces manual intervention.
- **Scalability and Flexibility:** IT infrastructure must be scalable and flexible to support the organization's growth and changing needs.

Chapter 5: Cybersecurity Leadership

- **Proactive Security Posture:** IT leaders must adopt a proactive approach to cybersecurity, anticipating threats and implementing preventive measures.
- **Incident Response:** Developing and maintaining a robust incident response plan is critical for minimizing the impact of security breaches.
- **Security Culture:** Fostering a culture of security awareness among employees is essential for protecting the organization's information assets.

Chapter 6: Data Management and Analytics

- **Data-Driven Decision-Making:** Leveraging data and analytics to inform decision-making is a key responsibility of IT leaders.
- **Data Governance:** Implementing strong data governance practices ensures data quality, security, and compliance.
- **Advanced Analytics:** IT leaders should explore advanced analytics techniques, such as AI and machine learning, to unlock insights and drive business value.

Chapter 7: IT Project and Portfolio Management

- **Project Alignment:** IT projects must be aligned with the organization's strategic goals to deliver maximum value.
- **Agile Methodologies:** Adopting agile methodologies enhances project flexibility and responsiveness to changing requirements.
- **Portfolio Management:** Effective portfolio management involves prioritizing and managing multiple projects to optimize resource allocation and achieve strategic objectives.

Mastering IT Leadership and Management, Strategies for Success in the Digital Age

Chapter 8: Financial Management for IT Leaders

- **Budgeting and Cost Management:** IT leaders must develop and manage budgets that align with business priorities while controlling costs.
- **ROI and TCO:** Understanding and communicating the return on investment (ROI) and total cost of ownership (TCO) of IT initiatives is essential for securing funding and support.
- **Financial Metrics:** IT leaders should use financial metrics to measure the success of IT investments and demonstrate their value to the organization.

Chapter 9: Building a Cybersecurity Strategy

- **Risk Assessment:** Conducting thorough cybersecurity risk assessments is the foundation of an effective security strategy.
- **Security Controls:** Implementing a layered approach to security controls protects the organization's information assets from a wide range of threats.
- **Incident Response Planning:** Developing a well-defined incident response plan ensures a swift and effective response to security incidents.

Chapter 10: Talent Management and Development

- **Recruiting Top Talent:** Attracting and retaining top IT talent is critical for building a high-performing team.
- **Continuous Learning:** Fostering a culture of continuous learning and development ensures that the IT team stays current with emerging technologies and trends.
- **Employee Engagement:** IT leaders must create an environment that engages employees, promotes growth, and encourages retention.

Chapter 11: Digital Leadership in the Age of Transformation

- **Visionary Leadership:** IT leaders must be visionary, guiding their organizations through digital transformation with a clear strategy and purpose.
- **Innovation and Collaboration:** Encouraging innovation and fostering collaboration across teams are essential for driving digital transformation success.
- **Ethical Leadership:** IT leaders must navigate the ethical implications of technology, ensuring that digital initiatives align with the organization's values and social responsibilities.

Mastering IT Leadership and Management, Strategies for Success in the Digital Age

Chapter 12: Financial Management for IT Leaders

- **Budget Alignment:** IT budgets must align with business strategy to ensure that investments drive the desired outcomes.
- **Cost Control:** Effective cost control measures help optimize IT spending and ensure that resources are used efficiently.
- **Value Communication:** IT leaders must effectively communicate the value of IT investments to stakeholders, demonstrating their impact on business success.

Chapter 13: IT Leadership in a Hybrid Work World

- **Supporting Remote Work:** IT leaders must provide the technology and infrastructure needed to support a hybrid workforce.
- **Security and Compliance:** Ensuring the security and compliance of remote work environments is critical for protecting the organization's data and assets.
- **Employee Well-Being:** IT leaders must prioritize employee well-being and work-life balance in a hybrid work environment.

Chapter 14: Talent Management and Development

- **Leadership Development:** IT leaders must focus on developing the next generation of IT leaders by providing opportunities for growth and leadership experience.
- **Retention Strategies:** Implementing effective retention strategies, such as career development and employee recognition, is essential for keeping top talent engaged and motivated.
- **Culture of Learning:** Fostering a culture of continuous learning and adaptation is key to building a resilient and high-performing IT team.

Chapter 15: The Future of IT Leadership

- **Strategic Partnership:** IT leaders will continue to evolve as strategic partners, driving business outcomes and innovation.
- **Emerging Technologies:** Staying ahead of emerging technologies, such as AI, blockchain, and quantum computing, will be critical for future IT leadership.
- **Ethical and Social Responsibility:** IT leaders must navigate the ethical and social implications of technology, ensuring that digital initiatives benefit society and align with organizational values.

Mastering IT Leadership and Management, Strategies for Success in the Digital Age

Chapter 16: Continuous Learning and Adaptation

- **Lifelong Learning:** Embracing lifelong learning is essential for staying relevant and competitive in the fast-paced world of IT.
- **Adaptability:** IT leaders must foster adaptability within their teams, ensuring that they can respond to change and seize new opportunities.
- **Preparing for the Future:** Proactive planning, scenario analysis, and continuous monitoring are key strategies for preparing for future challenges and uncertainties.

Chapter 17: Fostering a Culture of Continuous Learning

- **Fostering a Culture of Continuous Learning:** IT leaders should prioritize continuous learning by providing access to training, certifications, and real-world projects. This helps organizations stay competitive and encourages a mindset of growth and adaptation.
- **Cross-Training and Skill Diversification:** Encouraging cross-training and diverse skill development enhances workforce versatility, collaboration, and innovation, preparing teams for the rapidly changing IT landscape.
- **Data-Driven and Adaptive Learning Strategies:** IT leaders should use data to identify skill gaps and tailor learning programs to evolving business needs, ensuring the workforce remains aligned with organizational goals and ready for future challenges.

Conclusion

The journey of IT leadership is one of continuous growth, learning, and adaptation. As technology evolves and reshapes the business landscape, IT leaders must remain agile, forward-thinking, and committed to driving innovation and business success. By mastering the key concepts outlined in this book, IT leaders can navigate the complexities of the digital age, build high-performing teams, and position their organizations for long-term success. The future of IT leadership is promising, and those who embrace these principles will guide their organizations to new heights in the digital era.

Mastering IT Leadership and Management, Strategies for Success in the Digital Age

The Ongoing Journey of IT Leadership

The world of IT leadership is in a constant state of evolution, driven by rapid technological advancements, shifting business landscapes, and the ever-growing demands for innovation and agility. As we reach the conclusion of this book, it's clear that the journey of IT leadership is far from over. Rather, it is an ongoing process that requires continuous learning, adaptation, and a deep commitment to driving both technological and business success.

Embracing Lifelong Learning

In an industry that evolves as quickly as IT, lifelong learning is not just a recommendation—it's a necessity. The most effective IT leaders are those who continually seek out new knowledge, skills, and perspectives. They understand that staying ahead of the curve requires a proactive approach to education, whether through formal training, hands-on experience, or engaging with industry peers.

Lifelong learning is also about fostering a growth mindset within your team and organization. By promoting a culture where curiosity, experimentation, and continuous improvement are valued, IT leaders can ensure that their teams remain innovative and resilient in the face of change. This commitment to learning will enable IT leaders to navigate future uncertainties and capitalize on new opportunities.

Adapting to Change and Driving Innovation

The ability to adapt to change is one of the defining qualities of successful IT leaders. As new technologies emerge and business needs evolve, IT leaders must be agile and responsive, ready to pivot and adjust strategies as needed. This requires not only a deep understanding of current trends but also the foresight to anticipate future developments and prepare accordingly.

Driving innovation is at the heart of this adaptability. IT leaders are the architects of digital transformation, tasked with guiding their organizations through the complexities of integrating new technologies and reimagining traditional business processes. Innovation isn't just about implementing the latest tools; it's about fostering a culture that encourages creative thinking, risk-taking, and collaboration. By cultivating an environment where new ideas can flourish, IT leaders can propel their organizations to new heights and maintain a competitive edge in the marketplace.

Mastering IT Leadership and Management, Strategies for Success in the Digital Age

Building and Leading High-Performing Teams

No IT leader can succeed in isolation. The ability to build and lead high-performing teams is crucial to achieving organizational goals and driving successful outcomes. This involves not only recruiting and retaining top talent but also developing the skills and capabilities of team members.

Leadership in IT today goes beyond technical expertise; it requires emotional intelligence, effective communication, and the ability to inspire and motivate others. IT leaders must create an inclusive environment where all team members feel valued and empowered to contribute their best work. By investing in the development of their teams and fostering a strong sense of purpose, IT leaders can ensure their teams are aligned, engaged, and ready to tackle the challenges of the digital age.

Navigating Ethical and Social Responsibilities

As technology continues to permeate every aspect of society, IT leaders face increasing ethical and social responsibilities. Issues such as data privacy, cybersecurity, and the ethical use of artificial intelligence are at the forefront of public concern. IT leaders must navigate these complexities with integrity, ensuring that their organizations not only comply with regulations but also act in a manner that is ethical and socially responsible.

This responsibility extends to addressing the broader impact of technology on society, including the digital divide and the implications of automation on the workforce. IT leaders have the opportunity—and the obligation—to shape the future in a way that is inclusive, fair, and sustainable. By leading with a strong moral compass, IT leaders can build trust with stakeholders and contribute to a positive societal impact.

Preparing for the Future of IT Leadership

The future of IT leadership is both exciting and challenging. As we look ahead, it's clear that the role of the IT leader will continue to expand, encompassing not only technology management but also strategic decision-making, business transformation, and global impact. The leaders of tomorrow will need to be visionary, adaptable, and deeply connected to the needs and aspirations of their organizations and society at large.

Preparing for this future requires a commitment to continuous development—not just of technical skills, but of leadership capabilities, strategic thinking, and ethical awareness. IT leaders must be ready to embrace new roles and responsibilities, guiding their organizations through an increasingly complex and interconnected world.

Mastering IT Leadership and Management, Strategies for Success in the Digital Age

Conclusion

The journey of IT leadership is one of perpetual growth and evolution. It demands resilience, curiosity, and a relentless drive to push boundaries and explore new possibilities. As IT leaders, the responsibility to shape the future of technology—and its impact on the world—rests on your shoulders. By embracing the principles outlined in this book, you are well-equipped to lead your organization through the challenges and opportunities of the digital age.

The path ahead is filled with unknowns, but it is also rich with potential. As you continue your journey, remember that the essence of IT leadership lies not just in mastering technology, but in understanding how to harness its power to create lasting value, drive innovation, and make a positive impact on the world. The ongoing journey of IT leadership is yours to shape—one decision, one innovation, and one success at a time.

Mastering IT Leadership and Management, Strategies for Success in the Digital Age

Call to Action for Aspiring IT Leaders

As we conclude this book, it is important to recognize that the journey of IT leadership is not a destination, but a continuous path of growth, learning, and transformation. For those who aspire to take on the mantle of IT leadership, the road ahead is filled with challenges but also immense opportunities to shape the future of technology and its impact on the world. This is your call to action—to step forward, embrace the responsibilities of leadership, and make a meaningful difference in your organization and beyond.

Embrace Continuous Learning

The landscape of IT is ever-changing, and to succeed as an IT leader, you must commit to lifelong learning. Stay curious, seek out new knowledge, and never stop expanding your skill set. Whether it's mastering new technologies, understanding emerging trends, or developing your leadership capabilities, continuous learning is the foundation upon which your success will be built. Make a habit of regularly setting learning goals, attending industry events, pursuing certifications, and engaging with thought leaders in the field.

Cultivate a Visionary Mindset

As an aspiring IT leader, your ability to envision the future and translate that vision into actionable strategies is critical. Develop the skills to think strategically, anticipate trends, and identify opportunities for innovation. Learn to see the bigger picture and understand how technology can drive business success and create value. Cultivate a mindset that is not just reactive, but proactive—constantly looking ahead and preparing for what's next.

Build Strong Relationships

Leadership is not just about managing technology; it's about leading people. Focus on building strong relationships with your colleagues, stakeholders, and team members. Effective communication, empathy, and collaboration are key to fostering a positive and productive work environment. Invest time in understanding the needs and motivations of those around you, and work to build trust and rapport. By cultivating strong relationships, you'll be better positioned to lead, influence, and drive change.

Drive Innovation and Embrace Change

Innovation is at the heart of IT leadership. As you grow in your career, look for ways to drive innovation within your organization. Encourage creative thinking, take calculated risks, and be willing to experiment with new ideas. Embrace change as an opportunity to improve and evolve, rather than a challenge to be resisted. Your ability to adapt to new circumstances and lead your team through change will be a defining characteristic of your leadership journey.

Mastering IT Leadership and Management, Strategies for Success in the Digital Age

Uphold Ethical Standards

In today's digital age, the ethical implications of technology are more important than ever. As an IT leader, you will be responsible for ensuring that your organization's use of technology aligns with ethical principles and societal values. Commit to upholding the highest standards of integrity, transparency, and accountability in all your decisions and actions. Be a champion for ethical technology use, and lead by example in promoting responsible innovation and data protection.

Focus on Talent Development

One of the most important roles of an IT leader is to develop and nurture the talent within your team. Recognize the potential in others and invest in their growth and development. Create opportunities for your team members to learn, take on new challenges, and advance in their careers. By fostering a culture of continuous learning and development, you'll not only strengthen your team but also contribute to the long-term success of your organization.

Lead with Purpose

Finally, remember that leadership is about more than just achieving business goals—it's about making a positive impact on the world. Lead with a sense of purpose, and be guided by a vision of how technology can improve lives, create opportunities, and solve global challenges. Your leadership should be driven by a commitment to making a difference, whether that's through advancing your organization's mission, contributing to your community, or championing causes that matter to you.

Conclusion

The journey to becoming an IT leader is a challenging one, but it is also incredibly rewarding. As you take on this journey, remember that leadership is not a title, but a continuous process of learning, growing, and making a difference. The future of technology is in your hands, and with the right mindset, skills, and commitment, you can shape that future in ways that create lasting value for your organization and society as a whole.

This is your call to action: embrace the challenges, seize the opportunities, and lead with vision, purpose, and integrity. The world of IT leadership is vast and full of potential—step into it with confidence, and make your mark.

Mastering IT Leadership and Management, Strategies for Success in the Digital Age

Appendices

Appendix A: IT Leadership Frameworks and Models

In the rapidly evolving field of IT leadership, frameworks and models serve as invaluable tools for guiding decision-making, strategic planning, and operational management. These frameworks provide structured approaches to address the complex challenges IT leaders face, ensuring that technology initiatives align with business objectives and that organizations remain agile and resilient in the face of change. This appendix presents an overview of several key IT leadership frameworks and models that can be leveraged to enhance your effectiveness as an IT leader.

---

1. COBIT (Control Objectives for Information and Related Technologies)

COBIT is a comprehensive framework for managing and governing enterprise IT. It provides a set of best practices and guidelines for aligning IT with business goals, ensuring that IT investments deliver value, and managing IT risks.

- **Governance and Management:** COBIT distinguishes between governance and management of IT. Governance focuses on setting objectives, monitoring performance, and ensuring that IT aligns with business strategy. Management, on the other hand, involves planning, building, running, and monitoring IT processes to achieve organizational goals.

- **Processes and Domains:** COBIT is organized into five domains: Evaluate, Direct, and Monitor (EDM); Align, Plan, and Organize (APO); Build, Acquire, and Implement (BAI); Deliver, Service, and Support (DSS); and Monitor, Evaluate, and Assess (MEA). Each domain contains specific processes that IT leaders can use to effectively manage and govern IT.

- **Maturity Models:** COBIT includes maturity models for assessing the current state of IT processes and identifying areas for improvement. By using these models, IT leaders can set goals for process improvement and track progress over time.

Mastering IT Leadership and Management, Strategies for Success in the Digital Age

2. ITIL (Information Technology Infrastructure Library)

ITIL is a widely adopted framework for IT service management (ITSM) that focuses on aligning IT services with the needs of the business. It provides a structured approach to managing IT services, from initial design to ongoing operation and continuous improvement.

- **Service Lifecycle:** ITIL is based on a service lifecycle model that includes five stages: Service Strategy, Service Design, Service Transition, Service Operation, and Continual Service Improvement. Each stage addresses a specific aspect of IT service management, from defining service objectives to ensuring that services continuously meet business needs.

- **Processes and Functions:** ITIL outlines key processes and functions within each stage of the service lifecycle, such as incident management, problem management, change management, service level management, and capacity management. IT leaders can use these processes to ensure that IT services are delivered effectively and efficiently.

- **Value Creation:** ITIL emphasizes the importance of creating value for the business through IT services. By focusing on customer needs and aligning IT services with business objectives, IT leaders can ensure that IT contributes to the overall success of the organization.

3. TOGAF (The Open Group Architecture Framework)

TOGAF is a framework for enterprise architecture that helps organizations design, plan, implement, and manage their IT architectures. It offers a comprehensive approach to aligning IT with business strategy and ensuring that technology investments support long-term goals.

- **Architecture Development Method (ADM):** TOGAF's core component is the Architecture Development Method (ADM), a step-by-step approach to developing and managing enterprise architecture. The ADM includes phases such as Preliminary, Architecture Vision, Business Architecture, Information Systems Architectures, Technology Architecture, and Opportunities and Solutions.

- **Building Blocks:** TOGAF uses the concept of building blocks to represent the components of enterprise architecture. These building blocks can be reused across different projects, enabling IT leaders to create flexible and scalable architectures that adapt to changing business needs.

- **Framework Customization:** TOGAF is designed to be flexible and customizable, allowing IT leaders to tailor the framework to their organization's specific needs. This adaptability makes TOGAF a valuable tool for organizations of all sizes and industries.

Mastering IT Leadership and Management, Strategies for Success in the Digital Age

4. Balanced Scorecard

The Balanced Scorecard is a strategic management tool that helps organizations translate their vision and strategy into actionable objectives. It provides a comprehensive view of organizational performance by focusing on four key perspectives: Financial, Customer, Internal Processes, and Learning and Growth.

- **Strategy Mapping:** The Balanced Scorecard uses strategy maps to link organizational objectives across the four perspectives. IT leaders can use these maps to visualize how IT initiatives contribute to overall business goals and ensure that all activities are aligned with the organization's strategic vision.

- **Performance Metrics:** The Balanced Scorecard encourages the use of performance metrics to track progress toward strategic objectives. IT leaders can develop metrics for each perspective, such as IT cost efficiency (Financial), user satisfaction (Customer), process automation (Internal Processes), and staff training (Learning and Growth).

- **Alignment and Communication:** The Balanced Scorecard promotes alignment and communication across the organization by providing a common framework for discussing and measuring performance. IT leaders can use it to ensure that IT objectives are clearly communicated and understood throughout the organization.

5. Lean IT

Lean IT is an adaptation of Lean principles, originally developed for manufacturing, to the field of IT. Lean IT focuses on maximizing value for the customer while minimizing waste, improving efficiency, and driving continuous improvement in IT processes.

- **Value Stream Mapping:** Lean IT uses value stream mapping to identify and eliminate waste in IT processes. IT leaders can leverage this tool to analyze workflows, identify bottlenecks, and streamline processes to deliver value more efficiently.

- **Continuous Improvement:** Lean IT emphasizes the importance of continuous improvement (Kaizen) in achieving long-term success. IT leaders should foster a culture of continuous improvement by encouraging teams to regularly assess and refine their processes, practices, and tools.

- **Customer Focus:** Lean IT prioritizes delivering value to the customer. IT leaders must ensure that all IT activities are aligned with customer needs and expectations and that the organization is responsive to feedback and changes in demand.

Mastering IT Leadership and Management, Strategies for Success in the Digital Age

6. Agile

Agile is a framework for managing projects, particularly in software development, that emphasizes flexibility, collaboration, and customer satisfaction. Agile methodologies, such as Scrum and Kanban, enable IT teams to deliver projects in iterative cycles, allowing for continuous feedback and adaptation.

- **Iterative Development:** Agile promotes iterative development, where projects are broken down into small, manageable tasks completed in short cycles, known as sprints. This approach allows IT leaders to deliver value incrementally and make adjustments based on ongoing feedback.

- **Collaboration and Communication:** Agile emphasizes the importance of collaboration and communication among team members and stakeholders. IT leaders should foster an environment where open communication is encouraged, and cross-functional teams work together to achieve project goals.

- **Customer-Centricity:** Agile places the customer at the center of the development process, ensuring that products and services meet customer needs and expectations. IT leaders should focus on delivering high-quality solutions that provide real value to the customer.

7. DevOps

DevOps is a cultural and technical movement that combines software development (Dev) and IT operations (Ops) to improve collaboration, efficiency, and delivery speed. DevOps practices enable organizations to deliver software and services more rapidly and reliably.

- **Continuous Integration and Continuous Deployment (CI/CD):** DevOps promotes the use of CI/CD pipelines to automate the testing, integration, and deployment of code changes. IT leaders should implement CI/CD practices to reduce the time it takes to deliver new features and updates while ensuring quality and stability.

- **Collaboration and Shared Responsibility:** DevOps encourages collaboration between development and operations teams, breaking down silos and fostering a culture of shared responsibility. IT leaders should promote a collaborative culture where teams work together to achieve common goals.

- **Automation and Infrastructure as Code:** DevOps leverages automation and infrastructure as code (IaC) to streamline processes and reduce manual effort. IT leaders should invest in automation tools and practices to improve efficiency, reduce errors, and enhance scalability.

Mastering IT Leadership and Management, Strategies for Success in the Digital Age

Conclusion

The frameworks and models outlined in this appendix provide a solid foundation for IT leadership, offering structured approaches to managing technology, driving innovation, and aligning IT with business objectives. By understanding and applying these frameworks, IT leaders can enhance their strategic planning, improve operational efficiency, and ensure that their organizations are well-positioned to succeed in the digital age. Whether you are just beginning your journey as an IT leader or looking to refine your existing practices, these frameworks and models offer valuable insights and tools to guide your efforts.

Mastering IT Leadership and Management, Strategies for Success in the Digital Age

Appendix B: Tools and Resources for IT Leaders

In the fast-paced and ever-evolving field of IT leadership, having the right tools and resources at your disposal is crucial for success. Whether you're managing projects, driving digital transformation, or leading a team, leveraging the appropriate tools can enhance productivity, improve decision-making, and streamline operations. This appendix provides an overview of essential tools and resources that IT leaders can use to support their work across various domains, from project management and cybersecurity to continuous learning and strategic planning.

---

1. Project Management Tools

Effective project management is key to delivering IT initiatives on time, within budget, and according to scope. The following tools are widely used for managing IT projects, facilitating collaboration, and tracking progress:

- **Trello:** Trello is a visual project management tool based on the Kanban methodology. It allows teams to organize tasks into boards, lists, and cards, providing a clear overview of project status. Trello is particularly useful for Agile teams and those seeking a simple, intuitive interface.

- **Asana:** Asana is a versatile project management tool that supports task assignment, project timelines, and collaboration. IT leaders can use Asana to manage complex projects, track milestones, and ensure that teams are aligned and working efficiently.

- **JIRA:** JIRA is a powerful project management tool designed for software development teams. It supports Agile methodologies, including Scrum and Kanban, and offers robust features for tracking issues, managing backlogs, and planning sprints.

- **Microsoft Project:** Microsoft Project is a comprehensive project management tool that offers advanced features for scheduling, resource management, and budget tracking. It is ideal for large-scale IT projects that require detailed planning and monitoring.

Mastering IT Leadership and Management, Strategies for Success in the Digital Age

2. Cybersecurity Tools

Protecting an organization's digital assets is a top priority for IT leaders. The following cybersecurity tools can help safeguard your organization's data, networks, and systems:

- **Splunk:** Splunk is a security information and event management (SIEM) tool that provides real-time visibility into your IT environment. It collects, analyzes, and correlates data from various sources, enabling IT leaders to detect and respond to security incidents quickly.

- **CrowdStrike Falcon:** CrowdStrike Falcon is an endpoint protection platform that uses AI to detect, prevent, and respond to threats in real time. It provides advanced threat intelligence, malware detection, and incident response capabilities.

- **Cisco Umbrella:** Cisco Umbrella is a cloud-based security platform that offers protection against internet-based threats, such as phishing, malware, and ransomware. It includes secure web gateway, DNS-layer security, and cloud-delivered firewall features.

- **Nessus:** Nessus is a vulnerability assessment tool that helps IT leaders identify and fix security weaknesses in their IT infrastructure. It scans networks, systems, and applications for vulnerabilities and provides detailed reports on potential risks.

3. Data Management and Analytics Tools

Data is a critical asset for any organization, and effective data management and analytics tools are essential for leveraging this asset. The following tools can help IT leaders manage and analyze data to drive informed decision-making:

- **Tableau:** Tableau is a data visualization tool that enables IT leaders to create interactive, easy-to-understand dashboards and reports. It supports a wide range of data sources and provides powerful analytics capabilities for uncovering insights.

- **Microsoft Power BI:** Power BI is a business analytics tool that allows IT leaders to transform raw data into meaningful insights. It offers data visualization, interactive dashboards, and integration with other Microsoft products, making it a versatile choice for data-driven organizations.

- **Apache Hadoop:** Hadoop is an open-source framework for storing and processing large datasets across distributed computing environments. IT leaders can use Hadoop to manage big data and perform complex analytics tasks at scale.

- **Snowflake:** Snowflake is a cloud-based data warehousing platform that simplifies data storage, processing, and analytics. It supports multi-cloud environments and provides scalable, secure, and fast data management solutions.

Mastering IT Leadership and Management, Strategies for Success in the Digital Age

4. Collaboration and Communication Tools

Effective communication and collaboration are essential for IT leaders managing distributed teams or working in a hybrid environment. The following tools facilitate seamless communication and teamwork:

- **Microsoft Teams:** Microsoft Teams is a collaboration platform that integrates chat, video conferencing, file sharing, and project management features. IT leaders can use Teams to facilitate communication, host virtual meetings, and collaborate on documents in real time.

- **Slack:** Slack is a messaging platform designed for team communication and collaboration. It supports channels for different projects or teams, direct messaging, and integration with various productivity tools, making it a popular choice for IT organizations.

- **Zoom:** Zoom is a video conferencing tool that enables virtual meetings, webinars, and online events. It offers features such as screen sharing, breakout rooms, and recording, making it ideal for remote teams and virtual collaboration.

- **Miro:** Miro is an online whiteboard platform that supports brainstorming, planning, and collaborative work. IT leaders can use Miro to create visual representations of ideas, workflows, and projects, facilitating creative collaboration across teams.

5. Continuous Learning and Development Resources

To stay ahead in the IT field, continuous learning and professional development are essential. The following resources provide access to training, certifications, and knowledge sharing for IT leaders and their teams:

- **Coursera:** Coursera offers online courses and certifications from top universities and institutions in various IT-related fields, including cybersecurity, data science, and software development. IT leaders can use Coursera to upskill themselves and their teams.

- **Pluralsight:** Pluralsight is a technology-focused learning platform that provides courses on a wide range of IT topics, including cloud computing, DevOps, and programming. It also offers skill assessments and learning paths tailored to individual needs.

- **LinkedIn Learning:** LinkedIn Learning provides on-demand video courses on technology, business, and creative skills. IT leaders can access a wealth of content to enhance their leadership capabilities, technical knowledge, and soft skills.

- **ISACA:** ISACA is a global association for IT governance, risk management, and cybersecurity professionals. It offers certifications such as CISA, CISM, and CRISC, as well as resources like webinars, whitepapers, and networking opportunities.

Mastering IT Leadership and Management, Strategies for Success in the Digital Age

6. Strategic Planning and Decision-Making Tools

Strategic planning and decision-making are central to IT leadership. The following tools and frameworks can help IT leaders make informed decisions and align technology initiatives with business goals:

- **Balanced Scorecard:** The Balanced Scorecard is a strategic planning framework that helps organizations translate their vision and strategy into actionable objectives. IT leaders can use this tool to align IT initiatives with business goals and measure performance across multiple dimensions.

- **SWOT Analysis:** SWOT (Strengths, Weaknesses, Opportunities, Threats) analysis is a strategic planning tool that helps IT leaders assess internal and external factors that could impact their organization. It provides a structured approach to identifying areas of focus and potential challenges.

- **PESTLE Analysis:** PESTLE (Political, Economic, Social, Technological, Legal, Environmental) analysis is a framework for analyzing the external environment in which an organization operates. IT leaders can use PESTLE analysis to identify trends and forces that may influence their strategic decisions.

- **Gartner Research:** Gartner is a leading research and advisory company that provides insights, analysis, and tools for IT leaders. Access to Gartner's research reports, Magic Quadrants, and strategic planning tools can help IT leaders make informed decisions and stay ahead of industry trends.

Mastering IT Leadership and Management, Strategies for Success in the Digital Age

7. Leadership and Management Resources

Effective IT leadership requires a combination of technical knowledge and strong leadership skills. The following resources offer insights, best practices, and tools for developing leadership and management capabilities:

- **Harvard Business Review (HBR):** HBR is a renowned publication offering articles, case studies, and insights on leadership, management, and business strategy. IT leaders can use HBR as a resource for staying informed on leadership trends and improving their management practices.

- **MIT Sloan Management Review:** MIT Sloan Management Review provides research-based articles and insights on leadership, innovation, and technology management. It is an excellent resource for IT leaders looking to deepen their understanding of leadership in the digital age.

- **Books on IT Leadership:** Numerous books offer valuable perspectives on IT leadership. Titles such as The Phoenix Project by Gene Kim, Kevin Behr, and George Spafford, Leading Digital by George Westerman, Didier Bonnet, and Andrew McAfee, and Drive by Daniel H. Pink provide actionable insights for IT leaders.

- **Leadership Coaching and Mentoring:** Engaging with a leadership coach or mentor can provide personalized guidance and support for IT leaders looking to enhance their skills and navigate complex challenges. Many organizations offer coaching and mentoring programs to help leaders grow in their roles.

Conclusion

The tools and resources outlined in this appendix are designed to support IT leaders in their journey to drive digital transformation, manage complex projects, lead high-performing teams, and make strategic decisions. By leveraging these tools and continuously seeking out new resources, IT leaders can enhance their effectiveness, stay ahead of industry trends, and achieve success in their roles. Whether you are looking to improve your technical skills, develop your leadership capabilities, or stay informed about the latest developments in the IT field, these resources provide a solid foundation for ongoing growth and learning.

Mastering IT Leadership and Management, Strategies for Success in the Digital Age

Appendix C: Glossary of IT Leadership and Management Terms

Understanding the terminology used in IT leadership and management is essential for effectively navigating the complexities of the field. This glossary provides clear definitions of key terms and concepts frequently encountered by IT leaders. Whether you are new to the role or a seasoned professional, this glossary serves as a valuable reference to ensure clarity and comprehension in your daily work.

A

- **Agile:** A methodology that promotes iterative development, collaboration, and flexibility in managing projects. Agile methodologies, such as Scrum and Kanban, emphasize delivering value incrementally and adapting to changes quickly.

- **Artificial Intelligence (AI):** The simulation of human intelligence by machines, particularly computer systems. AI applications include machine learning, natural language processing, and robotics, and are used to automate tasks, analyze data, and make decisions.

- **API (Application Programming Interface):** A set of protocols and tools that allow different software applications to communicate with each other. APIs enable the integration of various systems and services, facilitating data exchange and functionality sharing.

B

- **Balanced Scorecard:** A strategic management tool that provides a framework for aligning business activities with organizational strategy. It uses four perspectives—Financial, Customer, Internal Processes, and Learning and Growth—to measure performance and achieve long-term objectives.

- **Big Data:** Large and complex datasets that are difficult to process using traditional data processing tools. Big Data technologies allow organizations to analyze and extract insights from these datasets, enabling better decision-making.

- **Blockchain:** A decentralized and distributed digital ledger technology that records transactions across multiple computers. Blockchain is known for its security, transparency, and ability to maintain an immutable record of transactions, often used in cryptocurrencies like Bitcoin.

Mastering IT Leadership and Management, Strategies for Success in the Digital Age

C

- **Change Management:** The process of managing the transition of an organization, team, or system from its current state to a desired future state. Change management involves planning, communication, training, and support to ensure a smooth and successful transition.

- **Cloud Computing:** The delivery of computing services, such as servers, storage, databases, networking, and software, over the internet (the cloud). Cloud computing offers scalability, flexibility, and cost savings by allowing organizations to access resources on demand.

- **COBIT (Control Objectives for Information and Related Technologies):** A framework for managing and governing enterprise IT. COBIT provides best practices for aligning IT with business goals, ensuring value delivery, and managing risks.

- **Continuous Integration/Continuous Deployment (CI/CD):** A practice in software development where code changes are automatically tested and deployed to production environments. CI/CD aims to improve software quality and accelerate the delivery of updates and new features.

- **Cybersecurity:** The practice of protecting systems, networks, and data from digital attacks, unauthorized access, and other security threats. Cybersecurity involves implementing measures such as firewalls, encryption, and security protocols to safeguard information.

D

- **Data Governance:** The process of managing the availability, usability, integrity, and security of data within an organization. Data governance ensures that data is accurate, consistent, and compliant with regulations and organizational policies.

- **Data Privacy:** The protection of personal and sensitive information from unauthorized access, use, or disclosure. Data privacy involves implementing policies and practices to ensure that individuals' data is handled securely and in accordance with legal requirements.

- **DevOps:** A cultural and technical movement that combines software development (Dev) and IT operations (Ops) to improve collaboration, efficiency, and the speed of delivery. DevOps practices include automation, continuous integration, and infrastructure as code.

Mastering IT Leadership and Management, Strategies for Success in the Digital Age

E

- **Enterprise Architecture (EA):** A comprehensive framework used to manage and align an organization's IT assets, processes, and projects with its overall business strategy. EA helps ensure that IT investments support the long-term goals of the organization.

- **Ethical AI:** The practice of developing and deploying artificial intelligence in a way that adheres to ethical principles, such as fairness, transparency, accountability, and respect for human rights. Ethical AI seeks to mitigate biases and prevent harm in AI applications.

- **Endpoint Security:** A cybersecurity approach focused on protecting network endpoints, such as laptops, smartphones, tablets, and other devices, from cyber threats. Endpoint security involves using tools like antivirus software, firewalls, and intrusion detection systems to safeguard data.

- **Encryption:** The process of converting data into a coded format to prevent unauthorized access. Encryption ensures that only authorized parties can read the data, typically requiring a decryption key to revert the data to its original form.

- **Enterprise Resource Planning (ERP):** Integrated software platforms that manage an organization's core business processes, such as finance, human resources, procurement, and supply chain management. ERP systems help organizations streamline operations and improve data accuracy.

- **Escalation Management:** The process of prioritizing and addressing critical issues or incidents that require immediate attention. In IT, escalation management involves moving a problem to higher levels of authority when it cannot be resolved at the current level.

Mastering IT Leadership and Management, Strategies for Success in the Digital Age

F

- **Firewall:** A network security system that monitors and controls incoming and outgoing network traffic based on predetermined security rules. Firewalls act as a barrier between a trusted internal network and untrusted external networks, such as the internet.

- **Framework:** A structured approach or set of guidelines used to organize and manage processes, projects, or systems. Frameworks provide a foundation for decision-making, planning, and execution, ensuring consistency and alignment with best practices.

- **Feasibility Study:** An analysis conducted to assess the practicality, costs, benefits, and risks of a proposed project or solution. IT leaders use feasibility studies to determine whether a project is viable and worth pursuing.

- **File Integrity Monitoring (FIM):** A security technology that detects and alerts on unauthorized changes to files, systems, and applications. FIM is used to protect sensitive data and ensure compliance with regulatory requirements.

- **Fault Tolerance:** The ability of a system or network to continue operating properly in the event of a failure or malfunction of one or more of its components. Fault-tolerant systems are designed to prevent data loss and minimize downtime.

G

- **Governance, Risk Management, and Compliance (GRC):** An integrated approach to managing an organization's governance, risk, and compliance responsibilities. GRC ensures that an organization operates ethically, manages risks effectively, and complies with relevant laws and regulations.

- **Gap Analysis:** A method used to compare current performance with desired performance. Gap analysis helps identify deficiencies in processes, systems, or resources and provides a roadmap for improvement.

- **Green IT:** The practice of implementing environmentally sustainable IT solutions and practices. Green IT focuses on reducing energy consumption, minimizing electronic waste, and promoting the use of eco-friendly technologies.

- **General Data Protection Regulation (GDPR):** A regulation enacted by the European Union to protect the personal data and privacy of EU citizens. GDPR imposes strict data protection requirements on organizations that process personal data, with significant penalties for non-compliance.

- **Governance:** The framework of rules, practices, and processes by which an organization is directed and controlled. IT governance ensures that technology resources are aligned with business goals, managed effectively, and used responsibly.

Mastering IT Leadership and Management, Strategies for Success in the Digital Age

H

- **Hybrid Cloud:** A cloud computing environment that combines on-premises data centers (private cloud) with public cloud services, allowing data and applications to be shared between them. Hybrid cloud offers flexibility, scalability, and the ability to optimize costs and resources.

- **Help Desk:** A support service that provides assistance to users experiencing technical issues with IT systems, software, or hardware. Help desks are often the first point of contact for resolving IT problems and ensuring user satisfaction.

- **Hyperconverged Infrastructure (HCI):** An IT framework that combines storage, computing, and networking into a single, integrated system. HCI simplifies data center management, improves scalability, and reduces costs by consolidating resources into a unified solution.

- **High Availability (HA):** The design and implementation of systems and networks to ensure continuous operation and minimal downtime, even in the event of failures or disruptions. HA is critical for maintaining the reliability and accessibility of mission-critical applications.

- **Human-Computer Interaction (HCI):** The study of how people interact with computers and other digital devices. HCI focuses on designing user-friendly interfaces and improving the overall user experience.

I

- **Incident Response:** The process of detecting, investigating, and responding to security incidents or breaches. Incident response involves a coordinated approach to minimize damage, recover from attacks, and prevent future incidents.

- **Information Security (InfoSec):** The practice of protecting information from unauthorized access, disclosure, alteration, and destruction. Information security encompasses a range of activities, including data encryption, access control, and security policies.

- **Infrastructure as a Service (IaaS):** A cloud computing model that provides virtualized computing resources over the internet. IaaS allows organizations to rent servers, storage, and networking infrastructure, eliminating the need for on-premises hardware.

- **Intrusion Detection System (IDS):** A security system that monitors network traffic for suspicious activity and alerts administrators to potential threats. IDS can detect a variety of attacks, including malware, unauthorized access, and policy violations.

Mastering IT Leadership and Management, Strategies for Success in the Digital Age

- **IT Service Management (ITSM):** The practice of designing, delivering, managing, and improving IT services to meet the needs of an organization. ITSM frameworks, such as ITIL, provide guidelines for aligning IT services with business objectives.

J

- **Just-in-Time (JIT) Access:** A security approach that grants users access to systems and data only when needed and for a limited time. JIT access minimizes the risk of unauthorized access and reduces the attack surface.

- **Job Scheduling:** The process of planning and executing tasks or jobs within a computing environment at specified times or intervals. Job scheduling is used to automate repetitive tasks, manage workloads, and optimize resource utilization.

K

- **Key Performance Indicators (KPIs):** Metrics used to measure the success of an organization, department, or project in achieving its objectives. KPIs provide insights into performance, progress, and areas for improvement.

- **Knowledge Management:** The process of capturing, organizing, sharing, and utilizing knowledge within an organization. Knowledge management enables employees to access valuable information and best practices, improving efficiency and decision-making.

- **Kubernetes:** An open-source platform for automating the deployment, scaling, and management of containerized applications. Kubernetes provides a robust framework for orchestrating containers across multiple environments, enabling organizations to manage complex workloads.

- **Kill Chain:** A cybersecurity framework that outlines the stages of a cyberattack, from reconnaissance to execution. Understanding the kill chain helps IT leaders identify potential attack vectors and implement defenses at each stage to prevent or mitigate breaches.

- **Key Risk Indicator (KRI):** A metric used to monitor the level of risk in an organization. KRIs provide early warning signals that allow IT leaders to take proactive measures to mitigate potential risks before they escalate into significant issues.

Mastering IT Leadership and Management, Strategies for Success in the Digital Age

L

- **Lifecycle Management:** The process of managing the entire lifecycle of IT assets, from acquisition to disposal. Effective lifecycle management ensures that IT resources are used efficiently, maintained properly, and replaced or retired at the appropriate time.

- **Lean IT:** An adaptation of Lean principles to the field of IT, focusing on maximizing value for the customer while minimizing waste. Lean IT emphasizes efficiency, continuous improvement, and the elimination of non-value-added activities.

- **Load Balancing:** The process of distributing network or application traffic across multiple servers to ensure no single server becomes overwhelmed. Load balancing helps improve performance, reliability, and availability of applications.

- **Log Management:** The practice of collecting, storing, and analyzing log data generated by IT systems. Log management is essential for troubleshooting, auditing, and ensuring security by providing a record of system activity.

- **Legacy Systems:** Older computer systems, software, or hardware that are still in use, often because they perform critical functions, but may no longer be supported or easily integrated with newer technologies. Managing legacy systems can be challenging due to their outdated nature and potential security vulnerabilities.

- **Low-Code/No-Code Development:** Platforms that allow users to create applications with minimal or no coding knowledge. These platforms use visual interfaces and pre-built components, enabling faster development and empowering non-technical users to participate in application development.

Mastering IT Leadership and Management, Strategies for Success in the Digital Age

M

- **Machine Learning (ML):** A subset of artificial intelligence that involves training algorithms to recognize patterns and make predictions based on data. Machine learning is used in various applications, such as predictive analytics, natural language processing, and image recognition.

- **Malware:** Malicious software designed to damage, disrupt, or gain unauthorized access to computer systems. Common types of malware include viruses, worms, ransomware, and spyware. IT leaders must implement robust cybersecurity measures to protect against malware threats.

- **Managed Services:** Outsourcing specific IT operations, such as network management, security, or data storage, to a third-party provider. Managed services allow organizations to focus on core activities while ensuring that IT services are managed effectively by experts.

- **Microservices Architecture:** An architectural style that structures an application as a collection of loosely coupled, independently deployable services. Microservices improve scalability, flexibility, and resilience by allowing different parts of an application to be developed, deployed, and maintained separately.

- **Multi-Factor Authentication (MFA):** A security mechanism that requires users to provide two or more verification factors to gain access to a system or application. MFA enhances security by adding an extra layer of protection beyond just a username and password.

Mastering IT Leadership and Management, Strategies for Success in the Digital Age

N

- **Network Security:** The practice of protecting an organization's network infrastructure from unauthorized access, misuse, and attacks. Network security involves implementing firewalls, intrusion detection systems, encryption, and other security measures.

- **Node:** A connection point within a network where data can be created, received, or transmitted. In distributed computing and blockchain, nodes are essential components that process and store data across the network.

- **Natural Language Processing (NLP):** A field of artificial intelligence that focuses on the interaction between computers and humans through natural language. NLP enables computers to understand, interpret, and generate human language, powering applications like chatbots, translation services, and voice recognition.

- **Network Attached Storage (NAS):** A file-level storage device connected to a network that allows multiple users and devices to access and share data. NAS provides centralized storage and is often used for file sharing, backup, and data archiving.

- **Normalization:** The process of organizing data in a database to reduce redundancy and improve data integrity. Normalization involves dividing a database into smaller tables and establishing relationships between them to ensure data consistency.

O

- **Operational Excellence:** The pursuit of efficiency, effectiveness, and continuous improvement in business operations. Operational excellence focuses on optimizing processes, reducing waste, and delivering value to customers.

- **Open Source Software:** Software that is freely available for anyone to use, modify, and distribute. Open source software encourages collaboration and innovation, allowing developers to contribute to and improve the codebase.

- **Orchestration:** The automated coordination and management of complex IT processes and workflows. Orchestration tools help streamline tasks across different systems, applications, and services, ensuring efficient and consistent operations.

- **Outsourcing:** The practice of contracting external organizations or individuals to perform specific business functions or processes. Outsourcing IT services can provide cost savings, access to specialized expertise, and increased flexibility.

- **Overhead:** The additional computing resources, such as memory, processing power, or storage, required to manage and execute tasks. In IT, overhead refers to the extra burden on systems or networks that can affect performance.

Mastering IT Leadership and Management, Strategies for Success in the Digital Age

P

- **Phishing:** A type of cyberattack in which attackers attempt to trick individuals into providing sensitive information, such as passwords or credit card numbers, by pretending to be a trustworthy entity. Phishing is commonly carried out through email, social media, or fraudulent websites.

- **Platform as a Service (PaaS):** A cloud computing model that provides a platform for developing, running, and managing applications without the complexity of building and maintaining the underlying infrastructure. PaaS allows developers to focus on coding while the provider manages the infrastructure.

- **Predictive Analytics:** The use of data, statistical algorithms, and machine learning techniques to identify the likelihood of future outcomes based on historical data. Predictive analytics is used to anticipate trends, customer behavior, and potential risks.

- **Private Cloud:** A cloud computing environment that is dedicated to a single organization, providing enhanced security, control, and customization compared to public cloud services. Private clouds can be hosted on-premises or by a third-party provider.

- **Project Management Office (PMO):** A centralized team or department within an organization responsible for defining and maintaining project management standards, practices, and governance. The PMO ensures that projects are aligned with organizational goals and delivered successfully.

- **Proxy Server:** An intermediary server that acts as a gateway between a user and the internet. Proxy servers can be used for security, anonymity, and content filtering by masking the user's IP address and controlling access to websites.

Mastering IT Leadership and Management, Strategies for Success in the Digital Age

Q

- **Quantum Computing:** An emerging field of computing that leverages the principles of quantum mechanics to perform complex calculations at unprecedented speeds. Quantum computing has the potential to revolutionize industries such as cryptography, materials science, and artificial intelligence.

- **Quality Assurance (QA):** The systematic process of ensuring that products, services, or systems meet specified requirements and standards. In IT, QA involves testing, reviewing, and validating software and systems to ensure they function correctly and reliably.

- **Query:** A request for information or data from a database. Queries are used to retrieve specific data by filtering, sorting, and aggregating information based on criteria defined by the user.

- **Quorum:** The minimum number of members or nodes required to be present for a decision-making process or transaction to be valid. In distributed systems, quorum is used to ensure consistency and fault tolerance by requiring a majority of nodes to agree on changes.

- **Quality of Service (QoS):** A set of technologies and techniques used to manage network traffic and ensure the performance of critical applications and services. QoS prioritizes certain types of traffic, such as voice or video, to prevent congestion and maintain service quality.

R

- **Risk Appetite:** The level of risk that an organization is willing to accept in pursuit of its objectives. IT leaders use risk appetite to guide decision-making and determine the appropriate level of risk mitigation.

- **Risk Assessment:** The process of identifying, analyzing, and evaluating risks to an organization's assets, operations, and objectives. Risk assessment helps IT leaders prioritize risks and develop strategies to manage them effectively.

- **Risk Management:** The systematic approach to identifying, assessing, mitigating, and monitoring risks that could impact an organization's ability to achieve its objectives. Risk management is a critical component of IT governance and business continuity planning.

- **Robustness:** The ability of a system or process to remain effective under a variety of conditions or in the face of unforeseen challenges. In IT, robustness often refers to the resilience of systems and networks against disruptions or attacks.

- **Roadmap:** A strategic plan that outlines the steps, milestones, and timelines needed to achieve specific goals or implement new technologies. IT roadmaps help

Mastering IT Leadership and Management, Strategies for Success in the Digital Age

leaders align technology initiatives with business objectives and ensure that resources are allocated effectively.

S

- **Scalability:** The capacity of a system, network, or process to handle increasing amounts of work or to be easily expanded to accommodate growth. Scalability is a key consideration in IT infrastructure and software design.

- **Scrum:** An Agile framework for managing and completing complex projects. Scrum involves iterative cycles known as sprints, during which teams work collaboratively to deliver increments of a product or solution.

- **Service Level Agreement (SLA):** A formal contract between a service provider and a customer that outlines the expected level of service, including performance metrics, response times, and responsibilities. SLAs are used to ensure that services meet agreed-upon standards.

- **Stakeholder:** Any individual, group, or organization that has an interest in or is affected by a project, decision, or outcome. IT leaders must consider the needs and concerns of stakeholders when making decisions and implementing changes.

- **Strategic Alignment:** The process of ensuring that IT initiatives and strategies are in line with the broader goals and objectives of the organization. Strategic alignment helps IT leaders demonstrate the value of technology investments and their contribution to business success.

- **Sustainability:** The practice of managing resources and operations in a way that meets current needs without compromising the ability of future generations to meet their own needs. In IT, sustainability often involves reducing energy consumption, minimizing waste, and adopting environmentally friendly practices.

Mastering IT Leadership and Management, Strategies for Success in the Digital Age

T

- **Total Cost of Ownership (TCO):** The comprehensive assessment of the direct and indirect costs associated with acquiring, operating, and maintaining an IT asset or system over its entire lifecycle. TCO analysis helps IT leaders make informed decisions about technology investments.

- **Transformation:** The process of fundamentally changing the operations, culture, or strategy of an organization, often through the adoption of new technologies. IT transformation is typically driven by the need to improve efficiency, competitiveness, and customer experience.

- **Threat Landscape:** The ever-evolving environment of cybersecurity threats that an organization faces. This includes the types of attacks, the methods used by attackers, and the vulnerabilities within the organization's systems and processes.

- **Two-Factor Authentication (2FA):** A security process that requires users to provide two different types of identification to access a system or account. 2FA adds an extra layer of security by combining something the user knows (like a password) with something the user has (like a smartphone or token).

U

- **User Experience (UX):** The overall experience of a person using a product, system, or service, particularly in terms of how easy and satisfying it is to use. In IT, UX design focuses on creating user interfaces that are intuitive, efficient, and enjoyable to interact with.

- **Uptime:** The amount of time that a system, service, or device is operational and available for use. Uptime is a critical metric in IT, as it reflects the reliability and performance of technology infrastructure.

- **Unified Communications (UC):** The integration of various communication tools, such as voice, video, messaging, and conferencing, into a single platform. UC solutions enable seamless communication and collaboration across different devices and locations.

Mastering IT Leadership and Management, Strategies for Success in the Digital Age

V

- **Vendor Management:** The process of overseeing and coordinating relationships with third-party vendors who supply products or services to the organization. Effective vendor management ensures that vendors meet performance expectations, comply with agreements, and deliver value to the organization.

- **Virtualization:** The creation of virtual versions of physical IT resources, such as servers, storage devices, or networks. Virtualization allows multiple virtual machines to run on a single physical machine, improving resource utilization and flexibility.

- **Vision Statement:** A clear and inspirational description of an organization's long-term goals and aspirations. In IT, a vision statement helps guide technology strategy and aligns IT initiatives with the overall mission of the organization.

W

- **Workflow:** A sequence of tasks or activities that are required to complete a specific process. Workflow management involves designing, automating, and optimizing these tasks to improve efficiency and consistency in business operations.

- **Wi-Fi:** A wireless networking technology that allows devices to connect to the internet or communicate with each other without physical cables. Wi-Fi is a critical component of modern IT infrastructure, enabling mobility and flexible working environments.

- **Workforce Analytics:** The use of data and analytics to evaluate and optimize the performance, engagement, and productivity of an organization's workforce. IT leaders can use workforce analytics to make informed decisions about talent management and resource allocation.

X

- **XML (eXtensible Markup Language):** A flexible text format used for structuring, storing, and transmitting data. XML is widely used in web services, data interchange, and configuration files, enabling interoperability between different systems.

Mastering IT Leadership and Management, Strategies for Success in the Digital Age

Y

- **Yield Management:** A strategy used to optimize revenue by adjusting pricing and availability based on demand and other factors. In IT, yield management can be applied to optimize the use of resources, such as cloud computing capacity or bandwidth.

- **Y2K (Year 2000) Problem:** A historical issue that arose from the use of two-digit years in computer systems, which caused concerns that systems would fail or produce incorrect results when the year rolled over from 1999 to 2000. The Y2K problem highlighted the importance of forward-thinking in IT system design.

Z

- **Zero Trust Security:** A security model that assumes that threats could exist both inside and outside the network, and therefore, requires verification of every request as though it originates from an open network. Zero Trust principles emphasize strict access controls, continuous monitoring, and the use of multiple layers of security.

- **Zigbee:** A low-power, wireless mesh networking standard designed for IoT devices, enabling communication over short distances. Zigbee is commonly used in smart home devices, industrial automation, and other applications requiring reliable wireless communication.

- **Zone of Possible Agreement (ZOPA):** In negotiation, the range within which an agreement is satisfactory to both parties involved. Understanding ZOPA is crucial for IT leaders when negotiating contracts, partnerships, or vendor agreements.

Conclusion

This glossary provides an essential reference for understanding the terms and concepts fundamental to IT leadership and management. As the field continues to evolve, staying familiar with this terminology will help you navigate the complexities of your role, communicate effectively with stakeholders, and lead your organization to success in the digital age. Whether you are leading a technology transformation, managing IT operations, or guiding your team through challenges, these definitions will serve as a foundation for informed decision-making and strategic leadership.

Mastering IT Leadership and Management, Strategies for Success in the Digital Age

References
Case Studies and Frameworks
1. **GM Case Study: The Transformation of IT Leadership**
   - Referenced in: Chapter 1, *The Evolving Role of IT Leaders*
   - General Motors Official Website
2. **Microsoft Case Study: IT Leadership in a Hybrid Work World**
   - Referenced in: Chapter 14, *IT Leadership in a Hybrid Work World*
   - Microsoft Hybrid Work Research
3. **Equifax Case Study: Building a Cybersecurity Strategy**
   - Referenced in: Chapter 13, *Building a Cybersecurity Strategy*
   - Equifax Official Site
4. **Honeywell Case Study: Navigating Digital Transformation**
   - Referenced in: Chapter 12, *Navigating Digital Transformation*
   - Honeywell Case Studies
5. **Cisco Systems Case Study: IT Project and Portfolio Management**
   - Referenced in: Chapter 9, *IT Project and Portfolio Management*
   - Cisco Systems Case Studies
6. **IBM Case Study: The Future of IT Leadership**
   - Referenced in: Chapter 16, *The Future of IT Leadership*
   - IBM Official Website
7. **AWS Case Study: Effective Communication in IT Leadership**
   - Referenced in: Chapter 5, *Effective Communication*
   - AWS Case Studies
8. **Intel Corporation Case Study: Financial Management in IT**
   - Referenced in: Chapter 10, *Financial Management for IT Leaders*
   - Intel Official Site
9. **GE Case Study: Digital Leadership in the Age of Transformation**
   - Referenced in: Chapter 11, *Digital Leadership in the Age of Transformation*
   - General Electric Official Website
10. **P&G Case Study: Managing Change Through IT Leadership**
    - Referenced in: Chapter 7, *Managing Change in IT*
    - Procter & Gamble Official Site
11. **TOGAF, COBIT, ITIL, Balanced Scorecard, Lean IT, Agile, and DevOps Frameworks.**
    Referenced in: Appendix A, IT Leadership Frameworks and Models
    - The Open Group - TOGAF, COBIT, ITIL, Balanced Scorecard, Agile
12. **Wlosinski, Larry G. *Cybersecurity Takedowns.***
    - *Referenced in: Appendix B, Tools and Resources for IT Leaders*
    - Published on November 15, 2019
13. **Nadella, Satya. "Transforming Microsoft: A Dual Approach to IT Leadership and Management."**
    - *Referenced in: Chapter 2, "IT Leadership vs. IT Management"*
14. **Mott, Randy. "The Transformation of IT Leadership at General Motors."**
    - *Referenced in: Chapter 1, "The Evolving Role of IT Leaders"*
15. **GE Case Study: "Digital Leadership in the Age of Transformation."**
    - *Referenced in: Chapter 11, "Digital Leadership in the Age of Transformation"*

Leadership and Strategy Resources
16. **Sinek, Simon. "Leadership is not about being in charge."**
    - Referenced in: Section on Leadership
    - Simon Sinek's Official Website

Mastering IT Leadership and Management, Strategies for Success in the Digital Age

17. **Sinek, Simon. *Start with Why: How Great Leaders Inspire Everyone to Take Action***
    - Referenced in: Chapter 1, *The Evolving Role of IT Leaders*
    - Simon Sinek's Official Website
18. **Drucker, Peter. "Management is doing things right; leadership is doing the right things."**
    - *Quoted in: Chapter 2, "IT Leadership vs. IT Management"*
    - Peter Drucker Institute
19. **Drucker, Peter. "The Best Way to Predict the Future is to Create It."**
    - Referenced in: Chapter 3, *Building a Vision for IT*
    - Peter Drucker Institute
20. **Kim, Gene, Behr, Kevin, and Spafford, George. *The Phoenix Project: A Novel About IT, DevOps, and Helping Your Business Win***
    - Referenced in: Leadership Resources
    - The Phoenix Project Book
21. **Kim, Gene, Behr, Kevin, and Spafford, George. *The Phoenix Project: A Novel About IT, DevOps, and Helping Your Business Win.***
    - *Cited in: Leadership and Management Resources Section*
    - The Phoenix Project
22. **Harvard Business Review (HBR)**
    - Cited as: A Key Resource for Leadership and Management Insights
    - Harvard Business Review
23. **MIT Sloan Management Review**
    - Referenced as: A Resource for Research-Based Articles on Leadership and Innovation
    - MIT Sloan Management Review
24. **Gartner Research**
    - Referenced in: Strategic Planning and Decision-Making Tools
    - Gartner Research

Cybersecurity Tools

25. **Splunk (SIEM Tool)**
    - Referenced in: Appendix B, *Cybersecurity Tools*
    - Splunk Official Site
26. **CrowdStrike Falcon**
    - Referenced in: Appendix B, *Cybersecurity Tools*
    - CrowdStrike Falcon
27. **Cisco Umbrella**
    - Referenced in: Appendix B, *Cybersecurity Tools*
    - Cisco Umbrella
28. **Nessus (Vulnerability Assessment Tool)**
    - Referenced in: Appendix B, *Cybersecurity Tools*
    - Nessus Official Website

Data Management and Analytics Tools

29. **Tableau (Data Visualization Tool)**
    - Referenced in: Appendix B, *Data Management and Analytics Tools*
    - Tableau Official Website
30. **Microsoft Power BI (Business Analytics Tool)**
    - Referenced in: Appendix B, *Data Management and Analytics Tools*
    - Microsoft Power BI
31. **Apache Hadoop (Big Data Processing Framework)**
    - Referenced in: Appendix B, *Data Management and Analytics Tools*

Mastering IT Leadership and Management, Strategies for Success in the Digital Age

- Apache Hadoop
32. **Snowflake (Cloud-Based Data Warehouse)**
    - Referenced in: Appendix B, *Data Management and Analytics Tools*
    - Snowflake Official Website

Learning and Development Resources

33. **Coursera (Online Learning Platform)**
    - Referenced in: Appendix B, *Continuous Learning and Development Resources*
    - Coursera
34. **Pluralsight (Technology-Focused Learning Platform)**
    - Referenced in: Appendix B, *Continuous Learning and Development Resources*
    - Pluralsight
35. **LinkedIn Learning (On-Demand Video Courses)**
    - Referenced in: Appendix B, *Continuous Learning and Development Resources*
    - LinkedIn Learning
36. **ISACA (Global Association for IT Governance, Risk, and Cybersecurity Professionals)**
    - Referenced in: Certifications and Training Resources
    - ISACA Official Website

Collaboration and Communication Tools

37. **Zoom (Video Conferencing Tool).**
    Referenced in: Collaboration and Communication Tools
    - Zoom
38. **Slack (Messaging Platform).**
    Referenced in: Collaboration and Communication Tools
    - Slack
39. **Microsoft Teams (Collaboration Platform).**
    Referenced in: Collaboration and Communication Tools
    - Microsoft Teams

Strategic Planning and Decision-Making Tools

40. **Gartner Research.**
    Cited as: A Leading Resource for IT Leadership Research and Strategic Planning
    - Gartner Research